'Rory Medcalf gives us a fast-paced ride around the world's newest, and most important, strategic arena. He has done more than anyone to introduce the world to the idea of the Indo-Pacific, and this book is a convincing manifesto for a new vision of connectedness. This is the world with all the difficult bits left in.'
—Bill Hayton, author of *The South China Sea: The Struggle for Power in Asia*, and Associate Fellow, Chatham House

'Rory Medcalf offers deep insights into the origin of the idea of the Indo-Pacific, deconstructs the power dynamics shaping the region and delineates potential pathways to limit the conflict. A rich and rewarding read for anyone interested in a region that promises to define the geopolitics of the twenty-first century.'
—C. Raja Mohan, Director, Institute of South Asian Studies, National University of Singapore

'Essential reading for any scholar or practitioner seeking to understand the geopolitics of a region that will define all our futures.'
—Michael J. Green, Center for Strategic and International Studies and Georgetown University, author of *By More Than Providence* and *Arming Japan*

'All of us struggling to understand great-power competition need to become ambidextrous if we are to develop policies to cope with a rising – or a collapsing – China, and learning from Rory Medcalf's book is a great place to start.'
—Kori Schake, Deputy Director-General, International Institute for Strategic Studies

INDO-PACIFIC EMPIRE

CHINA, AMERICA AND THE CONTEST FOR THE WORLD'S PIVOTAL REGION

RORY MEDCALF

Manchester University Press

Published by Manchester University Press by arrangement with La Trobe University Press, an imprint of Schwartz Books Pty Ltd.

Manchester University Press
Altrincham Street, Manchester M1 7JA
www.manchesteruniversitypress.co.uk

British Library Cataloguing-in-Publication Data
A catalogue record for this book is available from the British Library

ISBN 978 1 5261 507 83 hardback

First published 2020

The publisher has no responsibility for the persistence or accuracy of URLs for any external or third-party internet websites referred to in this book, and does not guarantee that any content on such websites is, or will remain, accurate or appropriate.

Typeset by Akiko Chan

For Eva

CONTENTS

PREFACE

The 2020s have arrived in a cloak of uncertainty. The world sees a crowded horizon of risk, ranging from the Middle East to Asian waters, from democracies in crisis to the burning impacts of climate change. So a book making claims about the future is a gift to fate.

But *Indo-Pacific Empire* is not just about today or tomorrow. It tilts the map to tell a history of international connection and contestation across the seas, tracing deep geopolitical currents to the 2030s and beyond. It ventures conclusions about the risks intrinsic to China's hasty regional expansion, the promise of multipolarity as middle players partner up, the staying power of the United States despite Trump and beyond him, and the value of many nations standing firm to help Beijing find a settling point. These judgements should be continuously contested. Each day brings new evidence for and against.

Amid their many travails, the middle players continue to gird themselves for resilience, solidarity and sovereignty. Japan, India and Australia strengthen their bonds with each other and in a quadrilateral with America.

But how long can such middle players hold their ground without American leadership? In late 2019, the US establishment was still saying things allies and partners wanted to hear, with the State Department declaring a 'shared Indo-Pacific vision', underscoring multilateral institutions and economic development rather than military confrontation with China. Yet the president was somewhere else: skipping the East Asia Summit while demanding South Korea and Japan pay more for US military presence. By the start of 2020, Donald Trump was mired in the rites of impeachment. With a desperate eye on political survival, he was striking a trade truce with Beijing while risking open war with Iran. A different administration – one that does not embody constant national emergency – is needed for global stability and managing strategic competition with China.

For Xi Jinping's regime will not stand still in combining extreme internal control with geopolitical struggle and reach. Trump's folly is Xi's opportunity. Yet the strains are showing for China too. Hints have emerged of internal dissatisfaction with some of Xi's largest schemes, whether the material expense of the Belt and Road or the moral cost of the mass incarceration of Uighur people. Hong Kong's defiance has set in. India, too, faces serious internal strife, with Hindu nationalism eroding long-term democratic strengths.

At sea, the contest of power and presence flows and ebbs. Indonesia and Malaysia have greeted the new decade with a stronger defence of their maritime interests against China. American and Japanese warships confidently sail the South China Sea. In the Indian Ocean, China asserts its presence by teaming up variously with Russia, Iran and South Africa for naval exercises. India and France share maritime surveillance information. India's navy expels a Chinese survey ship from its territories in the Bay of Bengal.

And smaller players cannot be dismissed. In a connected, contested Indo-Pacific, no island is an island. In Australia, the China debate has sharpened. The new leader of Sri Lanka asks China to hand back the Hambantota port and urges other nations to dilute China's influence, while celebrating a Chinese-built artificial island off Colombo. Taiwanese democracy is becoming a testing ground for freedom from Chinese Communist Party interference. In the South Pacific, a very different island votes resoundingly for independence – in this case from Papua New Guinea – in the shadow of its own 20th-century civil war. Bougainville is infrastructure-poor and resource-abundant. Here is one separatism Beijing may welcome – fresh terrain in the regional competition for influence.

These are a few examples from the eve of the 2020s. They do not signify trends. But they remind us it is far too soon to conclude that one country will map the future. Decision-makers must peer beyond the parochialism of the present and ask enduring questions about agency, influence, risk and power's many layers. It will be a long game.

Rory Medcalf
Canberra, January 2020

CHAPTER 1

OF NAMES, MAPS AND POWER

On 11 November 2016, as the globe reeled from Donald Trump's election as US president, two unlikely friends found themselves conversing aboard a *shinkansen* – a Japanese bullet train – between Tokyo and Kobe, speeding from sea to sea. Their journey is not yet diplomatic folklore, but it should be.

Aboard the Indo-Pacific express

Abe Shinzō, the Japanese prime minister, and Narendra Modi, his Indian counterpart, shared a reputation as strong leaders, driven and charismatic nationalists with a democratic mandate to rouse their sometimes slow-motion countries. Yet they hailed from different sides of the tracks. Modi was proudly from a modest merchant household in Gujarat. Hagiography has it he served chai by a railway station as a child. Abe was the scion of a patrician and conservative political family tied to Japan's imperialist past. Stereotypes separated their nations: Japan calm with wealth, technological perfectionism and its declining, ageing populace; India a colourful din of disorder, underdevelopment and a demographic of youth and growth. Even if these were cliches, Tokyo and Delhi surely remained in different worlds, with divergent problems and priorities. Through the modern era in which Modi-ji and Abe-san had grown up, their countries had little contact.

Yet the smiles and bear hugs of the Modi–Abe train ride that day in 2016 reflected a change in world affairs, less shocking but no less profound than what had just occurred in America. Deep shifts were accelerating in

Japanese prime minister Abe Shinzō and Indian prime minister Narendra Modi launch their Indo-Pacific partnership, November 2016

the structures of geopolitics – of power relations among states – influenced by the interplay of economics, strategy and geography over the previous two decades. The exact conversations between the leaders of Asia's second- and third-largest economies during the theatre of the train ride and the rest of that three-day summit are a state secret for those governments. From their published joint statement, all fifty-eight paragraphs, it is plain these were substantial talks.[1] While most eyes were understandably fixed on the American presidential drama, Japan and India were already shaping the future. For the sake of tact, the word China did not appear anywhere in the document, but it did not need to; it was a pervasive subtext.

Two things stood out. Once indifferent to each other, Japan and India were now agreeing to work closely together across the total range of issues: defence, diplomacy, economics, education, development, technology, energy, environment, culture and more. And they were naming a particular place for this cooperation: a wide arc of the world their leaders now chose to call the Indo-Pacific. For many people, that name was new. Even for seasoned watchers of diplomacy, its usage here was intriguing and significant. It was not a familiar term in current affairs, not the well-known Asia-Pacific or even Asia, but precisely the *Indo*-Pacific.

2

What was going on? Was this merely a choice of words to flatter India, or something more? Already another country, Australia, had formally renamed its region this way, and within a few years the trend had caught on. Today, an Indo-Pacific fever seems to have taken hold in governments from Washington to Jakarta, Delhi to Tokyo, Canberra to Paris to Hanoi to London. The term finds receptive audiences in almost every significant capital – except Beijing.

The purpose of this book is twofold: to make sense of the Indo-Pacific, past, present and future; and to explain how this region can cope with China's assertive power.[2] Where did this way of imagining much of the world come from? What does it mean for today's realities, the fates and fortunes of nations? And why does it matter for what comes next? At one level, the Indo-Pacific counts simply as an idea, describing and imagining a region that has become the global centre of strategic and economic gravity, just as the North Atlantic was for much of the 19th and 20th centuries. But there is a practical point too. Words shape the world. An imagined space on a map both reflects and influences real and palpable things like military deployments, patterns of prosperity, and calculations of risk among the world's most powerful states.

What's in a name?

The use of the term Indo-Pacific is no mere wordplay. It reflects something real: a changing approach by many nations to security, economics and diplomacy. Far from being an obscure account of words and maps, the narrative of the Indo-Pacific helps nations face one of the great international dilemmas of the 21st century: how can other countries respond to a strong and often coercive China without resorting to capitulation or conflict? This is a problem facing Japan and India, which have both in recent years confronted China on their borders in situations that could have led to war, and one day still could. But in more subtle ways it is a challenge for every other country too.

At a descriptive level, the Indo-Pacific is just a neutral name for a new and expansive map centred on maritime Asia. This conveys that the Pacific and

Indian oceans are connecting through trade, infrastructure and diplomacy, now that the world's two most populous states, China and India, are rising together. Their economies, along with many others, rely on the sea lanes of the Indian Ocean to ship oil from the Middle East and Africa, and myriad other cargoes in both directions, along the world's vital commercial artery.

But the Indo-Pacific is also about drawing strength from vast space, and from solidarity among its many and diverse nations. The term recognises that both economic ties and strategic competition now encompass an expansive two-ocean region, due in large part to China's ascent, and that other countries must protect their interests through new partnerships across the blurring of old geographic boundaries.

Some voices warn that the Indo-Pacific is actually code for geopolitical agendas: America's bid to thwart China, India's play for greatness, Japan's plan to regain influence, Indonesia's search for leverage, Australia's alliance-building, Europe's excuse to gatecrash the Asian century. Its more strident discontents claim it is nothing less than a terminological fabrication of 'Orwellian' proportions, 'as meaningless as the Atlanto-Pacific'.[3] Certainly China feels risk and discomfort in the term. It hears Indo-Pacific as the rationale for, among other things, a strategy to contain its power through a 'quadrilateral' alliance of democracies – the United States, Japan, India, Australia. Chinese foreign minister Wang Yi has gone to the trouble of publicly rejecting the Indo-Pacific as an 'attention-grabbing idea' that 'will dissipate like ocean foam'.[4]

Yet reality begs to differ. The irony is that what most makes the Indo-Pacific real is China's own behaviour – its expanding economic, political and military presence in the Indian Ocean, South Asia, the South Pacific, Africa and beyond. The signature foreign policy of Chinese leader Xi Jinping is the 'Belt and Road', a colossal scheme that takes a lot of explaining: part infrastructure-and-lending spree, part strategic powerplay, part marketing campaign. The 'Belt' refers to Chinese ambitions on land. The 'Road', however, is short for 'Maritime Silk Road' – which means the Indo-Pacific with Chinese characteristics. In this emerging empire, business brings risk as well as opportunity, warships and submarines stalk the sea lanes, soldiers and spies mix with merchants, and full-spectrum competition between China and other major powers overshadows their professed cooperation.

What's in a name? At first blush, the label Indo-Pacific may seem confected and jarring. It sounds like too much yet not enough, two adjectives without a noun, the sea without the land, Asia without its continent, a conflation of two oceans, each vast enough to be a region in its own right. For many years, people and governments have readily recognised terms like Asia or Asia-Pacific, so why add a new geographical descriptor? And what difference to people's lives – to their peace, autonomy, dignity and material wellbeing – does a new name for their part of the world make anyway?

Mental maps and material facts

In statecraft, mental maps matter.[5] Relations between states, competition or cooperation, involve a landscape of the mind. This defines each country's natural 'region' – what is on the map, what is off the map and why. It equates to what academics call a strategic system or a regional security complex: a part of the world where the behaviour of one or more powerful states has a strong and inescapable impact on the interests of other countries.[6] The importance of mental maps is as old as map-making itself.

What a nation imagines on the map is a marker of what that nation considers important. This in turn shapes the decisions of leaders, the destiny of nations, strategy itself. Maps are about power. How leaders define regions can affect their allocation of resources and attention; the ranking of friends and foes; who is invited and who is overlooked at the top tables of diplomacy; what gets talked about, what gets done, and what gets forgotten. A sense of shared geography or 'regionalism' can shape international cooperation and institutions, privileging some nations and diminishing others. For instance, the late-20th-century notion of the Asia-Pacific and an East Asian hemisphere excluded India at the very time Asia's second-most populous country was opening up and looking east. This was not just unfair; it was untenable. The Indo-Pacific fixes that, although it is important to correct the assumption that this way of seeing the world is all about India: it is principally about recognising and responding to China's widening strategic horizons.

There is no one right or permanent way of framing the world – nations choose maps that help them simplify things, make sense of a complex reality and above all serve their interests at a given time. For the moment, a Chinese description of much of the world as simply 'the Belt and Road' has become common parlance, though the meaning and purpose of this term is changeable, opaque and entwined with China's interests. For a long time, people have been accustomed to labels such as the Asia-Pacific, East Asia, South Asia and Southeast Asia, Europe, the North Atlantic, Eurasia and so on. Of an earlier set of politically loaded labels for Asia, the Far East and Near East are less recognised today, but the Middle East has endured.

These are all geographic constructs – invented terms that powerful states have at some time consecrated, with a self-centred political purpose.[7] Even Asia is not originally an Asian framework, but a term Europeans concocted and adjusted for their own reasons. Its imagined boundaries keep shifting. Asia began in ancient times as an Athenian label for everything east of Greece. In the 1820s, only half in jest, Austrian imperial statesman Metternich put the Europe–Asia boundary somewhere between Vienna and Budapest. In 2014, China hosted a conference that called for Asians alone to determine Asia's future, but with an interesting catch: its member states included the likes of Russia and Egypt, friends of China that are not categorically Asian, yet not Indonesia and Japan, unquestionably Asian countries but also powers that could make life difficult for China in the future.[8]

Like previous mental maps, the Indo-Pacific is in some ways artificial and contingent. But it suits the times: a 21st century of maritime connectivity and a geopolitics that is many-sided or, as the diplomats say, multipolar. A decade ago, the Indo-Pacific was almost unheard of in the discourse of international relations. Today we are seeing a contest of ideas in the mental maps of Asia being simplified down to the big two: China's Belt and Road versus the Indo-Pacific, championed in various forms by such countries as Japan, India, Australia, Indonesia, France and, as it gathers its wits, the

United States. Other nations are seeking to understand both concepts and identify how they can leverage, adjust, resist or evade them.

The term Indo-Pacific has thus become code for certain decisions of consequence. In part, it is a message to a rising China that it cannot expect others to accept its self-image as the centre of the region and the world. But it is also a message to America. It is a signal that China and America are not the only two nations that count, a reminder of the need to avoid the psychological trap of what veteran Singaporean diplomat Bilahari Kausikan calls 'false binaries' – such as the insistence that everything boils down to choosing between China as the future and America as the past.[9]

Of course, simple binary choices are a tempting way to make sense of some of the more mind-numbing headline statistics about the sheer size of the Chinese and American economies. In isolation, such data tells a compelling story: that China has either already overtaken America as the world's largest economy, or soon will, and not much else matters.[10] But it is illuminating to play with some other numbers – statistics that embed the two leading powers in a system of many substantial nations, the region we now call the Indo-Pacific.

This complex reality includes many 'middle players': significant countries that are neither China nor the United States. It is a core contention of this book that, working together, the region's middle players can affect the balance of power, even assuming a diminished role for America. Consider, for instance, the possibility of a different quadrilateral: Japan, India, Indonesia and Australia. All four have serious differences with China and reasonable (and generally growing) convergences with each other when it comes to their national security. They happen to be champions of an emerging Indo-Pacific worldview. And they are hardly passive or lightweight nations. In 2018, the four had a combined population of 1.75 billion, a combined gross domestic product, or GDP (measured by purchasing power parity, or PPP, terms), of US$21 trillion, and combined defence expenditure of US$147 billion. By contrast, the United States has a population of 327.4 million, a GDP of US$20.49 trillion and defence spending of US$649 billion. For its part, China's population is 1.39 billion, its economy US$25 trillion and its defence budget US$250 billion.[11] (This assumes, of course, that official Chinese statistics about economic growth and population size are not inflated, and there is reason for doubt.[12])

Project the numbers forward a generation, to mid-century, and the picture of middle players as potent balancers becomes starker still. In 2050, the four middle players are expected to have a combined population of 2.108 billion and a combined GDP (PPP) of an astounding $63.97 trillion. By then, America is estimated to have 379 million people and a GDP (PPP) of $34 trillion. China will have 1.402 billion people and a GDP of $58.45 trillion. Even just the big three of these Indo-Pacific partners – India, Japan and Indonesia – would together eclipse China in population and exceed it economically. By then their combined defence budgets could also be larger than that of the mighty People's Liberation Army (PLA). Include one or more other rising regional powers with their own China frictions, such as a Vietnam that may have about 120 million people and a top-twenty global economy, and the numbers are stronger still. Even the combination of just two or three of these countries would give China pause. And all of this, for the sake of the argument, excludes any strategic role whatsoever for the United States west of Hawaii. If added to the enduring heft of the United States, the alignment of just a few middle players would outweigh the Chinese giant. Moreover, size is not everything, and their maritime geography lends freedom of manoeuvre, a strategic advantage.

Of course, at one level this is all mere speculative extrapolation (albeit from existing numbers and assumed trends). But so is the widely propagated assertion that this unfolding century belongs to Beijing, that China will in every sense map the future. It is one thing to say that various coalitions of Indo-Pacific powers could balance China, provided they all stick together. In reality it would require breakthroughs in leadership, farsightedness and diplomacy for coalitions to harden into anything like formal alliances: arrangements that require mutual obligation among parties, underpinned by a willingness to take risks for one another. Moreover, it is difficult to see how loosely arrayed democracies can match authoritarian China's ability to mobilise its national resources. Still, the Indo-Pacific is at the early stages of a long game in which there will be many plausible combinations of nations that, in the right circumstances, could find their own kind of fortitude in numbers.[13]

Could the two train-travelling prime ministers of India and Japan herald such future solidarity? Certainly the now annual Abe–Modi summits are not unique: in anxious times, most everyone talks to everyone else. But in the Indo-Pacific particularly, a new 'security web' of dialogue and cooperation is being woven among many unlikely partners, as they meet in twos and threes and more. Japan and India are just more consequential and active than most. Abe and Modi have formed habits of trusted dialogue and cooperation about security and prosperity, about shared problems and the beginning of a shared strategy, once unthinkable for pacifist Japan and non-aligned India. These are not the usual scripted exchanges of busy heads of government, but open-ended and ambitious deliberations between leaders determined to cope with an assertive China and an unpredictable America. In November 2016, the Japanese and Indian leaders sat together to pore over maps of their two-ocean region, from California to east Africa, and considered how geography could help balance China's growing power.[14]

Breaking boundaries

Their answer? The two Asian leaders linked India's drive to 'Act East' with the 'Free and Open Indo-Pacific', a slogan unveiled by Abe a few months earlier in Africa.[15] Strikingly, in 2017 the United States adopted the same term to define its regional policy – a rare example of America willingly being led by others.[16] There may be subtle differences in what each country means by the label, but for both Japan and India, the Indo-Pacific is a way to navigate turbulence in Asian power politics in which Xi Jinping's China is disruptive, Donald Trump's America dysfunctional, and other countries are desperate to preserve what they can of peace, prosperity and sovereignty. And it does this by breaking through the late-20th-century mental boundary that separated the Pacific and Indian oceans, ossified into the once-useful but now outmoded idea of the Asia-Pacific.

Japan and India – Asia's most developed power and the one soon to be its most populous – seem to be joining forces across the seas, beyond the bromance of two political strongmen. The Indo-Pacific idea both explains and propels their new alignment. The signs are that this partnership is structural now, wired into both nations' bureaucracies, and will survive its political progenitors.[17] On its own, the Modi–Abe journey is not conclusive proof of how the world is changing. After all, the nature of diplomacy is a constant cycle of visits, talks and communiques, where everything seems important and little is what it seems. But plenty of data points and patterns suggest the map of Asia is being reimagined in consequential ways.

Hints of the contemporary Indo-Pacific idea appeared shortly after the turn of the 21st century.[18] Australia was the first country to formally name its region the Indo-Pacific, in a defence policy white paper in 2013, which included a map showing how the super-region was connected by sea lines of energy and trade.[19] But things really gathered pace once the United States declared the Indo-Pacific as its region of principal strategic interest – and the zone of a fast-intensifying contest with China – in its national security strategy of December 2017.[20]

The Indo-Pacific is now the standard American lens for the region. The powerful US military force based in Hawaii has been renamed Indo-Pacific Command. The new terminology threads policy speeches, strategic documents and legislation, from the White House to the Pentagon, from the State Department to Congress, where Republicans and Democrats now seem agreed on at least one major challenge: a long-term rivalry with China.[21] Donald Trump's use of the term Indo-Pacific is not exactly its best advertisement. He is far from the ideal advocate for this or any other foreign policy that involves allies.

But it attests to the resilience of the Indo-Pacific idea that so many other nations are embracing it anyway. Contrary to some claims, the Indo-Pacific is not an intellectual confection made in Washington and foisted on an unreceptive Asia.[22] Instead, it is an authentically regional approach to diplomacy, security and economics, with growing support in Asia and beyond. America has been a follower, not a leader, in lifting an Indo-Pacific banner.

In diplomatic summits, a domino effect has occurred, with many governments suddenly referring to the Indo-Pacific, even while China warned them away from such language. Indian prime minister Modi made it the animating theme of his keynote speech at an Asia security summit in Singapore in 2018.[23] And in June 2019, the entire ten countries of the Association of Southeast Asian Nations (ASEAN) agreed to an Indo-Pacific outlook on their relations with an enlarged region.[24] This confirms the Indo-Pacific is not an idea alien to Asia: indeed, it gives the middle players of ASEAN more centrality than they had in the past Asia-Pacific era, or than they would have in a world defined only by Beijing's Belt and Road. The Indo-Pacific has rapidly assumed almost totemic significance for a wide range of nations affirming their agency in an uncertain world.

Charting the past

Facing a new era means looking at the past anew. It turns out that the Indo-Pacific, or something like it, has a rich history. Recorded use of the term dates from around 1850.[25] The idea it connotes is of much greater vintage still. The first part of this book revisits the long and half-forgotten past of a two-ocean region at the heart of a connected world. This fresh telling of history affirms that maritime Asia has never been a China-centric region. Instead, the region is rediscovering its Indo-Pacific destiny. In this tempest of nations, the past is much more than prologue.

An integrated two-ocean perspective has an ancient pedigree. It is a more enduring way of understanding Asia than 20th-century notions like the Asia-Pacific. For a start, science has long recognised the Indo-Pacific as a connected region in the biogeography of marine species and ocean currents. Such connected marine ecosystems do not automatically make a chunk of the world a distinct region in economics and power politics. But the precursors of the Indo-Pacific in this geopolitical sense also go back thousands of years, to a proto-economy of regional maritime trade and migration before recorded history.

This was followed by the spread of Hinduism and Islam to Southeast

Asia, Buddhism to China, Japan and Korea, Chinese tributary relations to Southeast Asia and briefly the Indian Ocean, and European colonialism and consequent pan-Asian resistance across so much of the map. The contours of the Indo-Pacific were there all along in the cartography of exploration. From the 1400s to the mid-20th century, the typical map titled 'Asia' caught the sweep of the Indo-Pacific – the two oceans, India, Southeast Asia, China and beyond – in a single frame. A fresh appraisal explains how the age of empires broke then bound then broke the region again, concluding with the clash of America and Japan in the Indo-Pacific war that ended in 1945.

The prolonged flux in Asian security in the post-war era was a quest for structures of regional cooperation and identity. China and India were estranged – to the point of war in 1962 – and held back their own prosperity by closing their economic doors to the world. The Cold War further kept the region divided. A transient idea called the Asia-Pacific arose as a way to connect Japan and other Asian economies to America and Australia, and to keep Washington engaged across the Pacific even as the end of the Cold War gave it a reason to leave. But the structural re-emergence of an Indo-Pacific order was inevitable once China and India began to reform, trade and look out again. The stage was set in 1993, when China started depending on the Indian Ocean to transport the energy, resources and trade essential to its burgeoning prosperity. The Asia-Pacific project carried the seeds of its own demise: such a region could not be complete without China, yet China could not rise without looking south and west and across the Indian Ocean.

In the early 2000s, Indo-Pacific realities sharpened as China, India, Japan, the United States and others began to compete or cooperate across the Indian Ocean as well as the Pacific. The countries of Southeast Asia had sought to give structure to their region through a diplomatic forum called the East Asia Summit, but this ended up including a much wider range of countries, reflecting the new Indo-Pacific in all but name. Partnerships proliferated among the United States, India, Japan and Australia as many countries reimagined their diplomacy around two oceans. These diplomatic arrangements anticipated and reacted to material events, such as international responses to the devastating Boxing Day tsunami of 2004, the upsurge of Somali piracy, the historic return of China's navy to the Indian Ocean and the rapid extension of Chinese economic interests. The new shape of the region was locking in.

Contesting the present: many players, many layers

The second part of this book unveils some of the immense complexity of the contemporary Indo-Pacific moment and how nations are interacting in a great game with multiple participants and dimensions. China's expanding economic, military and diplomatic activity in the Indian Ocean marks an emerging Indo-Pacific strategic system, where the actions and interests of one powerful state in one part of the region affect the interests and actions of others. The Indo-Pacific power narrative intersects the interests of at least four major countries – China, India, Japan and the United States – as well as many other players, including Australia, Indonesia and the other Southeast Asian nations, South Korea and more distant stakeholders, not least in Europe. Russia, too, is making its presence felt. The Indo-Pacific is a multipolar system, in which the fate of regional order, or disorder, will not be determined by one or even two powers – the United States and China – but by the interests and agency of many. The region's foremost strategic challenges may be China-centric, but the region itself is not.

The power contest in the region has often been likened to the Great Game between imperial Britain and Russia in the 19th century. This time, though, there are more than two players. Academic theories and games of strategy help explain how nations interact when interests differ. But what if each is playing a different game? And if there is cooperation alongside competition? After all, there may be very different drivers – combinations of interests, values, identity – behind each state's actions in the region. Beyond narrow ideas about defence and security, these may involve nationalism, history, political legitimacy and of course economics, including the quest for resources and sustainability in a threatened natural environment.

For China, in particular, there is a troubling thread between the domestic and the international. For Xi Jinping and the Communist Party to maintain their grip on total power, they have found it necessary to raise the Chinese people's expectations that their nation will be great abroad, and will successfully handle any resistance. The result is not classic territorial aggression or wars of conquest – China is neither capable nor in favour of such crude and old-fashioned forms of imperialism – but instead enough assertiveness to make other countries look to their defences and consider ways of banding together. China's expansive policies mean that its problems overseas are accumulating, and the chances of a major misstep are thus increasing. In turn, this puts Xi and the Communist Party at particular risk, because China more than any other great power has staked much of the legitimacy of its political system on success abroad. When things go wrong, the whole Chinese system could suffer grievously – especially if crises of security, politics and economics intersect in ways hard to predict and impossible to manage.

Interaction between states occurs across many dimensions. Compounding the complexity of a multipolar region, a game with many players, is the reality that this is also a puzzle with many layers. Four stand out: economics, military force, diplomacy and a clash of national narratives. These blend in patterns of comprehensive competition – combined with elements of cooperation – that will shape the future.

Geoeconomics

Economics, especially demand for energy, propelled the rise of the modern Indo-Pacific. China, Japan, South Korea, Taiwan, Southeast Asia, Australia and India all depend acutely on the Indian Ocean sea lanes for energy and thus prosperity and security. Seaborne commerce is likewise making this maritime highway – carrying at least two-thirds of the world's oil and a third of the world's bulk cargo – the centre of gravity for the global economy. There are uncertainties about whether international supply and manufacturing chains will extend to South Asia, or remain more Asia-Pacific in character, or tangle and snap in new ways with trends in automation and 'onshoring' and the prospect of a disruptive 'decoupling' of industrial interdependence between America and China.

But there is also a race of connectivity. China and others are competing to build ports, road, rail, electricity and communications infrastructure to bind Asia and connect it with Africa, Europe and the Pacific. This extends to small island states, putting the South Pacific into the Indo-Pacific. Globally, meanwhile, the contest is on for the commanding heights of technology: artificial intelligence, quantum computing and 5G telecommunications. Contrary to turn-of-the-century dreams of globalisation, economic interdependence is no longer just about breaking down borders and letting all states rise together: it has become a tool of power and influence, captured in the newly popular catch-all of 'geoeconomics'.[26] This is partly about geography and partly not, though it is entirely about the nexus of wealth and power. It represents competition by states for power advantages through economics rather than military force, a continuation of both war and politics by other means.[27]

Whatever else it may prove to be – munificence or folly – China's Belt and Road spree of loans and infrastructure has become a geoeconomic powerplay, a strategy for pre-eminence.[28] The 'Road' is the Indo-Pacific with Chinese characteristics, a bid to extend influence into the Indian Ocean and the South Pacific. The 'Belt' of overland connectivity through Eurasia is of secondary importance, given that transport of bulk goods and energy by sea will remain cheaper and arguably no riskier – albeit slower – than by land. As pointed out by Cuiping Zhu, one of China's leading Indian Ocean experts, China needs sea transportation for 90 per cent or more of its imported oil, iron ore, copper and coal.[29] The strategic impacts of the Belt and Road warrant close attention, including a new colonialism – accidental or deliberate – in which Chinese coercion, political influence and security presence become consequences of connectivity. This does not mean that all such activity began as a grand strategy or – faced with complex local politics – that it will necessarily succeed. For instance, geographically pivotal places like Sri Lanka and Malaysia remain in play: their sustained dominance by China is not a forgone conclusion.[30] But as with the European empires of old, it is clear that the flag follows trade, and that security shadows economics, along with risks of conflict.

Force

The Indo-Pacific has a starkly military dimension. A pivotal moment has been China's turn to the sea. Its navy is expanding rapidly, in line with a 2015 proclamation by president, Communist Party general secretary, military chief and core leader Xi Jinping that the 'traditional mentality that land outweighs sea must be abandoned' when it comes to protecting China's interests. Instead, the new Chinese strategy is about 'offshore waters defence' and 'open-seas protection': euphemisms for deploying force in distant waters.[31] This is not just rhetoric. A massive shipbuilding program has been underway for years. Aircraft carriers are being commissioned, not primarily to patrol China's proximate waters or even the South China Sea, but to show force on the open ocean. The People's Liberation Army Navy (PLAN) showed up in the Indian Ocean with three warships to counter Somali piracy at the start of 2009, and has never left. For the first time since the voyages of Admiral Zheng He in the 1400s, China is an Indian Ocean power. This time, instead of sailing ships, it has destroyers, marines and submarines. These conduct exercises peaceful and warlike, backed by partnerships, port access rights and the Chinese military's first overseas base. This time China plans to stay.

Of course, China is not alone. To be fair, it has far-flung interests to protect and is hardly the only external power to fly the flag in Indian Ocean waters. Perhaps the real surprise is how long it took Chinese mariners to make their way back. The United States has long operated there, including at its base on the contentious UK possession of Diego Garcia. Japan opened a base at Djibouti before China did. European powers have been forth and back and forth again since the days of Vasco da Gama, the ruthless Portuguese adventurer who pioneered maritime empire-building five centuries ago. This century, almost every ocean-going navy, from Russia to Singapore, has sent forces to protect commerce from Somali-based pirates, a rationale for China's mission.

And the world's navies are converging not only west of the Malacca Strait, that strategic neck of water connecting the Indian and Pacific oceans. Indian, American and Japanese warships practise together from the Bay of

Bengal to the western Pacific. Almost every major navy joins Australia to train in waters north of Darwin. As China militarises artificial islands in the South China Sea, fleets both commercial and military from across the globe exercise their international legal rights by traversing this shared highway at the heart of the Indo-Pacific. The rights and wrongs of the South China Sea disputes are recounted elsewhere, but understandably there are rising fears of war in these contested and congested sea lanes. And, in this connected age, a war there would spread and resound far.

Militaries are modernising and deploying across the Indo-Pacific. The trend is towards what military jargon calls 'power projection': in plain language, a capacity to fight far away, across the seas. This means long-range and maritime capabilities: aircraft carriers, amphibious forces, destroyers, submarines, surveillance planes, satellites and missiles, combined with futuristic drone swarms and the unseen hands of cyber and electronic warfare.[32] The costly quest for advantage in undersea warfare is becoming a new peacetime fixation, an obsessive game of hide-and-seek, as China, India, Pakistan and North Korea imitate America, Russia, Britain and France in placing nuclear weapons on submarines.

Nearly all the region's powers are arming and making ready, but for what? Is it mainly about cooperation, on shared concerns like terrorism, piracy, illegal fishing, disaster relief in an age of climate change, search and rescue, peacekeeping, stabilisation of fragile states, evacuations of citizens from trouble spots? Is it to police the sea lanes, protect shipments of energy and commerce, and uphold international law? Or to deter, coerce, resist and, if need be, fight other nations in new wars, cold or hot? Underlying the military build-up is a gathering atmosphere of suspicion. No nation may plan outright aggression, but intentions are opaque. China does not take America at its word – and America, Japan, India, Australia and Vietnam, among others, are especially sceptical of China's.

Diplomacy

All this armed mistrust would seem an urgent call for greater attention to diplomacy, rules and respect in keeping the peace. The architecture of peace in the Indo-Pacific is woefully flimsy, and doubles as another arena in which nations can compete for influence. The region's multilateral diplomacy sometimes appears to be little more than an acrimony of acronyms, doing little in a practical sense to build cooperation or reduce risks of conflict. So-called confidence-building measures – the hotlines, rules and codes of conduct that helped keep the Cold War cold – are in short supply and little honoured.

The action is behind the scenes, with China, the United States and others competing to shape agendas. The regular diplomacy in the region remains bilateral: nations dealing with others one on one. This favours the strong. But another trend is about safety in numbers. That brings us back to middle players like Australia, India, Japan and Indonesia, building diplomatic ballast by strengthening their bonds with each other, typified by Modi and Abe on that bullet train.

Now a new diplomacy, called minilateralism, is gaining ground, where small groups of three or more countries form flexible coalitions based on shared interests, values, capability and willingness to get things done. The most controversial is the quadrilateral dialogue of the United States, Japan, India and Australia, which China sees as an embryonic alliance to counter its rise. But quietly and sometimes with more impact, a web of three-sided coalitions is arising: US–India–Japan; India–Japan–Australia; Australia–India–Indonesia; even a so-called Indo-Pacific axis of Australia, India and France, announced by French president Emmanuel Macron on Sydney Harbour in early 2018.

Critical questions remain. Can effective regional institutions take shape, some patchwork of diplomatic arrangements in which nations make genuine commitments to support peace and stability? Will new partners stand by each other if one finds itself in confrontation with China? And how much difference can middle powers really make when vital interests are at stake?

Narratives

The answer is partly about perception, for there is another level of contestation abroad – a struggle to shape perceptions, and therefore reality. Between Beijing and Washington, the many players in the middle are watching each other's responses to Chinese strength and assertiveness. The Indo-Pacific power competition includes efforts to shape attitudes and narratives among populations and decision-makers: a classic way to win without fighting, straight from the *Art of War* playbook of ancient Chinese strategist Sun Tzu. Not for nothing is a pilot Chinese think tank promoting the Belt and Road called the National Institute for Global Strategy. There is now a perpetual fight around perceptions and propaganda, a battle of the narratives. Warnings of 'political warfare' are sounded.[33] The reinterpretation of law or 'lawfare' plays its part. So does the reinvention of history. Just as the world is now fixated on the dangers of 'fake news', there are subtler risks from 'fake olds' – history fabricated to privilege one nation's interests over others'.

China is combining the 'soft power' of persuasion and attraction with the 'sharp power' of internal political interference, to neutralise opposition and reconfigure the Indo-Pacific game board, from Australia to Sri Lanka, Pakistan to the Pacific island states.[34] The narrative battle is no longer all going China's way. But there are risks in how America and others respond. Too blunt a pushback can be self-defeating, as one American official discovered when she likened competition with China to a 'clash of civilisations' in disturbingly cultural, even racial, terms. The reality is more like a clash of political systems, where Washington needs to maintain a diverse set of friends, not alienate them.[35]

Other countries are joining the 'soft power' race, with some like Japan, the United States and Australia promoting their own versions of the Indo-Pacific as an alternative to the Belt and Road. Universities, think tanks and media organisations can no longer imagine themselves detached observers and interpreters. Along with digital technologies, they have rapidly become part of the story: both terrain and instruments of strategic competition. Concerns about foreign interference, propaganda and espionage have resurfaced in new forms, and no longer sound like warmed-up Cold War paranoia. In recent years, a reality check on Chinese Communist Party influence in Australia, combined with revelations of Russian and Chinese activity in the United States, has set the tone for the wider global and regional debate. Future strategic competition in the Indo-Pacific will not be confined to seas and contested international boundaries, but will play out also on the home front. The great game will no longer be just between strategic elites. The opinions and sentiments of entire populations will be in play. People's very perceptions are being weaponised. Such tensions could threaten cohesion in many countries, even relatively small and managed societies like Singapore.[36] Multicultural societies and democracies will be especially vulnerable.

Securing the future: war and peace, survival and strategy

So what do the past and present tell us about the risks and opportunities ahead? The final section of the book focuses on plausible futures for the Indo-Pacific, and the choices nations can make to shape them, revolving around the question of how to manage coercion without it ending in conflict or capitulation. Relations between nations are a continuum from cooperation at one end, through degrees of coexistence, competition and confrontation, all the way to conflict at the other end, including outright war. Presently the Indo-Pacific dynamic is somewhere at the competition point on the spectrum, with rising risks of confrontation or conflict. The membrane between peace and war is not just porous, it is dissolving: strong nations are now in constant competition, and mistakes could have momentous consequences.

China and the United States have entered a state of comprehensive struggle, amounting to full-spectrum rivalry. The Pentagon publicly labelled China a strategic competitor, and a series of blunt speeches in 2018 and 2019 by US vice president Mike Pence confirmed that this assessment has permeated America's China policy. The situation could deteriorate further still, whether through miscalculation or confrontation. A small bit of good news is that, unlike Europe in 1939, no country wants war; all sides recognise it would be ruinous. But this alone is far from rendering war impossible.

There have long been four well-known flashpoints in East Asia: Taiwan, the South China Sea, the East China Sea and the Korean Peninsula.[37] But beyond these, there are now signs that conflict is increasingly conceivable in the wider Indo-Pacific. America is only one of China's potential adversaries: China–India and China–Japan relations will remain fraught and fragile. The flashpoints may not even be geographic, but could involve interventions in the information realm, such as cyber intrusions or disputes over freedom of expression. A conflict that begins in East Asia could escalate across the region, for instance through distant naval blockades, cyber attacks, economic sabotage, the disabling of nations' critical infrastructure and the pre-emptive destruction of communications networks, including in space. Future US–China crises could play out in the Indian Ocean and the South Pacific. Even some of Washington's more resolute national security voices warn about 'horizontal escalation' – widening the conflict to new places when limiting it to a confined location could be a losing strategy.[38] The argument is that horizontal escalation such as oil blockades could end up gravely harming both sides and the rest of the world. But that does not mean it won't happen. And if the regional situation takes on the character of a new cold war, then proxy wars become a possibility, for instance stronger states using weaker states as dispensable combatants or terrain for limited conflict.

The outcome of even a limited conflict in the Indo-Pacific is impossible to predict. Reasons include new technologies, economic connectedness, mutual vulnerability and random factors of decision and surprise. Ultimately, the catastrophic risks from nuclear weapons – right up to their actual use – cannot be discounted. But even if conflict ceased at a lower threshold, damage could be severe, including to the stability of states and the foundations of global prosperity and order. Fortunately, no state in the Indo-Pacific seeks war, and most tensions can be managed by other means. But fully fledged cooperation and conflict resolution are impossible under conditions of mistrust.

What can be done? It is difficult to imagine the region's powers accepting new diplomatic institutions and treaties or a meaningful role for the

United Nations in addressing their differences. Coexistence is the most reasonable expectation, and is an essential starting point for any loftier ambitions of institution-building and cooperation. But it may take an international near-death experience – the 21st-century Indo-Pacific equivalent of the Cuban missile crisis – to compel governments to get serious about the risk-reduction measures needed to keep the peace. Such a crisis could finally spook nations into making proper use of the existing but under-appreciated 'architecture' of rules and communication channels. Such crisis-management hotlines, along with arms control agreements and diplomatic summits, were used better in the Cold War because the gravity of the stakes was so clear. Scope also remains for today's Indo-Pacific governments to get much more serious about leveraging cooperation against common threats – like climate change, natural disasters, resource depletion, transnational crime, piracy and terrorism. This in turn could improve coordination and transparency in managing strategic mistrust.

But where to begin? And in a complex diplomatic impasse, how is it possible to choreograph compromise? Most governments now understand that they are struggling with a new regional security landscape – the Indo-Pacific – but lack a plan joining up the parts of the puzzle: geoeconomics, security, diplomacy and the domestic stage. The race is on for each nation to craft a comprehensive strategy. Progress is uneven. China's Belt and Road is the most advanced. Japan and the United States have their versions of a 'Free and Open Indo-Pacific'. India, Australia and Indonesia are working on their own pragmatic Indo-Pacific blueprints. Australia's 2017 foreign policy white paper, in particular, sketches the contours of a strategy for the emerging era, proposing a whole-of-nation response to regional uncertainty.[39] This is much easier said than done.

In this multipolar age, nations will not succeed in securing their interests if they pursue strategies in isolation. This includes the strongest powers, the United States and China. The region is too vast and complex for any country to protect its interests alone. There will be a premium on partnerships. An understanding of the special nature of the Indo-Pacific region – including its scale and diversity – helps identify the elements of a strategy for navigating likely decades of friction. These comprise a calibrated mix of diplomacy, development and deterrence, including contingency planning.

There is a need for sustained activism and solidarity among middle players like Australia, India, Japan, Indonesia and their partners in Southeast Asia and Europe, to show the way for an American strategy that is competitive but not confrontational, confident but not complacent. In dealing with Chinese power, old notions of 'accommodation' and 'containment' need to be discarded in favour of 'incorporation' or 'conditional engagement'. This would be about involving China as a legitimate great power based on mutual adjustment and mutual respect. There is nothing intrinsic about the Indo-Pacific idea that it should exclude China or, to use an outdated and misused Cold War term, 'contain' it. China is by definition a major player in such a region, and recognising this means acknowledging, for instance, its right to play a security role in the Indian Ocean. India has no more right to exclude China from the Indian Ocean than China has to shut out the United States from the western Pacific.

It is true that the Indo-Pacific idea dilutes and absorbs Chinese influence. That is much of the point. Yet this is not about shutting China out of its own extended region, but rather incorporating it in one that is large and multipolar. Others need to adjust to China and China needs to adjust to them, especially Asia's large middle players. Of course China has a major and rightful place, a status that is respected and prominent – just not dominant. A 'sphere of influence' approach, in which China is allowed to control East Asia while India in turn is allowed to dominate the Indian Ocean, will simply not work: China's seaborne oil dependence, and the security, economic and diaspora footprint of its Belt and Road, make it too late for that.[40] At the same time, given China's great strategic weight and temptations towards hegemony, the Indo-Pacific idea is empowering for other countries, encouraging them to build new and defensive partnerships across outdated geographic boundaries.

But such moderation of Chinese power will likely fail if middle powers do not seek solidarity but instead are cowed by the observation that there is little each can do to influence China on its own. Much will depend on how nations choose to use the current window of pan-regional awareness. For example, strategic solidarity and alliances have traditionally applied only to situations of armed conflict. But what if Indo-Pacific principles such as respect for rules and sovereignty began to translate into new forms of collective and non-military resistance to maritime bullying or economic coercion? Or if new region-wide standards for infrastructure were to limit the misuse of such investments for hostile purposes? Whatever happens, nations need to build their resilience and harness all elements of their power for a long phase of contestation. This requires not only attention to defence and diplomacy, but also bridging policy divides between economics and security. Governments will have to become more direct with civil society and business interests about what is at stake: the fact that no nation can hide from the world, that international tensions cannot be wished away and will touch everyday life.

A course can be charted between naivety and fatalism. There is no guarantee this will work. Still, the very nature of the Indo-Pacific – its connected vastness, its multipolarity as a game with many players – is part of the answer. This is a region too big and diverse for hegemony. It is made for multipolarity and creative new partnerships across collapsed boundaries. Its distances and riches and scattered strategic territories may tempt imperial overstretch – but correct it too.

Bridging and balancing, land and sea

Indo-Pacific ideas have their share of sceptics, not to mention outright critics.[41] The very speed with which Indo-Pacific thinking has arisen fuels doubts about its impact and staying power. After all, the countries that champion the term do not seem to agree precisely on what it means. America and Japan talk about 'free and open', with Indonesia and India emphasising inclusiveness and connectivity, and Australia somewhere in between. This may be a sign of deeper differences over how to respond to Chinese power and US–China tensions. For Americans, the Indo-Pacific is a signal that they are not leaving Asia and – even in spite of Trump – still have many friends there. For others it is a reminder that this region includes many nations, representing billions of people who are neither Chinese nor American, and that their views matter too.

Yet there is an underlying solidarity. All countries advocating the Indo-Pacific are using it to signpost what they want: economic connectivity that does not translate interdependence into one country's exploitation; rules and respect for sovereignty; the avoidance of force or coercion in resolving international differences. The question is whether this solidarity will translate into collective action and mutual protection if confrontation comes.

The Indo-Pacific is a work in progress. In keeping with the spirit of diplomacy, it makes a virtue of ambiguity: serving both as an objective description of geopolitical circumstances and the basis for a strategy. That is but one of its useful dualities, and Asian statecraft has long been comfortable with duality – a unity composed of differences, like the *Yin* and the *Yang* of Chinese philosophy. Indeed, the Indo-Pacific encompasses multiple dualities, the reconciliation of contrasting aspects within one idea. It is both inclusive and exclusive: it is about incorporating Chinese interests into a regional order where the rights of others are respected; but it is also about counterbalancing Chinese power when those rights are not. It is both economic and strategic: it has economic origins but profoundly strategic consequences.

The Indo-Pacific's boundaries are fluid – it is, after all, a maritime place – and this helps explain why various countries define it differently (and why that is no great problem). For example, is coastal east Africa part of the Indo-Pacific or not? Perhaps the answer depends on how the interests of key Indo-Pacific powers are engaged in African affairs. But the region's core is clear: the sea lanes of maritime Southeast Asia. As for the periphery, it is defined by connections, not borders. This is consonant with the ancient Asian concept of the *mandala*, originating from Hindu cosmology, which with many variations defined the universe according to circles and a central point. This informed ancient statecraft in India and Southeast Asia: polities were defined by their centre, not their boundaries.[42] In the *mandala* model, as opposed to the traditional 'middle kingdom' worldview of China, centrality does not automatically bestow superiority.[43] Rather, the model recognises a world of many places, many islands, each with their own qualities. In modern parlance, this equates to multipolarity, equal sovereignty and mutual respect – many belts and many roads.

This region is about Asia but also more than Asia. It includes and coexists with the old Asia-Pacific, even as it replaces it. And while the Indo-Pacific is a place, it is also an expression of global connectivity: the main highway for commerce and energy between Asia, Africa, Europe, Oceania and the Americas. It is the most globally connected of regions, literally the global region, a duality not a contradiction. Thus, in practical terms, not all the Indo-Pacific's chief stakeholders are necessarily resident or fully resident powers. And what happens there – including in the contested South China Sea – is all the world's business.

*

An overland rail journey may seem an odd way to begin a sea story, an account of a world moulded by connectivity and conflict in the maritime domain. But the Indo-Pacific idea is not just about the waterways. True, it reflects the dominance of the sea over the land. In economics, consider oil tankers and the absurdly low cost of shipping, which transports 90 per cent of everything.[44] In environment, consider fisheries, tsunamis and climate change, but also the vast potential for extraction of undersea resources; in security, think warships, nuclear-armed submarines and underwater drones. Sea power has the advantage in a competitive world: it has been decisive in major wars, helped empires rule the waves and has underpinned a rules-based order in more cooperative times. Little wonder that China and India – long deemed continental powers – have turned to the sea.

Yet a vital duality about the Indo-Pacific is that power and economics at sea are most effective when and where they connect with the land. This is illustrated by China's own Belt and Road – a mix of sea and land infrastructure. Ports are key but most useful when road and rail bind them closer to industry, to resources and to China itself: whether geographically or through political influence. Hence China's highway and railway ambitions through

Pakistan, or the China–Japan rivalry to build high-speed rail in Southeast Asia.[45] Japan, in turn, is helping modernise India's Raj-era railway system, with mass transit for urban populations and a *shinkansen* from Ahmedabad to Mumbai. The Indo-Pacific is a complement, not an alternative, to continental connectivity in Eurasia. Or, more accurately, Eurasia is the complement to the Indo-Pacific, given how the sea outweighs the land for range of power projection and cheapness of transportation.

Indeed, overland undertones help explain the first case of a country finding itself at home in a region defined as the Indo-Pacific. Australia has long combined the land and the sea in efforts to overcome its 'tyranny of distance' – both the scale of its territory (where even a defensive military deployment is an expedition) and its remoteness from allies and markets. The train connecting its east and west coast cities of Sydney and Perth is, naturally enough, named the *Indian Pacific*. For Australia, a multicultural democracy on a sovereign island-continent belonging neither entirely to Asia nor to what was once known as 'the West', the Indo-Pacific has a special quality. It defines Australia's place in the world. It is, quite literally, home. To comprehend this, we can take a leaf out of an old book.

Fittingly, it's a map.

PAST

CHAPTER 2

A SUBMERGED HISTORY OF ASIA

In 1845, Scottish soldier, surveyor and explorer Thomas Mitchell left Sydney on an expedition to find and map an overland route northwest across Australia. At the end of his epic journey, he proposed naming the north of the continent 'Australindia'. After all, a major reason for his mission was 'that a way should be opened to the shores of the Indian Ocean' – and thus the crucial sea lines of communication from northern Australia to Singapore, India and England. The colony of New South Wales had established a promising trade with British India, exporting cavalry remounts to the army of the East India Company. But the narrow Torres Strait between Australia and Papua New Guinea, where the Pacific and Indian oceans meet, made the voyage hazardous. More generally, the isolated and struggling colony wanted to find economic advantage in northern Australia's relative closeness to India, China and the 'Indian archipelago' or Indonesia – an imperative familiar to this day.

Pivoting the map

In his journal, Mitchell provided a creative twist to demonstrate the purpose of his journey. He pivoted the map. Little did he realise that his diagonally tilted map, in the 1848 publication of his journal, would foreshadow the Indo-Pacific shape of the Asia that matters in the 21st century.[1] It remains a refreshing and logical perspective. China, Japan, Southeast Asia and India are all equally conspicuous. Attention is focused on sea lanes to major populations and markets. It may not quite reach Hormuz or Honolulu, but it remains a telling depiction of the core Indo-Pacific. That first

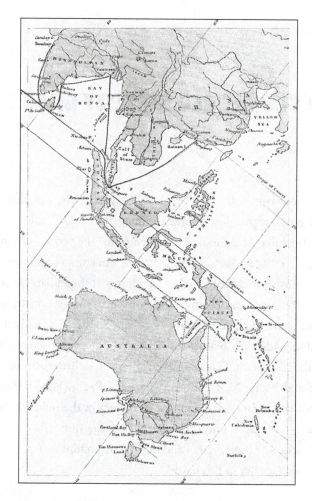

Thomas Mitchell's pivoted map, 1848

Australian map of the Indo-Pacific, and the overland odyssey that gave rise to it, was about an ambitious and pragmatic new society trying to get closer to its region; not trying to hide from it. Perhaps that helps explain why the Indo-Pacific concept has a special resonance for Australia, giving this unusual country – a democracy combining long Indigenous history, European political heritage and established multiculturalism – a home that is neither entirely Asia nor the West. Mitchell's map gives prominence to the coasts of what are now Western Australia and the Northern Territory, implying they are the continent's economic gateways (or security barriers) to the world. It's a contemporary message. A similar map today could usefully grace the office walls of resources companies in Perth, Tokyo or Shanghai, and of defence planners in Canberra – or indeed in Washington, Beijing or New Delhi.

Mitchell meets his modern match in Chinese cartographic researcher Hao Xiaoguang. The pivoted map has found fresh currency in today's Indo-Pacific, as captured in Hao's new Asia-focused world map authorised by the Chinese government (see inside back cover).[2] This powerfully reimagines the globe in a vertical frame. At a glance, it shows how today's China sees the world and illuminates Beijing's strategic ambitions – from economic connectivity to naval modernisation, from resource exploitation in Africa to a rapidly growing scientific footprint in Antarctica.

China and the Eurasian landmass are dominant, with Europe diminished from the distorted greatness of traditional Mercator projections. In a stunning visualisation of Chinese strategic wish-making, the western hemisphere is bisected and consigned to the edges. America is literally split and marginalised. Africa and even Antarctica receive much greater prominence. The projection shows Australia and Southeast Asia on the same angle Thomas Mitchell did in 1848. Most curiously of all, the map is centred not on China but on the Indian Ocean. Significantly, the map was released in 2013, the year that Xi Jinping gave speeches in Indonesia and Kazakhstan announcing what was to become his signature global strategy, the Belt and Road.[3] Thus the map reveals one of China's worst-kept secrets. Beijing's more audacious and overweening ambitions in the 21st century will play out not merely on China's maritime periphery of the western Pacific, but across the wider Indo-Pacific, of which the Indian Ocean is an integral, even central, part.

This follows a path charted by the rise and fall of nations and empires past. A telling of Indo-Pacific history readily shows that the Indian Ocean has long been much more than an empty space. When European adventurers arrived in 1498, the start of the long colonial Vasco da Gama epoch, it was already 'a densely interconnected world region'.[4] The Indian Ocean and the wider Indo-Pacific were the scene of a long pre-modern saga of cooperation, coexistence, competition, confrontation and conflict. It was a many-player game, a multipolarity that foreshadowed the struggle for this crucial region in the 21st century.

Within the complex cross-currents of Indo-Pacific history, patterns emerge. These carry lessons for the present and the future. Inter-civilisational contact by sea was an inevitable fact, and engaging with the wider region was more advantageous than hiding from it. Turning one's back on the oceans – and the opportunities and risks they delivered – was a mistake. The maritime highways were tempting vectors for would-be imperial powers. But the scale and multipolarity of the region they connected meant that hubris, overstretch and retreat were the sequence, time and again.

The narrative of maritime Asia and its contact with the world is also a submerged history of the Indo-Pacific. Of course, the Indo-Pacific aspects of that story – the connections across two oceans – are hardly the only element, or consistently the dominant one. Nonetheless, a voyage into history readily reveals that the idea of the Indo-Pacific has a long line of antecedents. It has been a far more enduring way of understanding the geography, geopolitics and geoeconomics of Asia than the artificial separation of East Asia and South Asia or the Asia-Pacific moment in the second half of the 20th century.

Deep history, broad horizons

Connections between the Indian and Pacific oceans run deep. Just ask the fish, as academic Tansen Sen reminds us.[5] The Indo-Pacific is an established term in disciplines ranging from marine biology to climatology, archaeology to zooarchaeology to biological anthropology. It has long been a useful concept for understanding the interactions between zones of the world, such as impacts on climate from ocean currents, the spectacular diversity of fish species where oceans meet, or the slow but unstoppable movement of early humanity across the globe.

Scholarly awareness is growing of the movement of people – and with them plants and animals – across the Indo-Pacific in prehistoric times. In 1941, Indian historian Kalidas Nag, who had done much to rediscover India's historic links with East Asia, identified the central role of 'the vast expanse of water extending from the Indian Ocean to the Pacific' in 'the earliest migrations of the world'. In his book *India and the Pacific World* he endorsed the characterisation of this region as 'the *Indo-Pacific* Domain'.[6] More recent researchers continue to identify seaborne migratory patterns linking culture, technology, genetics and language across indigenous populations – the 'Austronesian peoples' – in a vast area including Southeast Asia and Taiwan, extending west to Madagascar and the African coast and east to Hawaii and the islands of the South Pacific.[7] This was maritime Asia and more. Theories differ as to whether these travels had a central point of origin – one theory suggests Taiwan – or were 'a constantly communicating network transporting information and technology in many directions'.[8] And, while there is a growing recognition of the surprising degree of connectedness and contact across the prehistoric two-ocean region, much of the detail remains at phases of academic discovery or contention.[9] For instance, a theory of a unifying Indo-Pacific language or language group emerged in the 1970s but has since been widely challenged. The experience of Indigenous Australians – believed to have reached the continent in a very early phase of human migration out of Africa perhaps 65,000 years ago – is also distinct.

But what is increasingly clear is that more than 3000 years ago, a multitude of small communities of seafarers gradually transformed most of the Indo-Pacific region, from Southeast Asia to India to Africa, through countless courageous journeys, island-hopping and ocean-going in outrigger canoes. This helps explain much of the wide dispersal of domesticated crops and animals across Asia and Africa before recorded history, everything from bananas (possibly originating in Papua New Guinea) to chickens, pepper and mung beans (from India), millet (from China) and sandalwood (from Indonesia).

Then as now, obtaining, transporting and trading exotic goods over great distance was associated with luxury, status and power. There was a proto-economy of the Indo-Pacific long before any empire or nation disturbed these shared waters. As recounted in Bill Hayton's authoritative book on the South China Sea, the core of this early super-region was home to fishing and trading communities now labelled the Nusantao, who discovered its islands, navigated its waterways, recognised no state or boundary and belonged to no ethnic community recognisable today.[10] This casts a diffused light on the national claims of historical ownership underlying today's territorial disputes.

Subsequently, in recorded ancient history, the civilisations of Asia's varied subregions did not flourish in isolation. Economic, cultural and political interactions spanning all corners of maritime Asia go back millennia. Societies traded, negotiated, collaborated and sometimes clashed, oblivious to modern-day demarcations like South Asia, Southeast Asia, East Asia or even the totality of what we now call Asia. However unevenly, these patterns extended from the Mediterranean to China, via an ever-shifting mix of Arab, Persian, Indian, Malay, Chinese and European civilisations, ports and sailors. Continental contact and commerce mattered, but the sea mattered more; a pattern that has not changed.

Today's China has gone to great lengths to reinvent a historic narrative of commerce and cultural exchange, overland and maritime variants of a 2000-year-old 'silk road' between China and Europe. This reimagining of history – airbrushing anything at odds with a benign and enduring Chinese centrality – supports the economic and strategic agenda of the Beijing-centric Belt and Road. Of course, China was a major player in much early connectivity. But the persistent reality has been many belts, many roads, many centres.

Astrophysics offers a useful analogy for making sense of the way that powerful political centres of gravity compete and overlap. The barycentre is the centre of mass of two or more bodies that orbit each other. In an important article that reveals much about contemporary Chinese conceptions of geopolitics, scholar Zhang Wenmu has asserted that China is nothing less than 'the natural barycentre of Asia'.[11] This has an unfortunate similarity to some of the more unsettling geopolitical treatises from past eras of

European imperialism and fascism, implying a destiny of dominance by some kind of natural right. In fact, throughout history, the assertion that Asia is China-centric has been highly questionable. In all of the contending orbits of the pre-modern Indo-Pacific, if one place exerted more influence than others it was not China.

Instead, that central place belonged to India and its maritime environs, the northern littoral of the Indian Ocean. Of course, the India of times past – like China – was not a single or unified political entity matching the territory of the modern state of that name. But what is now India was unquestionably the core connective zone: 'literally central to the pre-colonial trading network' and 'on the way to everywhere'.[12] With its combination of resources, culture, power centres and strategic location, the coast of the Indian subcontinent attracted intense interest – traders, plunderers, explorers, pilgrims, proselytisers and emissaries alike – from all directions. Its own mariners and merchants, especially the ubiquitous Gujaratis, ranged from the straits of Hormuz to Malacca. Indian societies projected cultural influence too, as the grand Ozymandian ruins of Hindu realms across Southeast Asia silently attest. And, like ancient China with its famous strategist Sun Tzu, the antique Indian Mauryan empire left rich traditions of statecraft, purported to be devised by royal adviser Chanakya writing under the pen-name Kautilya. A millennium and a half before Machiavelli, Kautilya's treatise the *Arthashastra* urged an active foreign policy that would make the most of a multipolar setting, a pragmatic geopolitics of encircling alliances and the principle that the enemy of my enemy is my friend.[13] It holds clues to India's worldview and regional geopolitics today.

An Indian Ocean centre of gravity

From the vantage points of Rome, Greece, Egypt and Persia, India and its eponymous ocean were, unlike China, close enough to be a political and economic reality. In his *Histories* from the 5th century BCE, Herodotus records clear mutual awareness and a record of contact between the

Mediterranean world, the Indian subcontinent (identified as the most populous part of the world) and the 'Southern Sea' or Indian Ocean via Egypt and Persia.[14] Indians served in the army of Persian king of kings Xerxes I in his hubristic invasion of Greece, and India was the edge of the known world that Alexander of Macedon later sought to conquer in the other direction. But most contact across this 'Afroeurasian' network was about more peaceful pursuit of profit, knowledge or sanctuary.[15] As Indian historian K.M. Panikkar recounts, ancient Greek mariner Hippalus learned the secret of the monsoon route across the Indian Ocean from the Red Sea – the use of seasonal, highly predictable wind and currents for speed and navigation – and shared it with the Romans.[16] This was no discovery, but rather the transfer of knowledge long held by coastal Indian communities.[17] On those same winds, the Judeo-Christian world arrived in India in antiquity. The fall of Jerusalem to Rome in 70 CE sent exiled Jews in all directions, including to Cochin on the Malabar (Kerala) coast, although some traditional accounts put the first Jewish arrivals there centuries earlier still. Among some Indian and Sri Lankan Christian communities, lore has it that their faith arrived with the travels of Thomas the Apostle, said to have reached Kerala by sea a few decades after the crucifixion, and to have been martyred near modern-day Chennai. Whatever really happened, Christianity had a presence in India by the 6th century.

Ancient Indian civilisation projected as well as attracted. India is the one country to which China acknowledges a civilisational debt: an 'elder brother' providing 'gifts of singular and precious worth, which we can never forget'.[18] The spread of Buddhism from India in the first few centuries CE exerted a formative influence on cultures further east and north. Today's diplomats would call it soft power. Buddhist teachings travelled primarily overland, but also across the waters into and through Southeast Asia. There was already a cultural sea route from India to the Sinic world by the 5th century, when Chinese monk Faxian returned home from the Buddhist holy land by sea.[19] By the 8th century, Buddhism was also the faith for a stronghold of hard power at the heart of the Indo-Pacific, the Strait of Malacca connecting the two oceans. An early thalassocracy – a state reliant on sea power, of which the Indo-Pacific has known more than a few – was the Buddhist monarchy of Srivijaya. It embodied the Indian *mandala* concept of kingship, with core territory and leadership surrounded by a somewhat fluid periphery based on relationships of obligation and interest. This encompassed Sumatra, much of the Malay Peninsula, and at times parts of Java and the Bay of Bengal. Srivijaya engaged in diplomacy with imperial Chinese dynasties, warfare with India's Chola empire, and expeditions as far as Madagascar and Africa.

India's other major cultural export, Hinduism, initially reached Southeast Asia through seaborne commerce, but sometimes accompanied hard power too. For something like 1600 years, from the 3rd century BCE to the European medieval period, the Chola dynasty dominated south India. The Chola empire had diplomatic and economic relations with successive dynasties of its Chinese counterpart, which it would have perceived more as peer than superior. Moreover, it became a hub for extending sea power and cultural influence into the Indian Ocean and Southeast Asia, to parts of what are now Malaysia, Indonesia, Thailand, the Maldives and Sri Lanka. Hinduism became the adopted religion of civilisations across Southeast Asia, from Angkor in Cambodia and Champa in Vietnam to many centres across the Indonesian archipelago, culminating in the Javanese kingdom of Majapahit, which endured until the 1500s.

From the late 7th century, the trade winds of the monsoon also brought Islam eastwards, adding another major element to the Indo-Pacific cultural churn. Of course, Islam also arrived overland, with successive Muslim polities on the Indian subcontinent, from the Delhi sultanate in 1206 to the Mughal empire in the 1500s. Further east, Islam initially grew as a religion of seagoing traders. By the 1300s, some local political leaders were also adopting the Muslim faith. A sense of the maritime connections of the Muslim world across the Indian Ocean can be gleaned from the life of Ibn Battuta, a 14th-century Moroccan scholar whose adventures rival those of Marco Polo. He reached India overland, then recounted journeys to and from China by sea, with sojourns in Sri Lanka, Sumatra, Malacca and possibly Luzon. Scholarship is divided on whether he actually reached China, but his claims of hospitality from a network of Muslim rulers across much of maritime Asia are plausible.

In any case, by around 1400, Muslim power was a reality in the Malacca Strait, then as now a critical geoeconomic artery. This was when the sultanate of Malacca arose, based on the Malay Peninsula and dominating the space once held by Srivijaya. The sultanate was locally formidable – despite, or because of, its loose tributary relations with China's Ming dynasty – until its downfall at the hands of ruthless Portuguese adventurers (reportedly aided by pragmatic Chinese merchants) in 1511. As much as greed, commerce and discovery, a crusading zeal to defeat Islam was a major motivation for that opening phase of European colonialism. But Islam endured: the Malacca sultanate set the scene for other Muslim-dominated powers in maritime Southeast Asia, including the states that were to become modern Malaysia, Indonesia and Brunei.

For their part, the Malay and other peoples of maritime Southeast Asia were no mere passive recipients of imported culture. Skilled and adventurous mariners, they took advantage of their place at the fulcrum of the early Indo-Pacific system.[20] For centuries, Srivijaya and various port cities profitably mediated the commerce between the Chinese Pacific rim to their north and the Indian Ocean highway to their west. The privilege of location allowed them to derive great wealth and influence from transhipment: transferring cargoes originating from other places to their own vessels for part or even all of the journey. It's an advantage Singapore still tries to preserve. Before Srivijaya, historians have pointed to another transhipment power centre on the Mekong Delta, known by the Chinese as Funan. Other city states were scattered across the Indonesian archipelago. Their deference was provisional: tributary relations with China waxed and waned from dynasty to dynasty.[21]

China's first forays

All this provides a context for the important but surprisingly limited place of the Chinese empires in the old Indo-Pacific. Until the Song dynasty (960–1279), China chose to have little direct contact with the maritime world to its south, let alone beyond into the Indian Ocean, instead allowing its growing seaborne trade to be transhipped by the Srivijayans and earlier entrepreneurs. There is simply no record of Chinese shipping in the Indian Ocean before the 11th century. It seems China's first substantial turn to the sea was driven by necessity, when worsening land wars in the north and northwest shut down traditional overland trade routes, and pushed the population and capital south and to the coast. China cut out the middleman, hastening the decay of Srivijaya. It began direct trade with the merchants from the Arab world and India, with their ships allowed into its ports and its own growing merchant navy becoming prominent in Indian Ocean waters.[22] The Yuan (Mongol) dynasty that subsequently conquered China by land nonetheless valued the new maritime links, not least because they added a sea route to reach the Il-khanate, another and largely independent Mongol empire based in Persia. Marco Polo is remembered as an early European traveller to China by land, but in the late 13th century he recounts making the homeward journey by sea with a Chinese fleet, escorting the Mongol princess Kököchin to Persia, where she was being sent by the Yuan emperor Khubilai Khan to marry the ruler, the Il-khan, and thus renew familial bonds between the empires. The saga is a testament to the fragility of those early Chinese links with the world. The sea was chosen because the land route was so unsafe. Yet the voyage itself was slow and dangerous: it took two years, and many passengers – though thankfully not the resilient princess – perished.[23]

History may not repeat, but it rings with echo and premonition. Today we wonder at the scale and reach of China's economic and military ambitions: the Belt and Road of infrastructure and commerce across Asia, and an awe-inducing navy to match. It is easy to imagine this as the enduring reality. It is thus doubly worth recalling that, as tends awkwardly to happen with empires, the high point of that first Chinese bid to dominate the

Indo-Pacific came soon before that ambition vanished.

The animating spirit of today's official myth-making about Chinese sea-borne connectivity, strength and goodwill is Zheng He, the great admiral of the Ming dynasty. His seven voyages into the Indian Ocean between 1405 and 1433, with a gargantuan armada of ships and soldiers, were like nothing seen before or since. The Yuan dynasty had sent envoys to coastal Indian states to request submission in the late 13th century. But this amounted to mere invitations, not compulsion, to join the tributary system, and the responses were unsurprisingly uneven. The first Ming ruler, Zhu Yuan-zhang (known as the Hongwu or 'martial surge' emperor), was more demanding. He secured one-off tributes from the Indian states of Coro-mandel and Chola around 1371.[24] But the Zheng He voyages were something else – backing up the call for tribute with a show of force.

Zheng He remains an intriguing figure, the original hybrid of leader, warrior, adventurer, explorer and diplomat, with the resources of an empire at his call. He had the intrepidness of the outsider: a Muslim eunuch, a sur-vivor and servitor whose skill and reliability made him indispensable to a new leader, the third Ming ruler, the Yongle or 'perpetual happiness' emperor Zhu Di. This leader was both ambitious and desperate: he had come to power through force, and was at pains to affirm the legitimacy of his mandate. This may help explain the otherwise bizarre extravagance and overkill of Zheng He's naval expeditions: hundreds of ships, including nine-masted leviathans, carrying many thousands of soldiers (perhaps 30,000 in the 1410–11 voyage alone). It was an unusual way to come in peace.

Official Chinese lore today describes the purpose of those journeys as peace and diplomacy, 'win-win' and shared prosperity. The ships were called 'treasure ships', presumably more to reflect the gifts they carried from China to lesser places than the tributes they extracted. State propaganda and pseudohistory, typified by the popular writings of British author Gavin Menzies, have merged into claims repeated uncritically at the highest levels of government, such as the speech by President Xi Jinping to an interna-tional forum in 2017:

In the early 15th century, Zheng He, the famous Chinese navigator in the Ming Dynasty, made seven voyages to the Western Seas, a feat which still is remembered today. These pioneers won their place in history not as conquerors with warships, guns or swords. Rather, they are remembered as friendly emissaries leading camel caravans and sailing treasure-loaded ships. Generation after generation, the silk route's travellers have built a bridge for peace and East–West cooperation.[25]

In 2003, then Chinese president Hu Jintao told the Australian Parliament that Zheng He's fleet had even reached Australian shores – a claim without serious historical evidence – and identified this as the start of a long history of harmony in Australia–China ties.[26]

It is true the so-called 'treasure ships', though heavily armed, did not establish permanent colonies. But the record includes a quantum of coercion and conflict when local rulers failed to pay due respect. There's even a body count: thousands killed in what was left of Srivijaya; more casualties still in assaults to bring about regime change or obeisance in Java, Sumatra and Sri Lanka, where royal hostages were seized.[27] The historical account is uncomfortably at odds with the narrative of Zheng He proclaimed in Xi Jinping's 2013 Jakarta speech announcing the maritime part of China's new Belt and Road strategy: 'His visits left nice stories of friendly exchanges between the Chinese and Indonesian peoples, many of which are still widely told today.'[28]

What is recorded is that Zheng issued warnings that failure to submit would prompt extreme measures along the lines of the recent full-scale subjugation of Annam (Vietnam). Above all, these voyages seem to have been aimed at intimidating into submission populations across most of the known maritime world, thus boosting in the eyes of Chinese people 'the legitimacy and prestige of a ruler who had come to power via usurpation'.[29] In the 21st century, China's new Indo-Pacific strategy also seems to involve compelling the awe of foreigners to bolster the authority of the regime, and in particular the leader Xi Jinping, who has authored China's second great turn to the sea.

And the response? It is easy to imagine the 1420 equivalent of a modern international relations scholar telling the peoples of the Indo-Pacific that their only sane option was to tremble and obey the manifest strategic weight of the new hegemon. Yet China's seaborne dominance collapsed as dramatically as it had arisen.

The Yongle emperor died suddenly from illness in 1424, while at war in the Gobi Desert, and his successor, Zhu Gaochi of the 'vastly bright' or Hongxi era, immediately ceased preparations for Zheng He's next voyage. His rule was brief, and a year later the subsequent Ming emperor, Zhu Zhanji, permitted one last nautical foray in the years leading up to the eunuch admiral's death around 1433. And that was that. The new Xuande era meant 'proclamation of virtue', in which far-sea adventures were now deemed lacking. Within years, the building of ocean-going ships ceased; within decades the great shipyards were no more; and by the early 1500s, sailing afar was essentially criminalised.

It is hard to overstate the momentous impact of this retreat in Chinese imperial policy, which left the Indo-Pacific open for exploitation by much smaller European forces. Assessments differ as to the precise reason for this epochal policy shift, but tensions at home in China hold the key. These are said to have included protracted land conflicts in frontier regions, internal power rivalries, economic crisis, the need to fund domestic infrastructure, and the sheer cost of the armada – the lumber for all that shipbuilding may even help explain deforestation in China's southeast.[30] Apart from some resurgence of influence in the South China Sea in the 1600s, the notion of China as a sea power in the wider Indo-Pacific took six centuries to resurface.

Chinese culture and policy turned inwards, and new emperors – and new dynasties – no longer saw merit in contact with distant foreigners. For their part, European adventurers, beginning with Portugal's Vasco da Gama in 1498, soon saw merit and advantage aplenty.

Western winds: the colonial Indo-Pacific

The story of European imperialism in Asia has been told from many angles. In time, it was a catalyst of modernity, with all its mixed blessings. But this was no gift from West to East. The benefits were largely side effects of greed, brutality and cultural chauvinism.[31] Colonialism proceeded unevenly, in phases spread over several centuries, with combinations of commerce, conquest and ideological zeal differing from place to place, empire to empire.

A few years ago it would have seemed offensive to suggest that China's 21st-century ambitions abroad – the Belt and Road strategy – resembled elements of the colonial story. After all, China was prominent among the Asian civilisations to experience long humiliation and oppression from Western imperial powers. Surely it would not inflict the same on other nations? In a memorable speech to the United Nations General Assembly in 1974, the then Chinese delegation head, Deng Xiaoping, was so confident this would never happen, he urged that if China should ever turn into a superpower or 'play the tyrant', then the people of the world should identify this as imperialism, 'expose it, oppose it and work together with the Chinese people to overthrow it'.[32]

But it is increasingly common to point to European colonial parallels in Beijing's objectives and behaviour beyond its borders. Compellingly, the criticism of the Belt and Road as a new imperialism is coming from the former colonised – such as India and Malaysia – and not just from Western countries conflicted about their own past. The claimed parallels range from predatory use of seeming economic largesse to lack of respect for smaller powers and local cultures; from grand shows of political influence (with Xi's 2017 Belt and Road conference likened to Britain's 1911 imperial 'Durbar' in India) through to distant naval deployments and bases in strategic locations.[33] Chinese decision-makers themselves seem comfortable emulating some iconic acts of colonialism, such as the choice of a ninety-nine-year lease (modelled on Germany's imperial foothold in Qingdao and Britain's in Hong Kong) for control of ports as far afield as Hambantota in Sri Lanka and Darwin in Australia.

Key questions for the years ahead include whether China is actively pursuing the 21st-century equivalent of empire, or whether it is acquiring one inadvertently through a combination of ideology, sheer economic scale and dynamics it cannot entirely control. Is China's international footprint becoming an accelerated version of Western imperialism? How long can China restrain itself from deploying or using force when its interests and nationals encounter trouble? Are overstretch and decline inevitable – and if so, what disruptions will they bring? It is worth remembering that most of China's history is as an empire, albeit one that annexed its possessions by land rather than across the sea. The fact that the old fortified boundary that is the Great Wall of China is in the middle of the country today is immovable proof of just how much the borders have expanded.[34] It is reasonable to imagine that today's Chinese strategic analysts study empires past in part to identify how not to get their new one wrong.

A large part of the initial imperative of European colonialism and empire was commercial, not political – greed ahead of power. Two of the most influential entities were not strictly governments but companies, or more accurately what today could be seen as public-private partnerships, the British East India Company and its Dutch counterpart.[35] But, in the words of the first Asian historian of colonialism, K.M. Panikkar, 'exploitation was found to be more profitable than commerce'.[36] The degree of inadvertence was of course overstated by apologists for empire, captured in the classic line of 19th-century British historian John Robert Seeley that Britain had acquired or conquered much of the world 'in a fit of absence of mind'. Nonetheless, for the British, Dutch and French in particular, the typical pattern involved business first, colonialism later. Governments were sometimes reluctant to lift the responsibilities of governance and security from the private sector, as occurred in India after the gross misrule of the East India Company helped spark the 1857 uprising. But once they stepped in, as the India instance shows, imperial states took control in brutal earnest, and were loath to let go again, even at the risk of the overstretch that in time would doom those empires.

In its own violent way, Portuguese colonialism was more transparent from the start, with an openly military, religious and state-driven agenda.[37] This was nowhere more apparent than in one of the key turning points of history, the capture of the vital strategic port city of Malacca by the Portuguese general Afonso de Albuquerque in 1511. The impact of that fateful battle was manifold. Portugal seized the precious spice trade from its European rivals, notably Venice. The influence of Muslim powers was (however temporarily) weakened. And from one pivotal place – which it now quickly fortified – Portugal not only cemented its dominance of the Indian Ocean, but also won control of seaborne trade into China and the Pacific. With the conquest of Malacca, writes Panikkar, 'Albuquerque completed the structure of European maritime empire in Asia'.[38] If there was a pre-modern moment where the Indo-Pacific responded like a strategic system – with disruptions in one place affecting the interests of powers far and wide – this was it.

As remains the case in Indo-Pacific strategic competition, location carries consequence. The sultan's capital was at modern-day Melaka, on the southwestern Malayan Peninsula, overlooking the strait before it widens into the Bay of Bengal. The logic has been the same since the Chola–Srivijaya war more than a millennium ago: control of this maritime chokepoint would bring vast geoeconomic and security advantage. Thus Zheng He asserted China's authority here in the 1400s; the Dutch (with local Muslim ally the Sultan of Johore) in turn wrested Malacca from the Portuguese in 1641; and the British went one better in 1819 and established a new base on an island at the strait's eastern end, which was to grow into Singapore – in turn a critical target of imperial Japan's bid for dominance in the Second World War.

The 1511 fall of Malacca also dispelled any illusions about how colonialism would work when submission was not forthcoming. Where resistance was met and circumstances sufficiently favoured the Europeans, markets were opened through warfare, coercion and occupation. In 21st-century parlance, states deployed armed force to advance and protect the interests of their private-sector actors. The flag followed trade, and stayed. Most often this state-sponsored aggression was aimed at subduing Asian power – from the 16th-century Portuguese onslaught in India and Southeast Asia to Britain's coldly cynical Opium War along with its and other powers' humiliating 'gunboat diplomacy' against China in the 1800s.

This was not, however, a simple story about European strategic weight, technology, tactics or guile always winning the day. New research underscores the many-player complexity of the colonial Indo-Pacific. The colonial powers, often with inferior numbers or little military advantage, sometimes relied on local alliances.[39] Asian powers had agency and motive too, in working with the newcomers to weaken regional rivals. European states were not averse to working with Asian partners as they waged violent trade war on each other to gain the economic high ground in Asian waters: Spain against Portugal, the Netherlands usurping Spain, the British supplanting the Dutch and constraining the French. Yet though the Western powers were often pitted against one another, the major Asian civilisations were even more grievously divided. London's policy of divide and rule leveraged India's multitude of local rulers, whose differing interests and allegiances helped ensure the 1857 'first war of independence' only solidified the British Raj. Meanwhile, 19th-century China was devastated by the Taiping Rebellion, in which massive uprisings against the Manchu Qing dynasty were suppressed by Chinese imperial forces, sometimes employing European officers. This was a fourteen-year civil war that dwarfed America's, leaving tens of millions dead and what remained of a Chinese empire severely weakened.

Europeans did not invent the idea of an integrated region spanning the Indian and Pacific oceans. They encountered a web of maritime societies already connected, communicating and conscious of their own large horizons. And in some ways the colonial experience blocked, distorted or unravelled these links, severing the unity of the Indian Ocean trading system.[40] Colonies became artificially connected to other parts of the same global empires and estranged from their Asian neighbours.[41] In the words of India's first prime minister, Jawaharlal Nehru, in calling for Asian unity in 1947, 'One of the notable consequences of the European domination of Asia has been the isolation of the countries of Asia from one another.'[42]

But the forces of colonialism and empire also accelerated contact across distance, connecting the old Indo-Pacific region to an emerging global system. The cold economic logic of colonialism was not confined to extracting value from some particular territory abroad and then transferring it back to

Europe. The Portuguese and others soon after – Spanish then Dutch then British and French – multiplied their wealth and influence by entangling Indo-Pacific Asia in global webs of commerce and competition. Portugal had sought the sea route to the Indian Ocean to thwart European rivals – by cornering the all-precious spice trade – and outflank the Muslim world. But soon, as multiple European powers joined the geoeconomic fray in the 16th and 17th centuries, the Indian Ocean was of value mostly as part of a wider mercantilist maritime system, connecting the spices of the East Indies, the pepper and textiles of India, porcelain, silks and tea from China, and silver bullion from the Americas.[43] Later came other webs of colonial commerce, including the infamous British-directed trade to China of opium grown in India.

Along with all its oppression and injustice, the colonial system also left behind many of the characteristics and contours of contemporary Asia. Many of the region's national identities and borders – including their unresolved disputes – are a product not of pre-colonial Asian dynamics but of the boundaries of convenience drawn by colonial powers. The colonial-era efforts of Asian peoples laid the material foundations of Asia's place in the world trading system today, re-engineering local economies for export.[44] Many aspects of the region's economic and transport infrastructure – now often in desperate need of renewal – have colonial origins, as do most national systems of law and governance. Concepts of diplomacy and international law that now usefully respect the equal rights of small nations have their origins in European historical practice. Colonial contact introduced new routes of trade and migration, and even the signature ingredients of some Asian cuisines, such as chilli peppers (from South America). Cultural contact between Asian societies did not die during the colonial era; in fact Tansen Sen notes that connections between Indians and Chinese actually grew, with 'more intensive circulation of knowledge, goods and people'.[45] Along with oppression, colonial powers unavoidably fostered and transferred new ideas like liberalism, democracy, socialism, nationalism, scientific rationality and industrial modernisation. These influenced the pan-Asian liberation movements that ended Western dominance in the

20th century. So did the consciousness of a shared Asian identity, which arose largely in response to Western colonialism.[46] The empires could not help but further their own collapse.

Connected by cartography

The activities of European mercantilist trading companies, explorers, diplomats, missionaries and military expeditions were not confined to narrow 20th-century conceptions of Asia. Throughout colonial times, with extraordinary consistency from the 1500s to the early 1900s, European maps entitled 'Asia' encompassed an Indo-Pacific arc from the Indian Ocean rim, through Southeast Asia to China, Korea and Japan.

An integrated map of Asia was not solely a Western invention, of course. The Korean *Kangnido* map of the known world, for instance, dated to 1402, rendered a broadly accurate picture of a coherent region comprising two oceans and the Eurasian continent. It is informed by, but less China-centric than, the 1398 *Da Ming Hunyi Tu* map of the Ming empire and its neighbourhood. Both would have been informed by exchanges of geographic lore across Eurasia involving accumulated Chinese, Mongol, Muslim and European knowledge. These exchanges would also have influenced late-medieval European conceptions of the world, such as the stunning c. 1450 *Mappa Mundi* of Italian monk Fra Mauro, which puts south on top and is dominated by Asia, Africa and the Indian Ocean.

The colonial-era European maps, however, were distinct in several ways. Theirs was a maritime emphasis, with coastlines and ports typically receiving more detail and precision. Linked to this was a premium on cartographic accuracy, ahead of symbolic and aesthetic value: map-making aided and was aided by navigation and the advances in related technologies from the 16th century on. A breakthrough came with the great cartographer Abraham Ortelius of Antwerp. In 1570 he created the world's first modern atlas, the *Theatrum Orbis Terrarum*. A copy was brought to China by the Italian Jesuit Matteo Ricci in the late 1500s, as a precious gift for the Wanli emperor Zhu Yijun of the late Ming dynasty.[47] Its contents heavily influenced early Chinese cartography, including world maps produced for the emperor by Ricci himself.[48]

One of the most telling Ortelius maps, *Indiae Orientalis Insularumque Adiacientium Typus*, is centred on the islands of Southeast Asia (see inside front cover). This is strikingly modern and Indo-Pacific in its vision of a connected maritime space from the Persian Gulf to the coast of California. Less modern are its decorations with mermaids and sea monsters – but these vividly reinforce the overwhelmingly maritime character of the region. Ortelius presented a two-ocean visit, setting the trend for centuries of cartographic imagining. In the 17th century, French cartographer Alain Manesson Mallet depicted what he called *Asie Moderne*. Encompassing an oceanic arc including India, Southeast Asia, China and Japan, it is modern Asia indeed. Moving into the 1700s, German-British cartographer Herman Moll likewise produced influential maps and atlases of a whole Asia centred on India and the 'Indian Sea'.

Maps helped frame new concepts of place. Originally Asia had referred to anywhere east of ancient Greece. The maritime Asia of colonialism was also known as the East Indies, and by the mid-19th century more specific terms were arising to describe the parts of this vast region, such as the Indian Archipelago (what we now call Southeast Asia) and Eastern Asia. Then in 1850 a Singapore-based British lawyer and scholar, James Richardson Logan, introduced a new term, 'Indo-Pacific'.[49] This described the islands and language groups connecting Southeast Asia, Melanesia and the Indian Ocean. He later popularised the label Indonesia for the islands and people at the centre of this region.

Lines of empire

Maps were one thing, but a broad regional definition was also reflected in the hard realities of imperial practice, especially the British version. The trade arteries and military sinews of Britain's India-centric empire reached China and Australia via Singapore, and went west to Africa and Suez, as modern Indian strategist Raja Mohan reminds us.[50] No wonder that the

1840s Australia of Thomas Mitchell was interested in securing and mapping its lifelines to the world. British India not only gave the British empire a massive portion of its strategic weight and wealth, but also took on the character of an imperial centre in its own right. Figures like Lord George Nathaniel Curzon (viceroy from 1899 to 1905) emphasised the need for an Indian sphere of influence in its wider region, including as a check on imperial Russia in Eurasia and an anchor for Britain and its version of global order in the Indian Ocean.[51]

French territories extended across the two oceans, as did the residual empire of Portugal. Once the Dutch accepted the loss of much of their empire to Britain, they relied on British control of the Indian Ocean to help safeguard their remaining colonies in Indonesia. Spain, having in the 1500s seized the Philippines via the Pacific route from the Americas, proved to have the most tenuous hold in Asia of all the old European empires – as the rising United States was about to demonstrate.

Like Spain, the new great power of the United States built its strategic and economic footprint primarily across the Pacific Ocean rather than the broader Indo-Pacific region. America began seeking commercial and diplomatic relations with the voyage of the *Empress of China* from New York, via the Atlantic and Indian oceans, to Canton (now Guangzhou) in 1784. To begin with, it conceived of the region as the East Indies rather than East Asia, and pursued commerce in the Indian Ocean too, placing importance during these post–Boston Tea Party years upon its direct and untaxed tea trade with India. The United States also pursued interests in Southeast Asia – with its first use of force in Asia a punitive naval raid against pirates on the 'pepper coast' of Sumatra in 1832.[52] But as its business equities grew and its strategic ambitions gathered, the expanding 19th-century United States focused on China and Japan – opening them both for markets as well as a balance-of-power diplomacy intended to limit European empires and create space for America's own power and, sometimes, its ideology of republicanism, self-determination and Christianity. The Indian Ocean was of secondary importance not least because it already seemed so comprehensively the preserve of America's old enemy and emerging elder partner,

Britain. After America's continental expansion westward, the next step seemed a Pacific destiny.

By the turn of the 20th century, Washington was an established Pacific power, with a contradictory mix of extensive commercial interests and colonial possessions seized by war (the Philippines), and a diplomatic reputation as a reliable mediator among other powers.[53] This was backed by the kind of technologically advanced navy and network of coaling stations that any self-respecting empire of the old kind would appreciate. In 1908, under President Theodore Roosevelt, the Americans projected a manifestation of the kind of power they would become, with the world voyage of a Great White Fleet of modern battleships. Steaming westward to Australia, then Japan, then across the Indo-Pacific to Suez and home, the fleet gave pause to potential adversaries and friends alike.

An impetus for America's strategic naval debut was another momentous Atlanto-Indo-Pacific voyage just three years earlier: the doomed campaign of the Russian Baltic Fleet, sent round the world to punish the perceived upstart Asian power Japan.[54] The tsar's battleships ponderously crossed the Indian Ocean, struggling for coal, supplies and maintenance in a zone without friendly bases. Then, in a few unforgiving hours, the newly modernised navy of imperial Japan sank almost the entire Russian armada in the misty Tsushima Strait.[55] Imperial Japan had already defeated the ailing Manchu China in the war of 1894–95, but now it had humbled one of Europe's greatest empires.

The shock rolled out globally and down the decades. Russia had expanded overland through preceding centuries to become an Asian power as well as a European one. Defeat by Japan (with treaty negotiations mediated by America) did much more than set back Russian power in the Pacific. It also worsened domestic unrest, which led, via the First World War, to the 1917 Bolshevik Revolution, the fall of the Tsarist empire, the establishment of the Soviet Union and the seizure of state power by communist parties elsewhere. Japan's naval victory also awoke established empires, rising powers and new players alike to a shifting balance of forces and the need to look to their own defences: hence the Great White Fleet and even the origins of the Royal Australian Navy in 1911. And it was a signal flare for Asian societies to eject European colonialism.

Japan was ruthlessly pursuing its own interests – and, as became clear, its own cruel and unachievable version of a land-and-sea empire. But in the early 1900s, as the first modernised and sovereign Asian power, it was also the vessel for the hopes and schemes of others. Pan-Asian movements for self-determination – notably in India and Indonesia but even in China – saw admirable assertiveness. In the Kaiser's Germany, some also saw in Japan a certain inspiration (even though Germany itself had been a model for much of Japan's modernisation). Germany was the European great power which, as a latecomer, had missed most of the maritime spoils of colonialism: in the Indo-Pacific it made do with New Guinea and proximate islands. Already in 1908, a German military adviser in Japan named Karl Haushofer was seeing Japan as a proxy for Germany's own unfulfillable ambitions – and a future ally.

Arena of geopolitics

Haushofer later became a notorious (if now largely forgotten) figure, as geo-political advisor to the Third Reich.[56] He was one of several early geo-strategists to perceive and portray Asia – its continent and its two oceans – as a strategic whole. American seapower theorist Alfred Thayer Mahan and British continentalist geographer Halford Mackinder had already seen Asia as an integrated region. So would India's K.M. Panikkar during the Second World War and its aftermath.[57]

Under Haushofer, Indo-Pacific definitions of Asia came to prominence in the first few decades of the 20th century, but took a wrong turn: Haus-hofer's idea of geopolitics was primarily about justifying regional domination, and was thus drawn on by the Axis powers in the Second World War.[58] Inspired by Mackinder, Haushofer drew on his pre-1914 travels in Japan, China, Korea and India to come up with his own geographical determinism for world history. In his 1924 book, *Geopolitics of the Pacific Ocean*, described as 'a virtual text book' for Japanese naval strategy, he envisaged a world of four 'pan-regions', claiming that each warranted a dominant power.[59] The Indo-Pacific was already becoming a known term in ethnography and marine science. Applying it to his version of geopolitics, Haushofer saw this pan-region as the rightful preserve of imperial Japan, as Asia's rising maritime power, to be shared perhaps with Russia. Today's Indo-Pacific conceptions are precisely the opposite of Haushofer's: they are about finding ways to manage the intersection of multiple powers' interests in a vast common domain, rather than some imperial carve-up or life-and-death struggle.

Part of Haushofer's agenda was that imperial Japan and the Third Reich should form alliances of convenience with self-determination movements across Asia, including in China and India, to defeat the liberal democracies and the ailing British empire. Indeed, the political activists of Asian decolonisation, such as Rabindranath Tagore, the Indian writer and visionary popular in Japan and China, saw the region as a connected place, with such pronouncements as 'Asia is one'. With other Asian intellectuals such as Japan's Okakura Kakuzō, he 'sought to establish a cultural basis for Asia as a whole, stressing old maritime links, arts, and such shared legacies as Buddhism in India, China and Japan'.[60] Their ideals of pan-Asianism were appropriated and abused by Japan to justify its own imperial aggression in the 1930s. But the point here is that the reaction to colonialism, as much as colonialism itself, contributed to both the belief and the reality of a shared destiny for the peoples of Indo-Pacific Asia.

Along with the rise of Japanese power and self-determination movements in Asia, the First World War weakened the grip of European powers on their Indo-Pacific empires. That conflict was, from an Asian perspective, a European civil war, albeit fought across a global battlefield. Apart from hastening the re-emergence of Asian sovereignty and strength, the war included some Indo-Pacific aspects, notably the vital role of Indian expeditionary forces. The Asian nations of Japan and, from 1917, China and Siam (Thailand) also became belligerents, all on the side of the Allies (although Asian public opinion tended to be pro-German).[61] The Indian Ocean was critical to the worldwide war: by controlling those sea lanes, Britain could sustain a constant stream of troops and resources from the empire to the battlefronts of Europe and the Middle East. Across the strategic geography of the Indo-Pacific, security partnerships formed that would not be out of place in the 21st century.[62] For instance, in 1914 Japan was Britain's ally, and consequently a Japanese warship escorted Australian and New Zealand troop transports to the Middle East. This provided protection against Germany's East Asia squadron, originally based in Qingdao, China, from where the cruiser SMS *Emden* brought havoc to Allied shipping and ports in India and Southeast Asia. The Australian cruiser HMAS *Sydney* duelled and destroyed the *Emden* at Cocos Islands, then as now a crucial security outpost in the Indian Ocean.

The Indo-Pacific dimension to the Second World War was more substantial still. Japanese aggression had shattered Tagore's notions of Asian brotherhood. Clearly, this conflict was more than a European civil war. As Haushofer anticipated, imperial Japan saw its survival as requiring an Indo-Pacific footprint of domination and exploitation of resources. Singapore, the Malacca Strait and other Indo-Pacific sea lanes were vital objectives. Whether Japan ever seriously contemplated occupying substantial territory in the Indian Ocean beyond the overstretch of its Burma campaign, it certainly sought and achieved control of such strategic maritime zones as the Bay of Bengal, from bases in Burma, Malacca and the Andaman Islands.[63] Objectives included isolating India from Britain, and Australia from both the British and US-led Allied war effort.[64] Maps of the so-called Greater East Asia Co-Prosperity Sphere – Japan's ludicrously benign euphemism for its empire – underscored the importance of not only Southeast Asia but also South Asia and the Indian Ocean as sources of vital raw materials for warfare, empire and national survival.[65] The name was a misnomer in every sense; not only was it not about mutual prosperity (the wealth was all meant for Japan), it was about much more than East Asia. It was an Indo-Pacific sphere of control, an imperial and militarised distortion of pan-Asianism.

The so-called Pacific War was in some respects an Indo-Pacific war, not least when one considers the crucial role – and sheer scale – of Indian involvement. The British Indian army in the Second World War, the largest volunteer force in history, was essential to resisting and rolling back Japanese forces, with 700,000 troops in Southeast Asia alone.[66] Indian forces even occupied Japan. At the same time, other no less patriotic Indians served on the Japanese side. And the Allies recognised their theatre of operations against Japan as having something like an Indo-Pacific character. The British (with Indian troops) fought to regain Southeast Asia from their regional headquarters in what is now Sri Lanka. The South East Asia Command, based in Colombo (so not technically even in Southeast Asia), led British, American, Australian and Dutch forces in pushing imperial Japan out of the Indian Ocean and back to the Pacific. Indeed, the Indo-Pacific connection supported the defence of China against Japanese forces, with the United States and Britain supplying the Chinese nationalist army overland through Myanmar and Assam, in India, then later by air over the Himalayas.

Among the many discontinuities in the remade world after the cataclysm of the Second World War, the map of Asia was drawn yet again. The colonial empires did not return for long. India and China regained their agency. The United States became the dominant power, at least in the Pacific. The world's grim new strategic calculus of the Cold War became focused on Europe, even though so much of the violence was in Asia. And the seeds were sown for a whole new and hyphenated way of looking at the region, with America in and the Indian Ocean out.

Within a few decades, everyone got used to a place called the Asia-Pacific, as if it had been forever thus.

CHAPTER 3

ODYSSEY OF NATIONS: THE QUEST FOR A REGIONAL HOME

They converged from all over Asia and beyond.

Representatives arrived from the places that are now Sri Lanka, Myanmar and Malaysia. Indonesia's first prime minister, the brilliant young Sutan Sjahrir, led thirty-two delegates from his new nation, still fighting for its independence. Ten more came from the Philippines. A further nine attended from China, or more precisely Chiang Kai-shek's nationalist government, in the midst of its losing war with Mao Zedong's communists. Four representatives from independent Tibet 'had walked for 21 days over the windy plateau and mountain passes south of Lhasa' to join the meeting, and were accepted despite Chinese objections.[1] Delegations converged from Nepal, Bhutan, Afghanistan, Iran, Korea, Mongolia, Thailand (then Siam), Turkey, the Arab League, and the Hebrew University of Palestine (the modern state of Israel was yet to be). From Vietnam came Viet Minh insurgents. Their French adversaries – still in control of much of Indochina – would not be kept away. Five Soviet Central Asia republics were represented. There were observers from Australia, Britain, the United States and the United Nations. Most conspicuously absent was Japan. The US-led occupation preferred that the Japanese stay home and had imposed a travel ban.[2]

Best represented by far was India, still a few months before the searing summer of its independence. This was hardly surprising, since this unprecedented gathering of renascent Asia was taking place in New Delhi. The venue was the Mughal-era Purana Qila (literally, the Old Fort), overlooking a sea of trees and whitewashed Raj bungalows. The convener was India's soon-to-be prime minister, Jawaharlal Nehru.

False spring

The Asian Relations Conference in the Indian spring of 1947 was a truly historic assembly, yet is largely forgotten today. It was overshadowed by the 1955 Bandung conference of Asian and African states, convened by Indonesian president Sukarno to foster diplomatic non-alignment and radical anti-colonialism. The outcomes of the Delhi conference were largely symbolic: a message of Asian solidarity and self-determination, tempered with willingness to reconcile and cooperate with ex-oppressors. The backdrop was the unravelling of colonialism, the aftermath of global conflagration and the gathering atomic clouds of the Cold War. Topics for discussion were mostly social, cultural and developmental. Women's rights and empowerment were part of the program, inspired by Indian poet and activist Sarojini Naidu. Security and foreign policy were technically off the agenda, understandable given the conflicts unresolved or brewing among many of those represented. In today's diplomatic jargon, it was a '1.5 track' dialogue, a hybrid affair, not entirely official but no mere academic talkfest either. In an enormous temporary auditorium gathered 'professors and revolutionaries, economists, politicians, scientists, members of governments, feminists, high judicial and administrative officials'.[3]

This was a significant moment in world history: the first attempt to bring together the voices of a unified Asia.[4] It was the genesis of efforts to build Asian regionalism, a sense of shared purpose and identity informed by geography. This would be a story of churn and change for the next sixty years. India was the prime mover and nexus. In the words of Nehru, India was 'the compelling factor' and the 'meeting point' of Asia's subregions: north, south, southeast, east and west.[5] The diverse cast of attendees suggested an exceptionally inclusive definition of India's region – an Asia-centric combination of the Indo-Pacific and Eurasia, with a place for more distant

Gandhi addresses the closing ceremony of the Asian Relations Conference, New Delhi, 1947

maritime powers. Photographs from the conference show Mahatma Gandhi before a grand wall map lit by a flashing neon sign saying simply 'Asia'. Europe was a minor appendage. Crisscrossing lines marked air routes starting to connect the world. At the heart of the map was India.

Yet in the decades that followed, India became much less central to the international relations of Asia. By the 1980s, India was an afterthought in efforts to build a new 'Asia-Pacific' order focused on economics, East Asia and America. It was only around the cusp of the 21st century that the Asia-Pacific interlude came to an end, and the roll-call of Asia-centric diplomacy began to resemble that premonition of an expansive and inclusive region, the Indo-Pacific and more, as glimpsed in Delhi's Old Fort at the dawn of a new age.

Strife and separation

For 1947 proved a false spring for the unity of Asia, in any of its forms. The conference had steered clear of the region's many international disputes and internal conflicts. But that was precisely because the region was so fractured – and the divisions were about to get worse. India itself would know the trauma and communal bloodshed of Partition. This would be followed by the first of four wars with Pakistan, along with enduring separatist conflicts and insurgencies. Nationalist China had offered to host the second Asian Relations Conference, scheduled optimistically for 1949. But by then China had other preoccupations. The People's Republic was emerging victorious in a massive civil war, with the nationalist administration fleeing across the water to Taiwan, and the scene thus being set for the cross-strait tensions that remain a key regional flashpoint in the 21st century. China was going through the final carnage of its long internal conflict, followed by the killings of millions out of favour with the new communist regime, the further self-harm of the so-called Great Leap Forward – bringing famine and repression – and the civilisational implosion of the Cultural Revolution.[6] Indonesia's freedom fight was ending and Vietnam's multiple armed struggles had only begun. Korea was about to become the fiercest battleground of the Cold War. And by 1962 India and China were at war with each other.

In the mid-20th century, far from integration, Asia was torn by new waves of strife: internal, regional and global. Shortly after the hopeful Delhi conference, the region entered a new disorder. The Pacific and Indian ocean areas began a half-century of estrangement. One factor was the Cold War between the Soviet-led communist bloc and the American-led West. Victory over Japan had left the United States ascendant as a Pacific power: it was here to stay, and was building an informal empire of alliances to support not so much its economic interests as its national security strategy. This centred on containing Soviet power and the spread of communist ideology. But it also involved constraining regional powers such as Japan, the nationalist Republic of China (on Taiwan) and South Korea from provoking major land wars in Asia, so that the United States could focus on its primary theatre of security concern, Europe and the North Atlantic.[7] (This of course did not stop America becoming embroiled in its own terrible land war in Vietnam.)

For its part, the Soviet Union had regained territorial footholds in the northern Pacific, and seized on anti-colonial momentum as an opportunity to cultivate independence movements and new states created in friction with the West. Superpower tensions were centred on the North Atlantic region, the world's strategic and economic centre of gravity. Washington and Moscow saw Asia primarily through the prism of their global rivalry, and saw little value in helping to build Asian unity for its own sake. Where they constructed cooperative regional relationships, it was as an extension of global bloc-building: the US alliance system and the Soviets' fostering of communist movements and wooing of the non-aligned. The effect of much of this diplomacy was to deepen divisions between and within Indo-Pacific states, on grounds of ideological loyalty and strategic utility.

Nor was the region well prepared to pull itself together. Japan, the aggressive driver of earlier pan-Asianism, was held back in diplomacy and strategy by the preferences of its American former foe (now ally) and the wish of its own people to focus on reconstruction and the beginnings of prosperity. The notion of Japan leading in regional initiatives, especially those with a political or security character, was tarnished by the legacy of imperialism.[8] Only in trade and post-war reparations – the origins of its aid program – was Japan daring to reach beyond its borders. Commerce and development would nonetheless combine to propel a remarkable resurgence of a new and peaceful Japan as a leading player in a reimagined region – the Asia-Pacific – within a few decades.

Japan's former foe Australia, meanwhile, emerged from the Second World War haunted by the fall of British Singapore, where many Australians were taken into deadly captivity by Japanese imperial soldiers. Canberra sought new defensive arrangements with the powerful United States, alongside its own more active diplomacy. These imperatives manifested in the 1951 ANZUS (Australia–New Zealand–United States) Treaty and the 1950 Colombo Plan. The latter was a development and education initiative, spearheaded by Australia, focused on Southeast and South Asia.[9] It was 'the first multilateral aid scheme engaging the Asian countries themselves' and an effective 'Australian initiative to shape the region'.[10] And it was distinctly Indo-Pacific in character, expanding rapidly beyond its initial cast of British Commonwealth member states. The plan was launched in Colombo, involved India, Pakistan and most of Southeast Asia, and came to engage the United States and a rehabilitated Japan.

But Australia was still going out into the region primarily out of security motivations, seeking to weaken the appeal of communism and to bolster defences not only against the West's Cold War adversaries but more generally against larger Asian states. Australia, under its long-serving conservative prime minister Robert Menzies, remained overwhelmingly an Anglo-Celtic society culturally heavily influenced by Britain, with racially restricted immigration in place. Nonetheless, the Colombo Plan was not the only early glimmering of an Australia that, only a few decades later, would time and again seek to lead the building of an inclusive future for the region. On the eve of his death in 1951, former Australian Labor prime minister Ben Chifley gave what was to be his final press interview. It was with visiting Indian journalist J.N. Sahni, who wrote that Chifley:

> repeatedly got up from his desk to study a map of Asia ... Referring to the Indian-Pacific region, Chifley stated: 'we on this side of Asia, from Bombay to Sydney, could do a lot for mutual development and for helping each other in distress' ... he acknowledged and accepted Australia's geographic identity as belonging to the Indian-Pacific region.[11]

India and China: the giant divide

Central to Asia's fortunes were the choices of the two largest powers, China and India. How they opted to connect – or not – was critical to any real prospect of regional cohesion. Fatefully, they turned inwards and cast aside the opportunity to lead in Asia, either separately or together. Newly independent India and the People's Republic of China (PRC) rejected thousands of years of their own history as trading economies. They imposed autarchic systems that ended enterprise and largely closed off exports. Production in India was largely state directed; in China, entirely so. Regional trade was minimised. Massive neighbouring nations that could have supported each other's journeys to development had bewilderingly little to do with one another for the next fifty years. Their political ways, too, parted profoundly. India, for all its flaws, had gained independence largely though nonviolent pressure, and embarked on the experiment of being the world's largest democracy, albeit one dominated by the Congress Party and its dynastic leadership for many years. China, born in civil war, consolidated the dictatorship of one party and one leader, interested above all in survival through control.

There was an initial flush of seemingly constructive India–China diplomacy in the 1950s, culminating in a 1954 'trade' agreement between the two closed and struggling economies. The agreement's real importance was its supposed commitment to peaceful coexistence through non-interference. This largely meant Indian recognition of Chinese sovereignty over Tibet, where China had forcibly taken control four years earlier. The deal was celebrated with a Chinese song about an idealised history of peace and cultural exchange and an Indian poem with the refrain 'Hindi-Chini bhai-bhai' – Indians and Chinese are brothers.[12] The line has become immortalised more in irony than in earnest. A clue of trouble to come lay in the fact that the seizure of Tibet had pushed China's frontiers right up to India's, or the vague Indo-Tibetan boundary defined by the British empire, known as the McMahon Line.

Just eight years later, the breakdown in friendship was complete. In October 1962, as the world was transfixed by the nuclear near-death experience of the Cuban missile crisis between the United States and the Soviet Union, the Himalayan passes and valleys echoed with the gunfire of a brief and bitter war. This involved a rapid onslaught by Chinese forces right along the contested mountain border. Indian units were variously pushed back, cut off or defeated. China then withdrew its forces to previous positions, except in the substantial western sector called Aksai Chin, abutting Kashmir and Xinjiang, as if to signal that the conflict had been more about punishment than conquest.

From an Indian perspective, the China–India war of 1962 was a shocking betrayal of the principles of cooperation and coexistence: a surprise attack that humiliated India and personally broke Nehru (who died two years later).[13] China argued that its warnings had been ignored, and portrayed the actions of its PLA as a counter-attack following an Indian policy of lodging small units to hold 'forward positions' in contested areas; this view was backed in a book by an Australian journalist, drawing on a leaked internal Indian report.[14] Another interpretation suggests that the war suited Mao as an external distraction, helping restore pride and confidence in his regime after the disastrous famine his policies had inflicted on the Chinese people. Either way, India lost the fray. Its forces were unready and outgunned. Despite its non-alignment and solidarity with anti-colonialism, India found itself requesting and obtaining, briefly, moral and material support from the United States, Britain, Australia and Canada – a foretaste of Delhi's 21st-century tilt towards America and its allies.

Whatever the proximate cause, the war was influenced by China's determination to hold onto Tibet and to brook no equivalence with India as a fellow great power. It set the tone for decades of estrangement between the Asian giants. Two years later, China tested its first nuclear bomb, a step in the action–reaction cycle to India's own eventual nuclear weapons program, then Pakistan's. In the decades to follow, Chinese military support for Pakistan – including its nuclear and missile programs – hardened Indian mistrust. More than half a century later, the India–China border remains militarised and undemarcated. For most of the rest of the 20th century, the world's two most populous countries shunned one another in a cold peace.[15] A direct India–China commercial air link, for instance, had been a glaring gap on the wall map at that optimistic 1947 Delhi conference. It remained so until 2003. Moreover, from the late 1940s until the 1980s, India and China turned their backs on the sea and their long history of commerce across the waters of the Indo-Pacific. Their seaborne trade to anywhere dwindled. In the words of Indian strategist Raja Mohan: 'A deliberate de-globalization and de-emphasis on trade meant there was little scope for a maritime vision.'[16] With no long-range interests to protect, their under-resourced, technologically inferior naval forces were largely incapable of more than local and defensive operations.

The Cold War, the North Atlantic dominance of the world's weal and woe, and the inward-looking mutual indifference of India and China all helped keep Asia broken into multiple maps. These narrow horizons were clouded further by economic underdevelopment, limited trade, and populations still cut off from new technologies of travel and communication. (In the 1960s, there were still fewer than a million telephones in all of India, one for each 500 citizens, and China's landline telephone network was still being built.) Asian nations were consumed with internal needs and problems. And when they looked outwards, it was not at some expansive whole but across smaller neighbourhood spaces: East Asia, South Asia, Southeast Asia, Oceania. These new artificial concepts gained prominence, just as the outdated and Euro-centric habit of calling Asia 'the Far East' began to recede. But even though they used the term Asia, these new labels still in a way diminished the role of Asia in world affairs, by suggesting that it constituted disparate parts, not a weighty whole. Today we tend to imagine that these terms and compartments are the natural order of things, and it is true that terms like Eastern Asia or the East Indies have been around for centuries. But the label Southeast Asia was entirely invented by Western military planners in 1943. This was one of the constrained versions of regionalism that took hold in strategy, diplomacy and academia.[17]

The kernel of later efforts at region-wide diplomatic cooperation was the modest step taken by five countries – Indonesia, Malaysia, Singapore, Thailand and the Philippines – to set up a loose arrangement, devoted initially to little more than sovereignty, non-interference and anti-communism, in 1967. The Association of Southeast Asian Nations (ASEAN) was a harbour, a rare place of steadiness, in decades of flux and unrest in regional cooperation and identity. Generally, in the 1960s and 1970s, there was little awareness among nations of a wider region, let alone agreement on its name and character. Was it Asia, East Asia, South Asia, the Far East, the Pacific, Asia and the Pacific, Pacific Asia, the Asia-Pacific? Or something else entirely?

Indo-Pacific echoes and premonitions

Amid all this confusion, ideas connecting the destinies of the Indian and Pacific oceans retained a quiet currency, even though no country would successfully turn them into policy action for decades to come. In 1945,

K.M. Panikkar reflected on the war just ending to conclude that events in the Pacific would be crucial to his country's long-term quest for security and power.[18] Subsequently, the actual term Indo-Pacific gained low-key policy use in Britain and Australia as those countries sought to define their security links in a maritime region and a post-imperial age. In 1965 and 1966, defence analysts assembled at the Australian National University to assess their nations' security outlook in terms of risks and challenges across the 'Indo-Pacific basin'.[19] Gathering political and economic pressures would drive the United Kingdom to reduce its presence east of Suez. But behind the scenes, British foreign and defence policy planners were drafting a sensitive document, titled 'Indo-Pacific Strategy', providing options for their future governments to support UK and allied interests across this wide region.[20]

Britain's 1965 Indo-Pacific Strategy was a secret policy review document, long forgotten and now declassified.[21] It focused on supporting the United States, Australia and New Zealand in countering Soviet but especially growing Chinese power across the region. There are some striking 21st-century resonances, such as an anticipation of China as the primary source of region-wide threat, and the need for a strategy involving India and Southeast Asia. The British wanted to maintain an influence on US policy 'in an area where the conflict between America and China provides the most fertile ground for the seeds of a Third World War'.[22]

But largely this was a Cold War document, and some of its concepts are properly left in that era. Indonesia was referred to as another source of risk to Western interests. This would soon become an outmoded notion in the post-Sukarno era. There was reference to the Southeast Asia Treaty Organization, or SEATO, as a source of balancing against aggression. This organisation, with its motley membership that included Pakistan and the Philippines, was never much use, and dissolved in 1977. Nor was any government inclined to pursue the British strategy's more radical proposals, such as a multi-nation Indo-Pacific Nuclear Force, with a nuclear deterrent under international control (along the lines of NATO). There were also many references to the need for a crude 'containment' of China. Back then, containment was meant literally: it described the US policy to defeat the Soviet Union, involving warfighting alliances and economic strangulation.

The 1965 British strategy was far from fully implemented. But it proved ahead of its time in recognising that risks in Asia could not be compartmentalised to one ocean or another: with limited resources, a range of partners and wide-ranging maritime interests, some kind of two-ocean strategy was needed. The document was also practical about the limits of British power following the anticipated withdrawal of its remaining garrisons from Malaysia and Singapore. 'We need American support far more than the Americans need ours,' it said – a point that could be made by any number of regional partners, then or since.[23]

There were other Indo-Pacific premonitions around this time. As US president in the early 1970s, Richard Nixon would famously turn to China. This meant fundamentally realigning US policy to recognise the People's Republic instead of Taiwan and to leverage the Moscow–Beijing split to balance against the Soviet Union. Thus began decades of American support for China's spectacular rise in power and wealth. (Some have since argued that perhaps it was China that successfully turned to, and turned, America.) The Nixon administration, with Henry Kissinger as secretary of state, left plenty of unhappy legacies in Asia: the ignominious later phases of Vietnam, the bombing of Cambodia, failure to stem the Pakistani atrocities in what became Bangladesh, and even a coercive bid to discourage India's humanitarian intervention there, with the deployment of a US aircraft carrier to the Bay of Bengal. But before all this, ahead of his election, Nixon had experimented with rather brighter notions. In 1967 he had published a manifesto in the journal *Foreign Affairs*, titled 'Asia after Viet Nam'.[24] This referred to the emergence of 'Asian regionalism', the development of some key Asian economies, and an idea he later abandoned of building common cause with India, Japan, Australia and other democracies to balance Chinese power across a two-ocean version of Asia – a preview of partnerships now at last emerging.

And these precursors of a 21st-century Indo-Pacific were not solely American visions. Australia was reinventing itself and making independent choices to find a future in its region. In 1967, the Australian National University played far-sighted convener once again, hosting a dialogue of Japanese, Indian and Australian experts and former officials exploring scope for whether 'trilateral relations of significance could be brought into being'.[25] In the early 1970s, the ambitious government of Australian Labor prime minister Gough Whitlam – which dismantled the last vestiges of the White Australia policy – went a step further and proposed radical diplomatic institutions for Australia's region, nothing less than 'a new regional grouping that would potentially encompass all Asian countries from India to China'.[26] But to the Southeast Asian countries this looked too much like a rival to their own embryonic organisation. Whitlam downplayed his idea as a 'slow and delicate growth'.[27] It was decades before its time. What stuck was the need to bring ASEAN along with every emerging regional idea.

Still, individual Southeast Asian countries were not averse to their own omni-directional diplomacy. At least one was trying to weave a web of pragmatic Indo-Pacific partnerships from birth, even though it did not use that term. 'I had a selfish motive in wanting India to emerge,' stated Singapore's founding leader, Lee Kuan Yew, in 1974, adding: 'If India does not emerge, Asia will be submerged.'[28] Lee strove to enlist an initially reluctant India as a security partner, as part of the city-state's strategy of engaging multiple players to offset each other and its own vulnerability in the face of larger and none-too-friendly neighbours (Malaysia and Indonesia) and, of course, a looming China. India eventually got on board for its own reason. Delhi's Look East policy (from 1993), its later Act East strategy (from 2013) and its own economic opening had precursors in Singapore's example and encouragement.[29]

Across intellectual and bureaucratic horizons too, glimpses of the Indo-Pacific appeared. The UN Food and Agriculture Organization set up an Indo-Pacific Fisheries Council in 1948. In the 1970s, several academic associations and journals focused on history and archaeology dropped the antiquated and London-centric label of the Far East and renamed themselves after the Indo-Pacific. But mostly the Indo-Pacific was a submerged and fragmentary concept. The Asia-Pacific moment was at hand.

Asia, meet Pacific

The idea of merging Asia and the Pacific Ocean as one coherent piece of the world may seem natural now. Googling 'Asia-Pacific' brings up hundreds of millions of results, drowning the mere tens of millions from an 'Indo-Pacific' search. After all, the Asia-Pacific was the received wisdom at the start of the internet age. On the other hand, the Indo-Pacific turns out to be a more enduring idea. The term has had steady if low-key use in books since the mid-19th century. In contrast, the Asia-Pacific was a term that arrived in the mid-20th century, surged hare-like in the 1980s and was declining in usage by 2000.[30] But where did it come from?

The answer begins in the disarray of the 1960s. New Delhi and Beijing had abrogated Asian leadership. There were limits to what could be done by Tokyo or Washington. Japan, still hobbled by history, was rebuilding and re-emerging through the narrow frame of economics. The United States was torn between a genuine imperative to build regional order, the Euro-Atlantic focus of its Cold War struggle, and the widening gyre of its war in Vietnam. Along with a retrenching Britain, America quietly encouraged its Asian partners to move beyond their own differences and help or at least coexist with one another, not least to ensure no more fell into the Soviet or Chinese orbit.[31]

The initiative lay with five disparate and desperate non-communist states of Southeast Asia. Their tough histories made them unpromising soil for peace, trust and openness. Indonesia, still sensitive about its hard-won sovereignty, was barely past the anti-communist pogroms that brought military ruler Suharto to power. Malaysia, not long independent, had just stared down (with British and Australian military help) Indonesia's policy of armed confrontation. Singapore had peacefully separated from Malaysia, but each now considered the other a potential threat. The Philippines had a new president, Ferdinand Marcos, whose two-decade disfigurement of democracy would become a byword for corruption. The kingdom of Thailand was the successor to Siam, an island of Asian sovereignty during the colonial era, but now dominated by its pro-American military.

Yet in 1967 these five nations created Asia's first enduring diplomatic 'architecture'. At first, this did not seem a community in the making: little more than agreement among self-interested neighbours to meet, talk and do no harm. It was a far cry from the harmonised rules and diluted sovereignty that would become the European Union. The five governments were bound by little more than a determination to stay independent, free from excessive great-power influence, communist subversion and each other's meddling, and to remain at peace so as to pursue their own paths of economic development and political control. The evolution of ASEAN to become the neutral core for larger structures – an acronym within acronyms – would come much later. From the original five nations, ASEAN slowly expanded to take in the rest of Southeast Asia. Brunei joined upon independence from Britain in 1984, with Vietnam following in 1993 and Laos, Cambodia and Myanmar in the late 1990s as regional and internal differences stabilised. But the arrival of a greater regionalism, the Asia-Pacific, would require a second strand: cooperation across the Pacific Ocean.[32]

While ASEAN was all about peace and coexistence, Australia and Japan were at the vanguard of a push for regional cooperation driven by another engine: prosperity. These two countries pioneered an order that combined trade, wide regional horizons and the engagement of their crucial American ally. Beginning in the late 1960s, economists and policy-makers in these two anchor states pursued a new order driven by 'the high economic growth and interdependence among industrial economies of the Pacific Rim'.[33] This led to a series of Pacific economic councils, eventually bringing together North America, Australia, Japan, South Korea, New Zealand, Taiwan, Hong Kong, and the Southeast Asian and Pacific island states. These were early days in the quest for regional free trade, but the journey had begun. But this trend of Pacific dialogue had another consequence: the ASEAN states sensed competition. Was this a Western-led effort to marginalise less developed and more truly 'Asian' states? For their part, Pacific prime movers Japan and Australia had no wish to shut out their rapidly developing Southeast Asian neighbours. A growing market suited all.

It was only a matter of time before ASEAN and the Pacific push converged. Extra stimulus came from the sudden end of the Cold War and a new wave of concern about possible American withdrawal from Asia. By the

1980s, most countries recognised how much they had benefitted from US dominance since 1945. For all its flaws, the unintended American empire had – on balance – provided stability that was now supporting an extraordinary surge in economic growth, development and human welfare. There was also an emerging pattern of democratic and accountable government. Japan, Australia, New Zealand and their small Pacific neighbours were no longer the only outposts of democracy east of Malacca. South Korea, Taiwan, Thailand and the Philippines had all democratised to a dramatic degree, and others – notably Indonesia – would follow. To be clear, though, the new Asia-Pacific regionalism that was about to arise was about commerce first, security a close second and values a distant third. The early movers in regional cooperation were at pains to find ways to involve communist and other less than democratic states. The theory was that convergence in the quest for wealth and peace would occlude differences in political systems.

Australia found itself playing an outsized role. This unusual country's imperative to belong, its perpetual identity crisis (not Europe, not quite Asia), its opening economy, its security anxieties and its hyper-activist foreign policy – all these combined with a reputation as a trusted convener. The establishment of the Asia-Pacific Economic Cooperation (APEC) process in 1989, and its elevation to a leaders' meeting four years later, were high points of Australian diplomacy under the Labor governments of prime ministers Bob Hawke (until 1991) and then Paul Keating, with foreign minister Gareth Evans playing a key role.[34] From twelve initial economies being represented at the initial gathering in Canberra, APEC expanded to seventeen participants by 1993 and topped out at twenty-one in 1998.

Like all diplomacy, it was an imperfect endeavour. The agenda had artificial limits, centred on economics at a time when there was much else to do: after the Cold War, strategic problems were morphing rather than dissolving. There was a focus on aspiration rather than binding agreement, reflected in the institution's odd title, which Gareth Evans called 'four adjectives in search of a noun'.[35]

And then there was the problem of membership. APEC began with a number of obvious gaps, none larger than China, which had begun from

1978 to shift to a partly market economy. Beijing's decision to join APEC in 1993 was a crucial boost to the reality of an Asia-Pacific region and to China's own confidence and acceptance in a regional order. Beijing chose to tolerate the presence of Taiwan and Hong Kong as separate participants on the understanding that they were defined as economies not countries, and moreover that security was permanently off the agenda. But overall the roll-call of APEC was motley, as awkward as the leaders posing for photographs in the national 'silly shirts' they were gifted at each meeting. Russia, Mexico, Chile and Peru were in, but there was not a single South Asian participant, not even India, which itself was beginning to open up economically. As a reflection of 'Asia' or an Asia-centric region, APEC was unbalanced, unsustainable.

Moreover, the symbolism of China's entry into APEC – with President Jiang Zemin speaking in Seattle in 1993 of a 'more splendid new Asia-Pacific century' – obscured a much quieter and deeper turning point that same year, towards a quite different reality. This was about energy security: specifically, oil. It was the first and irreversible step towards China's destiny as an Indo-Pacific power. Just as with China's entry to APEC, the cause of this more structural shift was China's runaway economic growth, around 14 per cent that year alone. In 1993, China for the first time became a net oil importer. That vital fuel was from the Middle East and Africa. To get to China, it had to cross the Indian Ocean. The spirit of Zheng He was stirring.

The Asia-Pacific stage

Change inside China and India was finally propelling the two Asian giants to look outwards once more. For a decade from the late 1970s, China's experience was dominated by exhilarating reform at home – social as well as economic – and welcome pragmatism abroad as Beijing sought resources, partners and stability to nurture its growth. China seemed somewhat uninterested in taking a broad regional view, dealing in isolation with each of its border zones and often difficult relationships: the Soviet Union, India, Japan, Vietnam, the Koreas and so on. Indeed, China only began to catch

'Asia-Pacific fever' (*yatai re*) in the mid-1980s, and remained cautious about the associated Japanese and American agendas.[36]

Any path of Chinese international openness was gravely damaged by the events of 4 June 1989: the regime's use of the PLA to massacre students protesting for greater reform and democratic rights. Nonetheless, within a few years the narratives of economics and engagement were back. The United States and most other self-styled 'Asia-Pacific' nations saw priority in encouraging what they saw as a wary and weak China to join them in building regional cooperation. The vision was partly to help China develop, not out of altruism but for mutual enrichment. But it was also about peace and security. The idea was to build confidence, on all sides, that a strengthening China would not feel militarily threatened – nor threaten its neighbours. China had attacked Vietnam in 1979, in a failed re-run of its India war; violently seized an island from Vietnamese forces in 1988; and built small outposts in the contested South China Sea in the 1990s. Yet it was militarily behind not only the hegemon America but also Japan and even little Taiwan, whose American-equipped air force dominated the strait.

Thus, alongside APEC, a web of light-touch security talks was spun. Strongly encouraged by Australia and Japan, the ASEAN states became the core of what was styled an Asia-Pacific multilateral security dialogue, the first meeting of the ASEAN Regional Forum (ARF). Its original eighteen members met in Bangkok in 1994. They included the Southeast Asian countries and others entirely of their hemisphere – Japan, China, Australia, South Korea and New Zealand. But this was also a venue to engage global power with stakes in Asia: the United States, Russia and the European Union.

At least a regional security grouping now existed. Yet the first annual meeting of the ARF set the tone for many more: not much happened. The mandate involved sleep-inducing jargon about confidence-building and preventive diplomacy, constructive dialogue and consultation 'at a pace comfortable to all'. An ASEAN consensus rule meant that this was as slow and superficial as the preferences of the most reclusive participants, which came to include Myanmar, Cambodia and Laos. Dialogue turned out to be short set-piece statements at annual meetings of foreign ministers, who were expected to break the ice with a gala concert of their amateur musical skills and theatrical sketches, bringing a moment of levity to the topical issues they could have spent more time solving.[37]

This was nothing like the deep cooperation across Europe during détente and the aftermath of the Cold War: formal arms control agreements along with multinational institutions to push peace across borders. Asia was beginning from a low base of trust and integration. The prevention of renewed conflicts internally or between smaller countries was a priority; the Cambodia peace process (with the good offices of Australia and the United Nations) was a recent achievement. Seemingly the last totalitarian relic, North Korea, with its early efforts to build nuclear weapons, was ground zero for most fears about major conflict, and this appeared preventable through American-led policies: deterrence combined with appeasement packages of aid and civil nuclear cooperation. America was the answer to keeping regional peace when it came to China. Chinese coercion of Taiwan also seemed roundly deterred by a sail-past of US aircraft carriers in 1996. In any case, the global trend appeared to be towards economic interdependence, an 'end of history' convergence of political systems in favour of liberal democracy, and the obsolescence of war between powerful states. So, while some kind of Asia-Pacific regional security organisation was desirable, there seemed little it could do that a dominant United States could not.

The entry of China into regional organisations – first APEC and then the ARF – was widely considered a foundation for a new era of coexistence, even cooperation, across the Asia-Pacific. With China, the United States and Japan all agreeing to talk with one another via the unusual rites of ASEAN, the 1990s became the brief heyday of Asia-Pacific regionalism. The Asia-Pacific idea had needed China. But China's horizons were already wider.

India too was beginning to open itself to the world, and to look east. The socialist economic model, the dominance of the Congress Party and India's strategic partnership with the Soviet Union were already breaking down in the 1980s. A balance-of-payments crisis in 1991 was the catalyst to begin economic liberalisation: a greater acceptance of foreign investment and the easing of bureaucratic curbs on commerce. India finally began to realise the potential of its vast human capital. It was no longer oblivious to the rapid gains in wealth and living standards in much of East Asia. In 1993, the Congress government of Narasimha Rao complemented its business reforms with a diplomatic initiative called Look East, prioritising relations with ASEAN and trying to restore trade and investment links with South-east Asia for the first time since the Raj. India and Singapore even established defence relations, with a joint naval exercise in 1993. Lee Kuan Yew's patience was finally paying off.

India and ASEAN began formal dialogue in 1992, and India could not long be excluded from the new security forum. It was hardly credible for a supposedly Asia-centric council to include Europe, America and Russia but not India. In 1996, India was admitted to the ARF, despite some members' private concerns that this would inject India–Pakistan tensions (and out-spokenness) into the quiet halls of ASEAN diplomacy. And with the testing of nuclear weapons by India and Pakistan in 1998, and a new phase of con-frontation, it seemed the perils of the subcontinent would indeed cloud the optimism of the Asia-Pacific. India soon found its access to regional meet-ings double-edged, as they became venues for denunciation from other states, not just America's moralistic allies like Australia but also the old enemy China. Still, once India was in the ARF, there was no keeping out its South Asian neighbours Pakistan, Bangladesh and Sri Lanka.

Yet while China and India were finding their way into the ASEAN-centric meeting halls of Asia, a new momentum was gathering to exclude America and others seen as Western, or simply the wrong kind of Asian.

The East Asia push: miracle, mirage, misnomer

Without question, the long economic growth and interdependence journey from the 1960s to the 1990s was centred on East Asia. Underwritten in large part by US strategic superiority, trade and investment, this prosperity 'miracle' began with Japan, spread to the flying geese (or rising tigers) of Taiwan, Hong Kong, Southeast Asia and South Korea, then to China from the 1980s. Through their own enterprise, labour and thrift, hundreds of millions of people gained in dignity and wellbeing.

But with rapid growth came risk, with connectivity contagion. The Asian financial crisis of 1997–98 wrought vast harm on human welfare and political stability across the region, notably in Indonesia, where hardship hastened the downfall of Suharto and the breakthrough of democracy. It burst expectations of a relentless Asian economic ascendancy. But it also impelled second thoughts about the Asia-Pacific project.

The late 1990s brought a push for a narrowly East Asian model of regional dialogue and cooperation. Some voices in East Asia, such as Malaysian prime minister Mahathir Mohamad, had long extolled 'Asian values' such as collectivism, hierarchy, family loyalty and prudence, over supposed Western extremes of political freedom bordering on the anarchic. Although these 'Asian' values and their champions themselves struggled to keep traction amid a crisis they failed to forestall, there was also scope to blame the West. A defining photograph showed Suharto signing an International Monetary Fund bailout deal, with tough austerity measures, before an imperious-looking IMF official. The echoes of colonialism were humiliating.

And so, just as the frameworks of Asia-Pacific dialogue were taking hold, another idea resurfaced. Asia for the Asians was back, and in an exclusively East Asian form: limited to the ASEAN states (now ten) and the big three north Asian powers: China, Japan and South Korea. Hedging its bets, ASEAN had already begun dialogue with each of the three. The financial crisis motivated the thirteen to join a single conversation about what their version of Asia could do to prevent future turmoil. They also wanted to project their own collective voice and weight on the world stage, where Western blocs (like a strengthening European Union) and Western-dominated global institutions showed no inclination to put Asia first.

An 'ASEAN Plus Three' process gathered pace, with summit meetings and senior officials' talks on everything from finance to agriculture to social development. This looked logical at the time. The East Asian countries were finding their economies enmeshed through cross-border chains of production and investment – geared for growth in the good times, a corridor for contagion in the bad. Japan remained at the top of the tree of value-adding in manufactures, and all welcomed China's added weight, its seemingly endless supply of labour and skills in the lower and middle tiers. During the crisis, the Southeast Asians appreciated a Chinese decision not to worsen their plight when it resisted the temptation to defensively manipulate the value of its currency. Whether through optimism or obliviousness – and because China was not yet locked into an assertive path – the risks of China coming to dominate the new grouping did not figure. Indeed, such was the enthusiasm for a future minus the imagined outsiders – America, India, Australia, Russia and the rest – that ASEAN Plus Three soon commissioned a 'vision group' of experts and elders to examine how to turn mere dialogue into a fully fledged East Asian Community.

The study was driven by South Korea – a country hit hard by the financial crisis, seeking to make its own contribution to regional order, and squeezed by the rivalries of strong forces all around: China, Japan, America, Russia and its volatile northern twin. The panel of the good and the great reported back in October 2001, with a Panglossian blueprint for a true community of nations, 'a region of peace, prosperity and progress' in which 'the governments and the peoples of East Asia will work together for a common future'. It paid scant regard to enduring differences in security interests, political systems, levels of development or international relationships, emphasising that East Asian nations shared 'geographical proximity, many common historical experiences, and similar cultural norms and values'.[38] And the report was silent on the world south of the Sunda Strait, west of Malacca or east of Tokyo, as if East Asia were a sphere apart, flourishing in isolation.

This was all at odds with fast-emerging realities enmeshing East Asia in a wider place. India was becoming a nation to be taken seriously beyond the subcontinent. Japan and South Korea had long relied on the Indian Ocean sea lanes to ship their vital oil supplies from the Middle East. Australian resources were critical to their growth story. Now China's runaway economic growth was dragging it down the same paths of Indo-Pacific dependency.

Then there were the unpleasant realities of the security picture. While the vision group's report was in gestation, strategic differences heightened between China and the United States. The accidental bombing of the Chinese embassy in Belgrade during the 1999 NATO intervention in Kosovo led to state-directed rage against America on the streets of Beijing. In early 2001 came the collision of a Chinese fighter jet and a US surveillance aircraft in the South China Sea, with the US plane and crew detained in the first external crisis of the George W. Bush presidency. Although the terrorist atrocities of 9/11 diverted much American attention to Afghanistan and the misguided Iraq War, Asia remained a significant – and generally well-handled – priority through the Bush administration. That included managing tensions over Taiwan and North Korea, strengthening alliances with Japan and Australia, helping the Philippines and Indonesia suppress Islamist terrorism, and building security partnerships with Singapore and – most notably – India.[39] After a brief outcry over India's 1998 nuclear tests, the United States began a rapprochement with the world's largest democracy. After all, India was a country with which America was finding common cause against terrorism; it was a growing economy, and a power with the reason and capacity to help balance China's growing military might. In 2002, Indian warships rode shotgun for American ships passing through the Strait of Malacca to provide logistics support to the war on terror.

Some say pivotal moments in history are about leadership and initiative. Others watch for structural factors: shifts in population, wealth and power. But sometimes the story turns out to be one of unintended consequences when both elements intersect. So it was with the fate of the East Asia project, which ended with an overarching diplomatic institution that was Indo-Pacific in everything but name. In retrospect, the Asia-Pacific concept could not last without coming to terms with two factors that emerged in the 1990s. The first was the rise of India as a substantial economic and military power with interests beyond South Asia. The second was the increased connection between the economic powerhouses of East Asia and the Indian Ocean region, related to their demand for energy and resources.

The East Asia vision group recommended setting up an East Asia Summit, a regular meeting of national leaders to steer the region to a future of unity and cooperation. The assumption was this would be a simple evolution of the ASEAN Plus Three process into a standing forum of the thirteen East Asian states. A benign China and a realistic Japan would share preponderance, South Korea would feel satisfied, and the Southeast Asians would occupy the diplomatic driver's seat, reserving the prerogatives of the chair and guarding their grail of ASEAN centrality. If things worked, the East Asia Summit could supplant APEC as the pre-eminent vehicle of Asian regionalism, eclipsing the Asia-Pacific moment with a narrower East Asian future.

But this would have replaced one unnatural arrangement with another, distinguished only by the tighter geographic footprint of its member states and their somewhat manufactured sense of a shared identity, as if Indonesia had more in common with China than it did with India. It would shut the door on many countries with the right and reason to be part of the region.

Yet a very different outcome lay in store. In the early 2000s, there was an overlay of economic interdependence and hope about the kind of society China was becoming. But apprehensions were also stirring about what rising Chinese power could actually mean for others in the wider region. The more diplomatically adroit nations of ASEAN – Indonesia, Singapore, Thailand, Malaysia, Vietnam – were beginning to think harder about their freedom of action and how to play a balancing game in a new era. India, projected to become the world's third-largest economy, would no longer accept marginal status in the councils of Asia. After 9/11, the United States had postponed, but not abandoned, its need to limit some future China challenge. And, despite the apparent Asia-aversion of its conservative prime minister John Howard, Australia had not forsaken its geography after all.

Storm and summit

On Boxing Day 2004, a massive seismic event – an earthquake of 9.1 magnitude on the Richter scale – occurred in the Indian Ocean, at the northern tip of Sumatra. It sent tsunami waves east and west. It was a global catastrophe: more than 230,000 people were killed. The toll was greatest in Indonesia, Sri Lanka, India and Thailand. Many foreign visitors also lost their lives. The impact was felt as far away as Africa, the Antarctic and North America.

Amid the shock of this truly Indo-Pacific disaster, four countries took the decision to mobilise, rapidly and with military assets. It was a singular coalition. The United States, Japan, India and Australia. What did they have in common? Strictly speaking, only one was East Asian (and long suspected as having one foot in the West). One was South Asian, one Australasian with a permanent identity crisis, and one the global hegemon from the other side of the Pacific. But the four-nation coalition that led the humanitarian assistance and disaster relief effort had enough in common to make a difference: interests in a stable maritime region, capabilities close at hand, and a willingness to help populations and partner states in dire need. Their contribution was considerable: Australia alone provided $1 billion in support to its neighbour Indonesia. If the four had a shared geography, it spanned two oceans, just as the tsunami itself showed no distinction for 20th-century subregional boundaries.

Even as their forces were deployed on the ground, in the water and in the air at the juncture of the Indo-Pacific, Australia and India were also mobilising in a quieter way. In the smoggy Delhi winter and the arid Canberra summer of early 2005, officials in their respective foreign ministries were crafting diplomatic campaigns to join the region for good and gain admission to the new summit. To his credit, Australian foreign minister Alexander Downer, generally known more for self-styled realism than for vision or activism, persuaded Howard that Australia was better off in the regional tent than out. By the end of 2005, Australia and India – along with New Zealand – would take their places at the first meeting of the East Asia Summit. They joined with the help of such partners as Singapore, Indonesia and Japan, and despite active resistance from China, which realised this would be a room it could not dominate. The ASEANs kept the door open for the United States and, at Chinese insistence, Russia too. Both would formally join in 2010.

Thus a bid to shrink the region achieved the opposite. At the peak of efforts to build imagined regions of East Asia and the Asia-Pacific, a different structure was unveiled, reflective of the region's future as well as its submerged history. In December 2005, leaders gathered for the first meeting of the East Asia Summit (EAS) in Kuala Lumpur, on the Indian Ocean coast of a peninsula that for millennia had been at the hinge of two oceans.[40] It was at least as apt a meeting place of greater Asia as had been Delhi in 1947. And many of the same players, including India, were there – now as independent powers. The EAS was suddenly the top table of the Indo-Pacific.[41] After a six-decade odyssey of nations, something resembling a regional home was finally in view.

Manoeuvres in the rarefied sphere of diplomatic summitry were thus revealing the new shape of the region. In a physical way, the world's seafarers were soon to grapple with the same thing.

CHAPTER 4

RISE OF THE INDO-PACIFIC

Admiral Zheng He would have been proud. It was a send-off more befitting an imperial expedition than a police patrol. Uniformed sailors lined the wharf. The image, shaped by official media, was of a great and generous nation contributing order and safety to troubled waters far away. On 26 December 2008, three glittering warships departed China's naval base at Sanya, on Hainan island in the South China Sea, for a ten-day voyage across the Indian Ocean and into history.[1] Their stated mission: to protect Chinese and international shipping from the piracy plaguing the waters off Somalia. But an even greater expectation lay on the officers and crew of the destroyers *Haikou* and *Wuhan*, supported by the supply ship *Weishanhou*. At stake was China's pride, and its confidence in a fleet it had been quietly modernising for years. For this was China's first Indian Ocean naval foray in six centuries, a test of the PRC's readiness to be a power at sea.[2]

China's was one of many navies to converge on the Indian Ocean to fight piracy. The subsequent saga featured all the countervailing currents of connection and competition among nations that would shape the emerging era of the Indo-Pacific.

Pirates and partnership

Pirates have often provoked more than they bargained for. Throughout history, their attacks on merchant shipping have goaded continental states into finding their sea legs. The global military reach of today's United States began with campaigns in the early 1800s against the corsairs of North Africa, the Barbary pirates: hence the 'shores of Tripoli' in the hymn of the

US Marines. It is hard to imagine that the latter-day pirates of Somalia, desperate gangs in barely seaworthy skiffs, were planning to take on the elite of the world's navies, or give cause to China and other countries to make their Indo-Pacific destiny manifest by dispatching warships to far-off waters. Yet that is what happened.

In the world of 2008, piracy – like colonialism, or war between powerful nations – seemed so out-of-date. Global prosperity involved massive flows of seaborne commerce: energy and resources, inputs and finished products for markets from Indo-Pacific Asia to Europe, the Middle East to America. Critical sea lanes included the Gulf of Aden, connecting the Indian Ocean to the Mediterranean, via the Red Sea and the Suez Canal. Yet this artery was squeezed between strife-ridden lands: Yemen to the north, and to the south Somalia. In the wake of civil war, coastal communities found their own lawless methods for survival. Guns were abundant and there was nothing to lose. What little there was of local resources – the fish – was being plundered by commercial trawlers from far away. Yet just beyond the ragged shore lay the cornucopia of a globalising world: an otherworldly flotilla conveying a king's ransom, day after day.

The Somali pirates' haul in 2008 turned out to be a veritable United Nations of treasure and trouble. The pirates attacked vessels owned by or registered in Japan, South Korea, the United States, Germany, India, Malaysia, Singapore, Greece, Panama, Russia, France and Denmark. The targets ranged from yachts and tugboats to bulk carriers and a supertanker. Hijacked cargoes included oil from Saudi Arabia, chemicals from Singapore, palm oil from Malaysia, even a shipload of Russian tanks en route to Kenya. Hostages were grabbed without discrimination: sailors from Malaysia to Myanmar, Pakistan to the Philippines, Iran to India, Estonia to Egypt. An intrepid French couple on a yachting odyssey was kidnapped. Attempts were made to take cruise liners full of wealthy Americans and Germans. Fishing trawlers were seized with their crews, one Spanish and another, most consequentially, from China.

What made China's leaders reach that historic decision to send the PLAN into the Indian Ocean? The hijacking of the Chinese long-range fishing vessel

Chinese crewmen being held captive by Somali pirates on board the
FV Tianyu No. 8 *in 2008, the incident that sparked China's first modern*
naval deployment to the Indian Ocean

Tianyu No. 8 while trawling off the coast of Kenya on 14 November 2008 was likely a decisive factor. A photograph of the captured crew spread around the world and inside China, where social media was blooming. Chinese sailors squatted on the deck, held at gunpoint by African sea-bandits. This was national humiliation for all to see, only mildly redeemed a month later by the resourcefulness of another Chinese fishing crew, who held off armed pirates with nothing more than water cannon, beer bottles and Molotov cocktails until the Malaysian navy saved the day.[3]

Not that it was just public outrage – malleable in a one-party state – that drove China's decision. Stars had aligned. China could hardly get a neater rationale to test-drive its new ocean-going warships, to watch how other navies operated, or to begin performing what the leadership called its 'new historic missions'. These had been set out in a speech by President Hu Jintao in December 2004. As China turned into a global economic power, its military was now charged not only with protecting the Communist Party and national territory, or taking Taiwan, but safeguarding broader interests like economic development, even contributing to global peace.[4] Piracy was disrupting energy and trade: the foundations of economic and political stability, within China but also in a connected world. There was little risk of looking like a sheriff or vigilante in breach of the non-interference Beijing had long trumpeted. The United Nations Security Council had bestowed a global blessing, calling all capable states to defeat Somali piracy 'by deploying naval vessels and military aircraft'.[5] Many were already in action: the United States, its European and Canadian allies, the Russians, the Indians and the Malaysians – none averse to shows of force in guarding everyone's cargoes, shipping insurance premiums and the global public good. And more followed, spurred by China's example: South Korea, Japan, Australia and Indonesia. It was quite the Indo-Pacific armada. While the obscure worlds of diplomatic institutions and academia hesitated to name a new strategic system, facts in the water were starting to make one.

In 2007, at the height of globalisation and America's own preponderance, US naval leaders had called for a 'Thousand Ship Navy', an international fleet of all for one and one for all.[6] Navies were no longer about preparing for war, but jointly managing a future of peace and plenty: cooperatively policing the commons against crime, terrorism, environmental hazard and the smuggling of rogue nations like North Korea. Now it seemed the dream had come true in the waters off Somalia. National navies escorted each other's merchant shipping as well as their own. This was not altruism. It made essential sense in a market-driven world, where cargoes, ship ownership and registration were multinational. More than twenty countries, including China, coordinated their patrols with regular meetings, communications channels and even personnel exchanges. This had long been standard practice for the United States and its allies, but for emerging powers like China and India it was new.

There were hopes this signified things to come. The rapidly modernising Chinese navy could join the weary Americans and Europeans as a partner in world order. With vast economic interdependence, and an assumption that wealth and international interaction would accustom the Chinese people to political freedom, Washington's policy mantra was engaging Beijing as a 'responsible stakeholder'.[7] If China could work with America – or old rival Japan – in the Indian Ocean, then surely differences could be managed in other waters too.

Facts in the water: China's perilous edge

It was not to be. Just months after China began cooperating in counter-piracy far from home, a whole other dynamic – confrontation – began on its doorstep. The tale of tensions in the South China Sea and the East China Sea has been told elsewhere.[8] But the way this strife connects to the larger story of Indo-Pacific strategic competition is not widely understood. The South China Sea is at the heart of regional connectivity. Its control by one power could mean leverage right across the Indo-Pacific.

In March 2009, a US surveillance vessel, the USNS *Impeccable*, found its routine operations interrupted about 75 nautical miles south of China's Hainan Island, at the edge of the South China Sea.[9] The *Impeccable* was conducting hydrographic surveys to help future detection of submarines from China's growing Sanya base on Hainan: the same launch point as for the counter-piracy expedition a few months earlier. China and the United States had long differed over whether such surveillance activity was acceptable under international law: it was within China's 200-nautical-mile exclusive economic zone (EEZ), yet outside the more restrictive 12-nautical-mile limit of territorial waters. America cited its right of freedom of navigation under the United Nations Convention on the Law of the Sea (UNCLOS). Alongside the optimism of the responsible stakeholder policy, the US military still hedged against the possibility that a powerful China would be hostile to America, its treaty allies such as Japan, and Taiwan.

For the Pentagon, keeping watch on East Asia's maritime periphery – the South China Sea and the East China Sea – was an essential part of deterring China from disrupting a peaceful status quo. For China, it was unfriendly activity that had to end. America's confidence as sole superpower had been shaken by the global financial crisis. The Obama administration seemed faltering in strategic resolve. And China's strength kept expanding: an economy growing annually at double digits, with defence spending rising at least as quickly, 14.9 per cent in 2009 alone. The 2008 Beijing Olympics had projected a message of national greatness. China was poised to pass Japan as the world's second-largest economy. The

PLA already had a budget larger than that of any military except America's. China's bid for global dominance would come later, under Xi Jinping. But 2009 marked the start of a new assertiveness.

The crew of the USNS *Impeccable* thus witnessed an early warning. Their unarmed vessel was mobbed by a motley flotilla, all under the Chinese flag: fishing boats, coast guard, fisheries administration and a navy ship. The face-off was broadcast worldwide. There was risk of collision and loss of life. China lacked 'incidents at sea' agreements with other countries, protocols and hotlines to discourage such encounters or stop them escalating. Such rules had worked between America and the Soviet Union to keep the Cold War cold. But Beijing claimed no need, suggesting the solution was 'trust' – and the departure of America's navy.

China's seaward edge was suddenly perilous. For years, the South China Sea had been calm. Nations had agreed to disagree. Traditionally, this had been a shared space, vital to many societies through fisheries and Indo-Pacific trade routes – a pattern amplified in the 2000s, when it carried trillions of dollars' worth of trade, perhaps a third of global shipping.[10] Post-colonial boundaries, interstate struggles and the codification of international law made these waters contested in the 20th century. China, Taiwan, Vietnam, the Philippines, Malaysia and Brunei had overlapping claims. Indonesia preserved its own corner. China used a simple U-shaped and nine-dash line from a 1947 map, and vague claims of historic rights, to assert authority over much of the entire body of water.[11] In 1974 and 1988, Chinese forces violently wrested disputed islands from Vietnam. But as China seemed to accept the diplomatic bonds of Asia-Pacific regionalism in the 1990s, tensions had eased. A pause was called in the race to build makeshift outposts on disputed rocks and reefs. In 2002, China and the Southeast Asian nations even agreed in principle to negotiate a 'code of conduct' to manage differences. (By 2019, they were still negotiating.) There was talk of shared exploitation of fisheries and undersea oil and gas. It looked like the South China Sea was yesterday's issue, or a problem shelved for future generations.

Yet in 2010 Chinese officials began openly defining the South China Sea as a 'core interest', up there with Taiwan, Tibet and domestic stability as something for which the People's Republic would fight. A campaign of assertiveness began in the water, with case after case of ostensibly civilian (and occasionally military) Chinese vessels harassing foreigners, from Filipino and Vietnamese fishermen to prospecting energy companies. Boats were rammed, survey cables cut, threats issued, warning shots fired. India's navy and others traversing international waters were warned away, or given an unsought Chinese naval escort. Theories abounded as to why China was suddenly pushing long-dormant claims: was it about oil or fish or national pride? Could the shift have been brought about more by legal timelines, specifically the May 2009 decision by Vietnam and Malaysia to clarify their claims before a United Nations commission?[12] Was it maverick security agencies jostling for status?[13] Was China's real motive securing the sea as a bastion for nuclear-armed submarines, so it could deter America from aiding Taiwan in future conflict? Or was it about controlling the world's vital sea lanes so that China's shipping would be secure and others' kept at risk?

To confuse matters further, another front opened, this time further north, against Japan, over the waters, rocks and islands of the East China Sea. Again, at one level this was barely explicable: whatever their differences, China and Japan had calmly agreed to disagree over the East China Sea for decades. To be fair, Japan's right to the Senkaku Islands (or Diaoyu, to China) was open to dispute. It was a matter of pride on both sides, and to another claimant, Taiwan. But all claimants had long had better things to focus on. Materially, the possession of barren rocks would not matter if the countries agreed to share fisheries and seabed resources. And if the region's future was cooperation and peace, then the question of China's navy having uncontested passage past the islands in wartime need not arise. Depictions of Japan, Taiwan, Guam and the Philippines as a pro-American 'island chain' that blocked China from the open ocean surely belonged in the 1950s. Just as the new China had seemed intent on a peaceful rise and prosperous partnership with all, the Japan of 2009–2010 was swerving from its US alliance. After a rare change of government to the left-leaning Democratic Party of Japan, Prime Minister Hatoyama Yukio spoke of 'Asia first' and a

Tokyo more equidistant between Washington and Beijing.[14] The time was ripe for a Chinese charm offensive.

Instead, bewilderingly, by late 2010 China–Japan relations were all at sea. China held major naval exercises west of Japan, testing its latest cruise missiles intended to sink the American – or Japanese – fleets. Then, in September, a Chinese trawler collided with a Japanese coast guard vessel trying to prevent it fishing illegally near the contested islands. The Chinese skipper was arrested and there followed a spiral of confrontation, with face-offs at sea, nationalist protests on land and accusations that China was blocking the export of rare-earth minerals to hurt Japan's electronics industry. America reassured Japan that the Senkaku Islands were included in the treaty obliging Washington to help Tokyo in a military crisis. China had lost its chance to woo Japan. Two years later, tensions over the islands' sovereignty flared again, leading to years of near-war confrontation.

Pushback and pivot

Meanwhile, in 2012, the conservative Liberal Democratic Party returned to power with Abe Shinzō as prime minister, determined to prosecute his vision of a Japan protecting its interests across a broad region. Amid fears that China was preparing to dominate not only waters around Japan but also Japan's economic artery of the South China Sea, Abe envisaged out-flanking China's interests (and pre-emptively safeguarding Japan's) even further afield, in the lifeline of the Indian Ocean. He sharpened ideas from his previous brief stint in office in 2006–2007: a modernised military operating flexibility to support the US alliance; a novel partnership with India around a 'confluence of the two seas'; closer links, ideally a 'quasi-alliance', with an Australia that by 2015 was considering buying Japanese submarines; and a 'security diamond', a quadrilateral arrangement of the four democracies to support a rules-based order placing limits on Chinese power.[15] Some elements of an Indo-Pacific strategy were already visible.

The full extent of China's maritime ambition was unknown, but that early assertiveness did not pass unchallenged. Vietnam stood its ground.

Japan stepped up. The United States began reminding its allies and China of its own unique power and presence. In July 2010 it surfaced three of its most advanced submarines simultaneously off South Korea, the Philippines and Diego Garcia in the Indian Ocean: a signal of region-wide deterrence.[16] That same year, Secretary of State Hillary Clinton used regional forums to hold China to account and signal that America was 'here to stay'.[17] Encouraged by Australia and others, America finally joined the East Asia Summit. Caucusing among allies, Clinton made the ASEAN Regional Forum the venue for concerted criticism of China's new recklessness. The veil was off: so much that a senior Chinese official crudely warned his Vietnamese and Singaporean counterparts that China was a big state, others were small states 'and that's a fact'.[18] But there was still another big state on their horizons.

Washington sought to coalesce its revived focus on Asia with what became known as the 'Rebalance' or 'Pivot'.[19] President Obama addressed the Australian Parliament in November 2011, declaring that 'as a Pacific nation, the United States will play a larger and long-term role in shaping this region and its future'.[20] This raised plenty of questions. Was America executing an overdue correction, recommitting to its Asian allies after a decade's detour against terrorism in the Middle East? Had America ever left Asia? An under-recognised success of the George W. Bush administration – overshadowed by the war on terror and the disaster of Iraq – had been sustained commitment to Asia.[21] Did 'pivoting' to Asia mean retrenching somewhere else, like Europe? Was the rebalance meant to be economic, through the new free trade initiative of a Trans-Pacific Partnership? Was it largely diplomatic, with America making better use of partners and all those regional institutions? Or was it military? But if so, it was hard to see how such a policy could be credible, when it involved only small new force commitments, like lightweight 'littoral combat ships' operating out of Singapore and a few thousand marines being sent to Darwin, in northern Australia, for training. On the other hand, some observers worried that any expansion of America's security footprint in Asia was part of a needlessly provocative 'containment' of a China that still had good intentions until proven otherwise.[22]

And what region was the rebalance about anyway? Obama's Canberra speech referred variously to the Pacific, Asia, the Asia-Pacific and 'from the Pacific to the Indian Ocean'. Elsewhere, Secretary of State Clinton and the architect of the rebalance, her assistant secretary, Kurt Campbell, had begun referring to something else: the Indo-Pacific.[23] This was partly about the nature of the alliance with Australia, and a recognition that this key ally looked out on both oceans. But Obama had also noted that America welcomed India's larger role as an Asian power. After decades of estrangement, the world's two largest democracies were joining forces.

Eagle and elephant

When India tested nuclear weapons in May 1998, America led the condemnation. Since the end of the Cold War, the world, it was popularly imagined, had been relegating these most abhorrent of armaments to the dustbin of history, with cuts to superpower arsenals and a test-ban treaty. Yet here was a country defying the tide, prompting its rival Pakistan to do the same. Bill Clinton's administration initially spearheaded global moves to enforce a norm embodied in the Non-Proliferation Treaty: defining virtue in a double standard where possession of nuclear weapons was deemed legal only for the five powers that had tested them before 1967 – the United States, the Soviet Union (later Russia), China, the United Kingdom and France. Its outcry against the explosions in India's Thar Desert seemed just another bid to bar new players from the club.

Mistrust cut both ways. Delhi kept unhappy memories of American support for Pakistan and the anti-Indian postures of Nixon and Kissinger. State Department orthodoxy had long cast India as troublemaker, a 'hardline' member of the non-aligned movement, close to Russia, ambivalent about market economics, and enamoured with the UN mostly as a place to obstruct America's version of order. Outdated stereotypes of poverty, chaos, caste and bureaucracy fed a smug superiority towards India among many countries' policy elites.

Yet India was changing, and far-sighted observers saw opportunity.

Within just a month of its token atomic anger, Washington began secret talks with New Delhi to find common ground. In justifying nuclear weapons, India's prime minister, Atal Bihari Vajpayee, wrote to President Clinton of a 'deteriorating security environment', with 'an overt nuclear weapon state on our borders, a state which committed armed aggression against India in 1962'.[24] He meant China. While thirty-four years may seem a long time in diplomacy, India sustained mistrust 'mainly due to the unresolved border problem' – and the fact that China had helped Pakistan acquire nuclear arms of its own.

America's incentives to tolerate a nuclear India were complex. An immediate goal was peace between India and Pakistan. For the next five years, India–Pakistan relations hovered hazardously between peace and war, with the intense but localised Kargil conflict in 1999, frequent cross-border terrorism emanating from Pakistan, and a million-soldier mobilisation following a terrorist attack on the Indian Parliament in December 2001. American shuttle diplomacy – back and forth visits to convey trusted messages between New Delhi and Islamabad – helped defuse India–Pakistan confrontation in 2002. This averted war, and allowed America and India to concentrate on fostering their new friendship.

The US government was realising the absurdity of telling India to abjure nuclear weapons while China and Pakistan showed no intent of doing the same. And there were other currents. India was becoming a serious economic player: despite diverse troubles, it was attaining growth rates around 7 per cent, with forecasts of better ahead. While it had opened up later than China, and had much reform to finish, the Indian market held global promise: credible projections were that it would become one of the world's three largest economies, part of the new BRIC (Brazil, Russia, India, China) phenomenon (later to become the BRICS with the addition of South Africa in 2010). Migration had made Americans of Indian origin a large, skilled and wealthy community, a lobby alongside Israel and Taiwan in influencing Washington. Rather than shatter US–India relations, the 1998 tests might have cured a long malady, a crude nuclear medicine.

Relations flourished, with visits by successive US presidents, cooperation in defence and counter-terrorism, and even America's leadership of a radical new agenda – this time to give India special status as a legitimate partner in the nuclear energy industry worldwide. In 2005, the United States initiated a controversial nuclear deal to signal new trust. India's coalition government, led by the centre-left Congress party, now prioritised friendship with the once-suspect United States. The prime minster, soft-spoken economist Manmohan Singh, gambled on it as his signature foreign policy.

By the early 2000s, in a complete reversal, the United States was helping India become a major world power.[25] In the aftermath of the September 11 terrorist attacks, America had in a sense joined India's own long war with jihadist terrorism. But the real glue behind US–India friendship turned out to be China.[26] Both sides were careful not to accentuate the China factor in their public statements, but the reality was plain to America's chief architects of the new relationship, Ambassador Robert Blackwill and his neo-Kautiliyan adviser, Ashley Tellis.[27] Certainly that is what the Chinese saw.[28]

Elephant and dragon

At the turn of what looked set to become an Asian century, America was not India's only suitor. At this stage, Chinese foreign policy was pragmatic, and there were signs of a fresh attempt to build common cause with Asia's other civilisational power. Perhaps China was seeking to neutralise India before it could become a rival or too close to America. Perhaps the win-win of commerce was the thing. After the 1998 nuclear tests, India encountered a double game from its strengthening neighbour. On the one hand, China refused to legitimise India's nuclear weapons. Having signed the Non-Proliferation Treaty in 1992, and despite its own illegal nuclear assistance to Pakistan, China instructed its diplomats to deplore India with a convert's zeal. Beijing also kept up support for Pakistan's military.

On the other hand, China did not take Pakistan's side in the crises of 1999 and 2001–2002, allowing India to concentrate on one adversary.

And in 2003 China bestowed the modest 'gift' of recognising Indian sovereignty over Sikkim, formerly a tiny Himalayan kingdom over which the two powers had clashed in 1967. Hints were dropped that a solution to the wider border dispute was at hand.[29] Larger gains beckoned: these were now the world's two fastest-growing economies, and trade was taking wing in more ways than one. Direct flights between the two countries finally began. The 1950s rhetoric of China–India *bhai-bhai* resurfaced, not entirely with irony, along with a new term: 'Chindia'.

Yet this new pan-Asianism soon withered. In 2005, Delhi and Beijing found themselves vying for influence in Nepal amid political crisis in that neighbouring monarchy. Their own border tensions flared again and both sides reinforced their militaries in the mountains. On issues like water and energy, where such huge developing countries may have sought to meet needs together, a competitive dynamic emerged: China outbid India for energy supplies in Africa and the Middle East. Concerns grew that Chinese dam building in Tibet would rob Indians of a basic necessity, restricting the flow of the Brahmaputra River, a mainstay of Indian agriculture. China and India may not have become fully fledged rivals – for a start, that would have required China to recognise India as a peer – but relations would stay stuck at competitive coexistence. Phases of cooperation would end in confrontation. Xi Jinping's opening dialogue with Narendra Modi in 2014 was interrupted by a Chinese submarine foray to Sri Lanka and tensions on the Himalayan border – the foretaste of a confrontation between Chinese and Indian troops on the Doklam plateau in 2017.

China seems to have concluded as early as 2005 that India had fallen categorically into the US camp. The nuclear deal was a transformational gesture China could not match, and proof that America was co-opting India in constricting China's rise. This perception was reinforced by a new camaraderie among the American and Indian security establishments. Plans were announced – however aspirational and painfully negotiated – in areas like defence equipment, space programs and missile defences.

Four's a crowd

Some of the most tangible signs of US–India alignment were on the water, where China's own ambitions, interests and vulnerabilities were growing. In 2002, an Indian patrol vessel took on escort duties for US military cargoes from Singapore through the Malacca Strait.[30] Next came the rapid combined mobilisation of India and American forces – along with Australia and Japan – to deliver relief after the December 2004 tsunami. Since 1992, India and America had modest annual naval drills, called Malabar. Now these exercises expanded in ambition, with submarines and aircraft carriers. In 2005, they simulated a month-long war at sea. The next year the US marines played too. In 2007, Malabar was held twice. First, it extended into the Pacific, bringing Japan into the fold. Indian, American and Japanese forces trained together off Okinawa. In September, a second round of wargames brought in warships from Australia and Singapore. More than twenty-seven vessels converged in the Bay of Bengal, with three aircraft carriers and more than 200 aircraft.

It was a strong signal – too strong. A month earlier, mid-level officials from the United States, Japan, India and Australia had met for a mere forty-five minutes on the sidelines of an ASEAN Regional Forum meeting in Manila to talk about lessons learned from their shared tsunami relief operations. Perhaps they also exchanged a few views on other matters of shared interest, such as China.[31] Now the five-nation naval exercise in the Bay of Bengal was being conflated with that first 'quadrilateral' dialogue: perhaps not surprisingly, given that the quad's first champion was Prime Minister Abe of Japan.

China reacted with public outrage and diplomatic pressure, conducting formal démarches in all 'quad' capitals. Its officials and media portrayed that brief consultative meeting as a plot to forge an 'Asian NATO' – a firm alliance to gang up on China and 'contain' it, just as the Soviet Union had been crushed.

The reality was very different. The exercise had been a one-off, and commitment to the dialogue was fragile. Japan's attachment weakened after Prime Minister Abe suddenly left office in ill health. India was lukewarm, its coalition government disrupted by leftist parties angry at anything resembling military alignment with America. Close US–India relations were Prime Minister Singh's priority, one reason he could ease off on the quad. Enter Australia's new Labor government in late 2007 under Kevin Rudd, who voiced great ambitions for diplomacy in Asia. The Mandarin-speaking prime minister subsequently received almost all the blame, somewhat unfairly, for the demise of that first incarnation of the quad.[32] That said, it was more than a bad look for the embryonic four-party solidarity when his foreign minister, Stephen Smith, revealed Rudd's intent not to continue with the quad, while standing beside his visiting Chinese counterpart at a press conference.

The end of Quad 1.0 was, however, only a minor distraction in the larger picture of realignment among the four maritime democracies. Bit by bit, they identified convergent interests across the two-ocean region, with misgivings about China a significant driver. Indeed, by concentrating its wrath on the quad, a phantom menace, China was missing the main game.[33] Bilateral security relations were strengthening: the United States and India, but now also Japan and India, even Australia and India. New security triangles were forming too: dialogues, intelligence sharing and complex military exercises among Australia, the United States and Japan were now joined by consultations with Delhi. A web of trusted security relations in every other permutation among the quad members had the same effect of preparing to manage Chinese power, even if the four nations never met in the same room again.

Presence and pearls

Back in the Indian Ocean, the fight against Somali piracy was turning into a contest for national advantage. One of the last works of the celebrated Australian international relations scholar Dr Coral Bell was a 2007 paper titled 'The end of the Vasco da Gama era', in which she foreshadowed emerging multipolar competition among nations. 'The Indian Ocean,' she wrote, 'is likely to become an arena of complex naval rivalries.'[34]

As the foreign naval presence persisted, piracy declined. The international fleet marked plenty of wins, such as the mission of American Navy SEALs retold in Hollywood movie *Captain Phillips*. But there was little clear link between naval action and the drop in piracy. Of greater impact was improved policing and governance on land, and private military companies starting to put hired guns on merchant ships.[35] Yet even as the original pirate threat began to dissipate, foreign navies kept using it as a rationale for visiting the Indian Ocean – and staying. Counter-piracy was turning into an excuse for more strategic missions. If foreign militaries still had something to watch for in the Indian Ocean, it was each other.

America and its European allies were already familiar with Indian Ocean waters, given their long operations in the Middle East. Australia's navy had been present almost continuously since 1911. India was hardly going to neglect its own maritime backyard. What was surprising was the new tenacity of East Asian powers. Since 2001, Japan had creatively interpreted its 'peace constitution' to send ships to the Indian Ocean in support of US-led action against terrorism in Afghanistan and elsewhere. Now, along with regular counter-piracy rotations by its destroyers, Japan began flying surveillance aircraft, initially out of a US facility in Djibouti and then, after 2010, from its own. However small, with just 180 troops, this was the first overseas Japanese military base since 1945. Even South Korea – a country preoccupied with the grave problem to its north – showed it meant business when defending its economic lifeblood. South Korea's dependence on energy imports was even more acute than China's or Japan's. In 2011 it despatched a destroyer and commandos to take lethal action against pirates and recapture a chemical tanker. And from 2009 it had quietly kept a special forces unit in the United Arab Emirates.[36]

China's new security presence was on a different scale entirely. A three-month mission turned permanent. By the end of 2018, the Chinese navy had rotated its forces thirty-one times, providing long-range experience for 100 warships with more than 26,000 sailors, escorting more than 6600 merchant ships and rescuing seventy.[37] It augmented its Indian Ocean patrols with submarines – a capability of limited use against piracy, but

ideal for intelligence collection, deterrence and war. In 2014, Chinese submarines began turning up in Sri Lanka.[38] That same year, Chinese warships
began annual combat exercises in another part of the ocean, the northeastern corner near Indonesia's Sunda Strait and Australia's island territories,
which made for bracing news in Canberra.[39] China was making itself at
home in the Indian Ocean. Some of this activity was welcomed or even
encouraged by local nations. Chinese forces worked cooperatively with
Australia and many other nations in searching for missing Malaysian air-
liner MH370. And China's navy evacuated its own and other countries'
nationals from strife-torn Yemen. But China's security planners had a lot
more than constabulary missions on their minds.

As far back as 2004, American security analysts were warning of a new
Chinese strategy they colourfully termed the 'string of pearls'.[40] They cited
a little-known 2001 agreement between China and Pakistan to build a deep-
water port on the desolate sands of Gwadar, a fishing village on the Arabian
Sea. This, it was claimed, was part of a grand plan to build Chinese naval
bases, access points and energy infrastructure across the Indian Ocean, thus
protecting China's seaborne oil supplies in some future clash with America,
with the dual benefit of strangling nascent rival India in its own eponymous
ocean. This was widely dismissed as fanciful and paranoid, at a time when
fashionable thinking about international affairs dwelt on market-based
global cooperation, the obsolescence of major war and the unity of all
civilised states against terrorism. Surely the new China was all about what
it professed: peaceful development and win-win cooperation in a harmonious world.

At the start of China's counter-piracy operations, its official line was
a firm denial of any intent to set up overseas bases. Yet soon prominent
Chinese strategists were flagging that such a global military footprint was
no longer an idea to shun.[41] Within a few more years, negotiations had
begun with local authorities to build a significant Chinese military facility
in Djibouti, not far from existing French, American and Japanese bases.
The location could hardly be more strategic, next to what had become
the Chinese-operated container port of Doraleh and overseeing the

Bab el-Mandeb chokepoint between the Red Sea and the Gulf of Aden. American pressure had headed off a similar bid by Russia in 2014, but failed to block the audacious Chinese move. So in 2017 Chinese forces raised the red flag in a fortified site capable of housing perhaps 10,000 troops. Whatever their job, it would be about much more than policing piracy. After all, China was already establishing a 'second continent' in Africa, where its investments, aid projects, resource exploitation, peacekeeping deployments and diplomacy had grown dramatically, along with the migration of more than a million Chinese nationals.[42]

In the Ming era, Zheng He had rejected the idea of leaving garrisons far from home. The new China was on an altogether different voyage.

Follow the Maritime Silk Road

It was the first time a foreign leader had addressed the Indonesian parliament, but Xi Jinping's speech of 2 October 2013 made waves for another reason too. 'China and Indonesia face each other across the sea,' he said, referring to historic visits by Zheng He and the 'nice stories' left behind. Xi went on to declare:

> Southeast Asia has since ancient times been an important hub along the ancient Maritime Silk Road. China will strengthen maritime cooperation with ASEAN countries to make good use of the China–ASEAN Maritime Cooperation Fund set up by the Chinese government and vigorously develop maritime partnership in a joint effort to build the Maritime Silk Road of the 21st century.[43]

The term Maritime Silk Road had suddenly entered China's lexicon. It sounded like a big deal. A month earlier, Xi had made an analogous announcement in Astana, Kazakhstan: 'To forge closer economic ties, deepen cooperation and expand development space in the Eurasian region, we should take an innovative approach and jointly build an "economic belt along the Silk Road".'[44] Together, these two speeches framed what would soon be Xi's signature initiative, his mark on history beyond China's borders. It was a grand design that soon became officially known as 'One Belt, One Road' (*Yi Dai Yi Lu* in Chinese). Later, Chinese officials sought to change the English translation to the Belt and Road Initiative (BRI), in a belated effort to counter perceptions that the whole thing was precisely what it was: a China-centric vision of dominating both the land (the belt) and the sea (the road).[45]

Many who paid early attention to the Jakarta and Astana speeches – including China's own bureaucrats – were baffled. Were such expansive infrastructure ambitions and messages of neighbourly goodwill really all that new? If this was primarily about economic cooperation – investment, development assistance and infrastructure – then China had been moving in this direction for years. It was already a growing investor in the region, with good reason: it had capital and others needed it. China was rising in respect and impact as a provider of aid, alongside established donors like Japan and Europe. As China's own countryside developed, it could export infrastructure: Xi's Jakarta speech rightly boasted of the Chinese-built bridge spanning the 5.5-kilometre sea gap between Surabaya and Madura. But some other Chinese projects had brought disappointment or controversy: unfinished oil and gas pipelines; a massive dam halted by local protests in Myanmar; shiny sports stadiums soon in disrepair.[46]

Having attained the leadership less than a year before, Xi was ruthlessly consolidating his power and authority. Instead of focusing on domestic issues, he had surprised foreign observers by staking his reputation on international ambitions. Any self-preserving Chinese bureaucrat or business figure knew the new leader's words were not to be disputed. Instead, they were to be leveraged: for Communist Party apparatchiks, provincial authorities and red capitalists alike, One Belt, One Road was one big opportunity. New initiatives could be cast as fulfilling the leader's vision. Existing pet projects could be rebadged as having been part of it all along. Everything from ports to bridges, highways to high-speed rail, pipelines to oil refineries, through to minor building works and production plants, even a tyre factory in Serbia: it was all being labelled as part of China's 'project of the century'.

The Belt and Road gathered shape and pace. It was many objectives rolled into one: geoeconomics, the use of economics for national power and advantage. As China's economy began to slow, here was boundless scope to keep production going and export excess capacity, notably in steel and cement. Chinese capital could generate returns or, where recipients could not service the debt, the acquisition of far-flung assets like ports through 'debt for equity' swaps. Here was a chance to replace Western countries at the top of value chains, setting the standards in production and transaction that would lock in long-term advantage for Chinese manufacturers and traders. New employment beckoned for Chinese workers on sites from Asia to Africa. Another goal was the projection of Chinese soft power: an image of altruism, whether aid projects in the field or educational placements for foreigners in the motherland. But this was accompanied by harder and sharper forms of power: influence over foreign elites, where economic leverage through debt, dependence and personal corruption could one day translate into support or silence on matters like diplomacy and defence.

Initially, the PLA was shy about what, if anything, the Belt and Road meant for security. But it soon became impossible to pretend security was separate. The Belt and Road traced the web of China's energy dependence, especially across the waters to Africa and the Middle East. It meant the expansion of China's economic interests, and these would need protecting, in places far away. Moreover, the whole show coincided with the rapid modernisation of a Chinese military able and expected to deploy at distance. Above all, the journey of the BRI bandwagon converged with worsening tension between states as the United States, India, Japan and others become more openly suspicious of how Beijing intended to use its accumulating strength. The vagueness of the geography of what had begun as 'one' belt and road only compounded the uncertainty: different interpretations had it taking in Africa, Europe, the South Pacific, even South America. The official version, formalised in a vision document in 2015, defined the Maritime Silk Road – the seaborne part of the BRI – as crossing the South China Sea through the Indian Ocean to Europe, with a branch line from the South China Sea into the South Pacific.[47]

By the time the developed world finally began noticing the BRI juggernaut, it was already all things to all people. But certain messages about Xi's China stood out. China now saw its wealth and influence as inseparable from its control of regional connectivity, and Xi saw his own legacy and the Party's legitimacy as entangled with his expansive ambitions abroad. One European observer, Bruno Maçães, defined the Belt and Road as nothing less than a Chinese goal of building a new world order.[48] If China's shift to the Indo-Pacific had commenced with its reliance on seaborne oil, now the infrastructure plans of the Maritime Silk Road were entwining China's fate and ambition further with the Indian Ocean and the lands along the sea lanes.

This made it notable that, not long after President Xi began proclaiming the virtues of the BRI, China closed ranks against other visions of the region, especially the emerging Indo-Pacific formulation. In the years before Xi took the helm, Chinese academics had evinced a courageous diversity of views about their country's interests and diplomacy. In 2010, for instance, some were frankly telling foreign counterparts – including the author – that their country's new assertiveness in the South China Sea was wrong and counterproductive.[49] Some Chinese scholars experimented with new Indo-Pacific formulations – *Yin Tai* in Chinese – to make sense of a changing regional order, their country's expanding interests and ways to ensure peaceful coexistence.[50] In June 2013, a senior researcher for the International Department of the Central Committee of the Communist Party, Minghao Zhao, even endorsed a new 'Australian' concept of 'Indo-Pacific Asia', noting it:

> has inspired many Chinese strategic thinkers and planners to begin to look at China's grand strategy across a wide Indo-Pacific swath ... The United States, India, Japan and other players are seeking to collaborate to build an 'Indo-Pacific order' ... China is not necessarily excluded from this project, and it should seek a seat at the table and help recast the strategic objectives and interaction norms that bind all participating states.[51]

But shortly afterwards, One Belt, One Road became the Communist Party orthodoxy, and other nations' visions of regional order became unwelcome. China's official line was now to reject the Indo-Pacific concept as an American or Japanese plot to co-opt India and exclude China from the regional order, even though the Maritime Silk Road was the same region by another name.[52]

Australia names its place

In adopting the term Indo-Pacific Asia, Minghao Zhao had noted that 'Chinese strategists keep a very close eye on the research outlets and debates within Australia.'[53] Australia again found its voice amplified in the regional debate.

The term Indo-Pacific was aired by a few foreign policy observers from around 2004–2005. For example, Canadian naval scholar James Boutilier and New Zealand academic Peter Cozens enlisted it to explain the way the region's maritime security had evolved over the preceding decades. Veteran Australian journalist Michael Richardson used it to describe the new East Asia Summit about to convene in Malaysia. Around the same time, the author of this book, then an Australian government intelligence analyst recently returned from a diplomatic posting to India, was one of several officials to be an early adopter. The logic that Australia's region was changing to a two-ocean system, with China turning south and west and India turning east, accorded both with the evidence and the need to define Australia's place in the world.

Influential voices shared the cause. One of the nation's most respected former political leaders, Labor's Kim Beazley, pushed an Indo-Pacific perspective, which made particular sense in his home state of Western Australia. Another West Australian, foreign and defence minister Stephen Smith, became a decisive convert to this view, influenced by one of the sharpest minds in policy, Peter Varghese, who went from being head of the nation's peak intelligence analysis agency to High Commissioner to India, then secretary of foreign affairs. In 2009, Prime Minister Rudd announced an

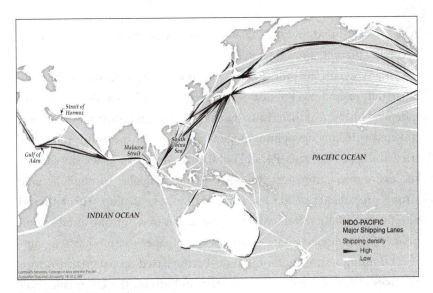

Indo-Pacific shipping lanes

ambitious plan to double the submarine fleet, including for a greater role in the Indian Ocean. But it was his successor, Julia Gillard, whose government fulsomely endorsed a new regional vision. In 2011, she ended a ban on uranium exports to India, closing decades of distance between two Indian Ocean democracies. In 2012, her 'Asian Century white paper' affirmed Australia's region was now the global centre of economic and strategic gravity. It referred to an emerging Indo-Pacific terminology and showed how Australia's economic reliance on China, Japan and South Korea rested in turn on their Indian Ocean supply lines.[54] In early 2013, the Gillard government went further. A new defence white paper, with an iconic map of the sea lanes, officially designated Australia's region of strategic interest the Indo-Pacific.[55]

Lively debate ensued. Critics noted that such a maximalist operating area was unrealistic for Australia's limited defence force acting alone. Some warned the new map overplayed India, excluded China and diminished Asia, worsening regional instability by supporting US-led naval strategy.[56] Others deemed it the last kind of help America needed, calling it 'wrongheaded and dangerous' to encourage the United States to extend forces across two oceans instead of concentrating them to deter China in East

Asia.[57] Never mind that the Indian Ocean was precisely where China was becoming present, and vulnerable.

In any event, an Indo-Pacific imprint was here to stay. It became bipartisan orthodoxy. Political leaders recognised it as authentically and independently Australian. Initially, shadow foreign minister Julie Bishop tinkered with this new phraseology bequeathed by the political foe: she tried 'Indian Ocean Asia-Pacific'. But then as foreign minister, she and her successive prime ministers, Tony Abbott and Malcolm Turnbull, became strong proponents of the Indo-Pacific. By 2017 Bishop, Turnbull and new foreign affairs secretary Frances Adamson were turning mindset into policy. They released a foreign affairs white paper (with bipartisan support) framing a strategy for the Indo-Pacific based on partnerships with the likes of India, Japan and Indonesia, to buttress the US alliance and manage the risks of China's rise.[58] This remained the pattern for the successor conservative government of Prime Minister Scott Morrison, elected in 2019.

Words across the water

Other nations were undergoing their own geopolitical reimaginings, with a cross-pollination of ideas. The American military's Hawaii-based Pacific Command had long called its area of operations the Indo-Asia-Pacific, 'from Hollywood to Bollywood'. American scholars and think tanks were recognising China and America at sea as the new great game; some were ahead in describing the new horizon as the Indo-Pacific.[59] Now US leaders and officials were interspersing such ideas amid old Asia-Pacific rhetoric. President Obama linked his 'Rebalance' to India's 'Act East'.[60]

In 2013, Indonesian president Susilo Bambang Yudhoyono added '*Indo-Pasifik*' to his country's adaptable language. His foreign minister, Marty Natalegawa, called for an 'Indo-Pacific Treaty of Friendship and Cooperation' to safeguard the regional engine of global growth from great-power rivalry.[61] Such non-aligned initiatives could hardly be dismissed as an American plot. A year later, new Indonesian president Joko Widodo defined his archipelagic nation as a nexus of two oceans, a global maritime fulcrum.

India too was charting its own course. In 2014, new prime minister Narendra Modi declared Look East was now Act East, with India stepping up defence links, trade and diplomacy with Southeast Asia, Japan and Australia. He told the Australian Parliament that the dynamic 'Asia-Pacific and Indian Ocean region' was 'the key to this world's future; and Australia is at its cross-currents'.[62]

His predecessor, Manmohan Singh, had already innovated with Indo-Pacific terminology, and soon this would be standard issue for Delhi's normally staid foreign service. After all, Indian analysts had been among the first to imagine the new Asia as a two-ocean system. Eminent strategist Raja Mohan evoked the Hindu myth of *Samudra Manthan* – the churning of the oceans – to convey a gathering contest between China and India as powers at sea.[63] Chief diplomat Shyam Saran saw India's future security interests extending to the Pacific.[64] Naval officer Gurpreet Khurana used the Indo-Pacific to describe early Japan–India security links in 2007.[65] It was much as their forerunner Panikkar had foreseen.

Japan and India took inspiration from one another. Japanese prime minister Abe had long envisioned a bond between Asia's two largest democracies and in 2007, in a speech to the Indian Parliament, offered the poetic 'confluence of the two seas' – *futatsu no umi no majiwari* – as the place where Japan would work with partners like India to promote a rules-based order.[66] Upon returning to power in 2012, amid worsening concerns about China, Abe and his advisers such as Yachi Shōtarō and Kanehara Nobukatsu began putting more prosaic elements of an Indo-Pacific strategy in place, with a reaffirmation of the US alliance, modernisation of Japan's navy, programs for quality infrastructure to win friends in South and Southeast Asia, and active diplomacy towards Indonesia, Vietnam, the Philippines, India and Australia.[67] In early 2016, Japanese scholar Shiraishi Takashi said: 'It is on the Indo-Pacific region that Japan has staked its future.'[68]

Age of uncertainty

Stakes were rising. Strains mounted on the post-1945 liberal international order of institutions, rules and non-coercion. American paramountcy was ending and great-power competition was back, as the likes of Coral Bell had anticipated. Not only China but even more forcefully Russia was showing its authoritarian and revisionist colours. Disrupting and damaging the existing order, advancing national self-interest at the expense of others: these were not side-effects of normal great-power behaviour but central strategic objectives. American leadership and credibility were in question, through both the actions of adversaries and the indecision coming out of Washington. Already in the South China Sea America had lost a chance to stop China's coercion against the Philippines at Scarborough Shoal.[69] Moscow and Beijing were emboldened by Obama's 2013 'red line' over Syria – warning that use of chemical weapons against its own people by the noxious Assad regime would be met with force, then backing down. There followed Russia's aggression against Ukraine and heightened Chinese reck-lessness in the South China Sea, including confrontations with passing American warships. China and Russia gave the impression of coordinated strategies, with showy meetings between Xi and Russian president Vladimir Putin casting the shadow of a possible future alliance across Eurasia. In any case, America couldn't concentrate on great-power competition: no sooner had President Obama suggested closure to a 'long season of war' in 2014 than the terrorist threat had morphed into the black-bannered caliphate of Islamic State.[70]

At least in the East China Sea, Japan's sustained defiance and America's support had made China think twice. Resolve and deterrence had worked. So China returned its gaze south. In early 2014, China deployed a mobile oil rig to claim resources off the coast of Vietnam. This met resistance. The strategy changed, from risky confrontations to a passive aggression that proved brilliantly effective.[71] China began building islands across the South China Sea, in a massive and environmentally devastating campaign of land 'reclamation' on rocks and reefs. Xi Jinping assured Obama there was no intent to 'militarise' such construction. Satellite imagery exposed the falsehood: runways, hangars, missile batteries. China was manufacturing an archipelago of militarised islands: unsinkable aircraft carriers to control the whole disputed sea. The burden of risk shifted. Now China would accuse other nations like America or Australia of disturbing the peace by sailing or flying close to its new 'islands', even though their actions upheld longstanding freedoms and practice in international waters and airspace.

America and the region's smaller powers used regional meetings to deplore such intimidation, to little effect. The Philippines kept faith in law: in 2013 it had brought a case against China to the international Permanent Court of Arbitration. It persisted with the case through to a resounding outcome in July 2016, which found China had no legal basis to claim historical rights over the South China Sea. But China rejected the ruling: it was writing its own laws. And soon a new government in Manila, under volatile populist Rodrigo Duterte, was walking away from the hard-fought legal victory and weakening hopes for Southeast Asian solidarity.

More storm clouds gathered. Amid reports of Russian interference, Donald Trump was elected president of the United States in November 2016. Trump had no experience in international policy, a record of disparaging America's allies, and no commitment to a rules-based order or American leadership abroad. He scrapped the Trans-Pacific Partnership, the free trade pillar of Obama's Asian rebalance. It was time for the middle players to step up.

The Indo-Pacific tide

Kenya is a long way from Tokyo, but a fitting place for an origin story. In August 2016, Abe Shinzō went to Nairobi to open a conference on African development, with a narrative about two oceans as well as two continents:

> When you cross the seas of Asia and the Indian Ocean and come to Nairobi, you then understand very well that what connects Asia and Africa is the sea lanes ... Japan bears the responsibility of fostering the confluence of the Pacific and Indian Oceans and of Asia and Africa into

a place that values freedom, the rule of law, and the market economy, free from force or coercion, and making it prosperous.[72]

He was unveiling Japan's 'Free and Open Indo-Pacific' strategy. This linked integration across the water with economic and social development. It was forthright about democratic values. The word China did not need to appear in Abe's speech. Tokyo had taken the contest all the way to Africa. Not that this was Japan's lone stand; Abe and India's Modi were accelerating their Indo-Pacific partnership, as they would announce together after their train ride the week of Trump's election win. India was hardening its stance against China's Belt and Road: boycotting a grand BRI summit in 2017 and declaring exhaustive conditions – of environmental sustainability, financial rectitude and good governance – on any future acceptance of Chinese infrastructure projects.

With the advent of Trump, global uncertainty became instability. Political polarisation, policy paralysis and self-harm curtailed American influence. Opponents of the US-led international order sought to lock in their gains. Trump's capricious confrontation on the Korean peninsula raised the spectre first of conflict, then of capitulation. Whatever their claims to the contrary, America's friends were anxious. They contemplated how long they would need to band in 'middle power coalitions' to sustain order until America's fever passed.[73]

But instead of fatalism, a new activism infused the diplomacy of US allies, notably Australia and Japan. Their watchword was 'Don't panic, don't relax'. On trade, Turnbull and Abe salvaged the Trans-Pacific Partnership such that America could one day rejoin. On security, Tokyo and Canberra worked assiduously across the US system to remind America of its equities in Asia and the risks of weakening the order that had brought peace and prosperity. The web of diplomatic triangles came into play, with Tokyo, Delhi and Canberra conferring among themselves and each cross-bracing the other's advice to Washington. The model was a set of independent yet interlocking schemes to hedge between Chinese power and American unpredictability. The thinking was expressed in Australia's November 2017 foreign affairs white paper, which directed closer cooperation among democracies to achieve 'a balance in the Indo-Pacific favourable to our interests'.[74]

And America did not entirely disappoint. In November 2017, the quadrilateral dialogue reconvened at last: now with a broader agenda of strategic issues – obviously China – and a determination by all four countries that this time their consultations would persist. Then, during the annual Asia-centric summit season – APEC and the East Asia Summit – the American rhetoric called for a Free and Open Indo-Pacific, the very term Abe had unveiled in Africa. Was America endorsing Japan's plan or just applying the same label to its own? At the very least, Abe had proven persuasive in bringing the difficult occupant of the White House some way to a worldview acceptable to America's friends and its foreign policy establishment. The world's media noticed the Indo-Pacific terminology for the first time, and wondered what it meant: some assumed it was somehow all about lifting India up and shutting China out.[75]

But Donald Trump made an unconvincing champion for an agenda meant to respect rules, inclusiveness and allies. His speech to APEC in Da Nang, Vietnam, awkwardly juxtaposed such sentiments with the trade protectionism of his domestic slogan, 'America First'. The common ground was an accentuation of national sovereignty. Thus, Trump said, America saw the region as 'a place where sovereign and independent nations, with diverse cultures and many different dreams, can all prosper side-by-side, and thrive in freedom and in peace'.[76] That, at least, was hard to disagree with.

Still, responses were mixed, including scepticism that Trump's America truly intended to compete with China for influence, or had the smarts to do so constructively. Allies were buoyed, albeit mildly. With Trump, they had set their sights low. A month later the United States released a National Security Strategy describing China and Russia in threatening terms and ranking as a top American priority the 'geopolitical competition between free and repressive visions of world order ... in the Indo-Pacific region'.[77] America was now talking the talk of the Indo-Pacific, but the jury was out on whether it would walk the walk in defence, economics and diplomacy.

Analysts warned that the Trump administration was offering more a 'conceptual bumper sticker' than a strategy.[78] At an Indo-Pacific Business Forum, Secretary of State Mike Pompeo applauded decades of foundational American business investment in Asia – then announced embarrassingly meagre funding to support new technology partnerships. The pivot had been uncomfortable enough: now Washington was promising even more and at risk of delivering even less.

Others were not investing all their hopes in America. Indonesia urged its fellow Southeast Asian countries to try to take to control of the emerging Indo-Pacific idea if they wanted to preserve the centrality of their precious ASEAN.[79] By mid-2019 the Southeast Asians had agreed to an 'Indo-Pacific outlook' document that defined their shared interests in rules, sovereignty and non-coercion across the two-ocean region, while also warning of the risks from US–China rivalry: they saw danger on either side.

A year earlier, Chinese foreign minister Wang Yi had openly dismissed the Indo-Pacific as an 'attention-grabbing idea' – perhaps because he saw it undermining other nations' support for the Belt and Road.[80] Yet this did not stop French president Emmanuel Macron, speaking at a naval base on Australia's Sydney Harbour, from invoking the Indo-Pacific as 'a geostrategic reality in the making' and the basis for a new balance of power to discourage hegemony; he even suggested a new 'Paris–Delhi–Canberra' axis.[81] At the 2018 Shangri-La Dialogue, an international security summit in Singapore, the Indo-Pacific was in almost every speech, beginning with the keynote from India's Prime Minister Modi. Some commentators breathlessly heralded a new era in regional diplomacy.[82]

This may have been somewhat premature: Indo-Pacific mania was not universal. Some governments remained reluctant. New Zealand gradually got on board, with a nuanced policy of referring to the Indo-Pacific in forums that involved India, but sticking with Asia-Pacific or just the Pacific in other venues.[83] Even as their governments were expanding their policy horizons, some foreign policy elites still found the Indo-Pacific too vague a concept.[84] America and Japan spoke of 'Free and Open', whereas others such as Australia, India and Indonesia were creatively promiscuous with their adjectives: free, fair, open, inclusive, transparent and more. Yet the terms of diplomacy in Asia were indeed shifting.

Whatever the unpredictability of Trump, American foreign policy was taking a definite stance on China – bipartisan and tough. Soon allies would find themselves wanting to moderate American confrontation with China, not encourage it. Talk turned to comprehensive strategic competition, economic 'decoupling', technological rivalry, even a new cold war. Years of state-directed Chinese cyber infiltration and intellectual property theft had the unintended consequence of rewiring American doves into hawks. The business community, tech sector, State Department and Democrats were now joining Republicans, the Pentagon, intelligence agencies and human rights organisations in seeing Xi's authoritarian party-state as a relentless source of risk. Concerns over political interference and influence by the Chinese Communist Party had gained prominence in Australia, and now spread to America and beyond.[85] Vice President Pence condemned the Belt and Road as 'debt diplomacy', and claimed America would form 'new and stronger bonds with nations that share our values across the region, from India to Samoa'.[86] In June 2019, the Pentagon released an Indo-Pacific Strategy report. This affirmed the Indo-Pacific as the priority theatre for the US military. It set out plans to combine multiple elements of power – military force, diplomacy, governance and geoeconomics – and to support a network of allies and partners in competing with the 'repressive' vision of a 'revisionist' China.[87] This built on a vote by Congress to support defence spending to compete with China across the region.[88]

After an unsteady start, America, Japan and Australia were joining forces with promised infrastructure investments such as electricity and undersea cables to contest Chinese geoeconomic influence over smaller countries. This was especially so in the South Pacific, no longer a strategic backwater but an extension of the Belt and Road, complete with alleged ambitions for a Chinese military base.[89]

Only a decade had passed, but the new era of power rivalry was a world away from the optimism of globalisation, China's peaceful rise, the all-together Thousand Ship Navy and the obsolescence of major-power conflict. The Indo-Pacific had become the global centre of gravity, in wealth and population, but also the heartland of military might and latent conflict. Confrontation was trumping cooperation. From the Gulf of Aden to Papua New Guinea, the board was uncomfortably set for a great game with many layers and many players.

PRESENT

CHAPTER 5

GAMES AND GIANTS

The contemporary power competition in the Indo-Pacific has been likened to the 'Great Game', the 19th-century imperial rivalry in the frontiers of India and central Asia.[1] It's an evocative echo. One of Britain's goals back then was to prevent rival Russia from securing access to the Indian Ocean and the Gulf. The modern parallel substitutes the Russian and British empires for China and its various potential adversaries – America, India, Japan – and replaces the mountainous with the maritime. Depicted in Rudyard Kipling's classic novel *Kim*, the Great Game 'never ceases day or night'; it is so large 'one sees but a little at a time', the action is all about positioning, rumour, shadow plays, espionage, merchants, agents of influence and local proxies as much as it is about armies and raw power.[2] Strong states seek advantage not outright conflict. They want to win without war.

Power games

The game metaphor can be played further in today's Indo-Pacific. As China, America and others build a mosaic of bases, partnerships and capabilities across the region's strategic real estate, the obvious analogy is a chessboard. The right asset in the right location delivers a certain effect: intelligence, deterrence, attrition, decisive harm. Even more apt is the ancient Asian strategy game of Go, or *Weiqi*.[3] This originated in China, spreading to Korea and Japan, where it was refined in its modern form. This Asian origin manifests in a fluidity and ambiguity that fits a maritime setting. The board game is more strategy than tactics, more prolonged outflanking than decisive confrontation or manoeuvre. It involves endless feints and patience, a long view where triumph and defeat can look deceptively alike right to the end. Success requires balance; the players poise constantly over a fine line between victorious encirclement and self-defeating overreach.

The emerging power contest in the Indo-Pacific combines all three – the Great Game, chess and Go – but with added dimensions of complexity. It is a game with many layers: military strength, to be sure, but also the economics of wealth, trade, investment and infrastructure.[4] Technology offers the new commanding heights. Diplomacy and intelligence play their part, but so do propaganda and political interference: in some ways the narrative *is* the battle.

Compounding the confusion, this is a game with many players. It is not a simple contest of China against the United States, or even of China and its supposed friends (such as Russia) against a US-led system of allied democracies. Multipolarity, a many-sided dynamic, is a defining feature of the region and its evolution: both in terms of there being many prospective centres of power, and of the potential for groups of them to band together to prevent one power dominating. Whichever way you measure them – population, economies, militaries, technology, geography, diplomacy – multiple countries have agency. The future will not be mapped by China or, for that matter, by the United States, either alone or together. Rather, it will be charted by the choices of many.

The next two chapters survey this game of many players. Six are examined in depth. Of these, three have claim to be giants into the future: China, India and the United States. Their moves will have global repercussions. A fourth, Japan, is battling relative decline but remains a resilient nation, holding its place as one of the world's largest economies. There is endless debate about what constitutes a 'major' or 'great' power – loosely, a nation that has global interests and impact, and can not only protect itself but compel others too. America and China are undoubtedly in the front rank. But, at least within the Indo-Pacific region, India and Japan are important too, perhaps best defined as a cross between major powers and middle players: India with its population, growth path and military (including nuclear) strength; Japan with a sizeable economy, a quietly formidable military and the 'quintessential smart power' of using limited resources to good effect.[5]

Within a generation, by the 2040s, these four may well be joined by a fifth: Indonesia. These will be five of the most consequential nations, all in the world's pivotal region. It is also worth scrutinising a sixth country, Australia, due not only to its core Indo-Pacific geography or its active role in shaping the region, but also its status as a bellwether, an example for other middle powers – countries that will need to mobilise all their wits and resources to navigate a region dominated by the contest, or cooperation, of giants.

Nations are not billiard balls

Of course, the game analogy has its limits. It is distasteful to reduce power relations among states – with all their implications for the survival and well-being of humanity – to a mere game. Nor is the situation all about winning and losing. There are gradations of victory or defeat, and success in one domain – such as attaining sheer volume of trade or a rigid protection of sovereignty – can have negative effects in another.

Words like competition, contest, clash, confrontation and conflict are sometimes interchangeably thrown about in commentary on world affairs. But precision is needed. Why do nations interact in one way and not another? What are the stakes that motivate them: survival and other vital interests, or something more negotiable? How much are large nations willing to risk in rivalry, or small ones in resistance? Can countries compete at one level while cooperating at others, and how does such diplomatic counterpoint resolve? The answers to such questions are essential to comprehending the dynamics of any relationship between states, let alone the intricate and many-sided powerplay of the Indo-Pacific. Ultimately, what is being described is more a many-dimensional puzzle than a game.

Academic constructs can only go so far to help us here. In the 20th-century field of international relations, a well-worn path follows so-called Realist theories. These are all about relative power. International affairs is explained as a kind of anarchy: even if differences are managed, there is no truly empowered arbiter. In power lies security and thus survival, so all states seek to maximise theirs. The ultimate prize is 'primacy' or 'pre-eminence', a top spot in a global or regional pecking order. But as one state gets stronger than another, the declining power's insecurity rises. Competition intensifies. Incentives grow for confrontation, in which one side either backs down or is defeated; either way, the power hierarchy changes. In its starkest form, such 'Offensive Realism' casts conflict as fairly much inevitable, a tragedy replayed ever since Thucydides recounted the mortal struggle between Athens and Sparta in ancient times.[6] Defensive variants argue that states really just want to protect themselves, but that this can still cause others to take fear and fight. Related theories define major states as either revisionist – having overriding interests in changing the existing order – or status quo. Lesser countries end up having to choose between siding with a rising great power ('bandwagoning') or balancing against it: a model for why alliances form or dissolve. In its own depressing way, it is reassuringly neat.

In the Realist universe, rules, law, norms, international institutions and common global interests – the currency of alternative 'liberal' theories – count for little in the end. Forget the better angels of our nature; prosperity is about fuelling a zero-sum contest for power, not the win-win paradise so many economists have predicted. This is of course something of a caricature of some prominent theories of how nations behave. Each has its merits and explanatory literature. And there are other theories too, such as constructivism, which highlights social practices, identity and history in shaping state actions.[7]

But by their own admission, international relations theories have limited connections with reality. It is fine to say the actions of nations are about their interests and power, but quite another thing to recognise that each country may see its interests and power in quite different ways. All nations may have security interests, but what exactly does that mean? Do large nations have to aim for 'primacy', or is self-protection enough? What if they don't see primacy in identical ways?

When it comes to power, the theories often have vague and variable definitions. Is it about population, territory, natural resources, economy, armed forces, technology? What of leadership, culture, organisation, resolve, mobilisation, agility, diplomacy, intelligence, the ability to attract allies, or some less tangible influence that can be measured only after it has been used?[8] The Soviet Union seemed powerful, until one day it collapsed and patently wasn't. Is power about compelling another state to do something, or about being able to resist such pressure, or both?[9] Expert jargon refers variously to variants of power that are hard (military), soft (cultural), sharp (coercive and covert infiltration) and smart (an effective use of whatever little one has). Simple readings of power based only on gross domestic product or military spending do not account for the many times less well-resourced states have defeated seemingly stronger ones, or the fact that populous states need to expend so much wealth in production or protection. Alternate measures of 'net' rather than 'gross' power suggest that China and India will remain weaker and America (and other long-developed countries) stronger than popularly imagined.[10]

In any event, no real-world government tries to make sense of its interaction with other states purely in the abstract. That's why they have diplomats and intelligence agencies. Their job is precisely to understand what makes each nation different, to look behind the border and inside the engine, at political systems and societies, at personality and dysfunction, at cultures, ideologies and histories, at the dictates of geography, at the differing dependence of particular places on flows of energy and resources, at contrasting attitudes to people, ideas and values.

For leaders make a difference. Decisions count. Surprise, initiative and unpredictability are strengths unto themselves. Mistakes happen and accidents matter. Size is not all. Small and middle nations have agency too. Nations are not billiard balls, reacting identically to shocks through some immutable physics.[11] Values, national identity and domestic politics shape their choices. The origin of tragedy as a dramatic art form in ancient Athens was an appeal to wisdom, a warning not to repeat mistakes – not a prophecy of doom.[12] Elegant theories crafted to explain world affairs in earlier eras warrant constant retesting with contemporary facts and changing conditions, such as new trends in technology, connectivity, interdependence and even the distinct character of each state. Capital-R 'Realism' suggests the very structure of the international system determines whether war or peace will prevail – as if the game plays itself. This needs to be tempered with other approaches. A mix of diplomacy and deterrence can reinforce coexistence, discouraging conflict and creating space for experiments in cooperation, which can deepen under the right conditions. And to have even a chance of getting their policy settings right, governments need an inside-out approach to reading their rivals or partners: to understand the other players from within.

Of course there are some commonalities across nations. It is fair to assume that all states seek some share of prosperity, peace, security and sovereignty. But they may not seek all in equal measure or at any cost. Real differences arise in nations' definitions of their interests and their compatibility or otherwise with the interests of others. The complexity of the current era – with linkages among issues and across borders – may also exacerbate the challenge that not all of a nation's interests are consistent. Sometimes the tragedy in foreign policy is not that a nation's many interests clash externally, with those of another nation, but that they clash internally, with each other. What happens if a country's interest in preserving peace is at odds with its interest in protecting sovereignty, or when the foreign investments that fuel a nation's near-term prosperity also bring long-term risks to its security?

The next two chapters open a window on the players in the new great game of power and influence in the Indo-Pacific. Who are they and what do they want? What are the national interests at stake? Which interests converge or clash with others? Why do the nations do what they do? Are they even engaged in the same game? How can we make sense of the mix of imperatives in play: what combination of prosperity, security, politics and pride? In short, what are the drivers of change and risk in this globally crucial region? Only by illuminating distinct national motivations do we have a chance of forecasting the contours of conflict and the opportunities for a sustainable peace.

There are good reasons to begin with China. This is not only about scale but also about the fact that so many of the actions of other players are in response to China's moves. No guide to the region's future will make sense unless it examines what China seeks and why.

China

The People's Republic of China is an Indo-Pacific power. Its interests and actions extend across the two-ocean region, affecting all other countries. It is investing in a region-wide strategy, involving all levers of power, from military to economic to political. But why? The answers have two foundations: China's sheer scale (a given) and the entwining of its authoritarian politics with its external ambitions (a choice).

China's leaders will be first to say their country is different. There is size: more than 1.4 billion people, the largest population of any nation in history, occupying vast continental territory. This gives China enormous economic and strategic bulk, but also gigantic challenges of development and social order matched only by India's: the requirement for a single government to somehow meet the needs and aspirations of so much of humanity. It is history's largest experiment in expectation management.

China's economy is far and away one of the world's two largest, rivalling only the United States'. By the purchasing power parity rate, which accounts for differing costs of living within countries, China is already the world's biggest economy. By more traditional exchange rate measures, China is the second-largest, and expert projections differ markedly as to when – or, most critically, whether – it will one day overtake the United States.[13] After all, China has slowed greatly from its dizzying economic growth rate of 10 per cent a year; it has achieved spectacular growth at high costs, and 'the costs are rising while growth is slowing'.[14] Serious doubts about the reliability of its data suggest growth may long have been less than claimed: is it now six per cent, five, four? Nobody knows for sure.[15] But even if China stops growing tomorrow, it is still an economic behemoth. And that wealth has become acutely dependent on international systems of trade and investment. These involve commerce and infrastructure, including flows of energy and resources, across land and especially sea.

Yet alongside this present-day global economic enmeshment, when it comes to culture and history, China sees itself apart: a 5000-year-old civilisation with a sense of centrality and superiority reflected in its Mandarin name: *Zhongguo*, the 'middle country' or 'middle kingdom'. China's history is much less uniform and unified than today's official view. Its borders have moved forcibly with each dynastic era. Regions such as Tibet, Xinjiang and Taiwan were 'incorporated into the Chinese empire only temporarily' or at a relatively late point in history.[16] China has also sometimes been open to foreign or minority influences and rulers (Mongol and Manchu). It has had experience of civic freedoms and moments when it could have taken that road.[17] Taiwan's alternative path, combining democratic rights with prosperity, is a hint of what might have been – one reason why the regime in Beijing has inculcated such an obsession with 'reunification' and ultimately the undoing of the freedoms that make Taipei (and Hong Kong) different.

Still, modern China projects a monolithic sense of national uniqueness. Even a phenomenon so Western in origin or global in evolution as socialism is officially modified to bestow it supposed 'Chinese characteristics'. Despite claims that its national unity reflects some tapestry of consent and consensus among diverse ethnic groups – such as minority Buddhist Tibetans and Turkic Muslim Uighurs – China has an overwhelmingly Han society and culture: more than 90 per cent of the population have Han ethnicity. Despite ostentatious shows of multiculturalism – such as through folk costumes at national gatherings – Han culture is widely and sometimes forcibly promoted as the only true Chinese culture, as shown through repression of the Uighurs' religion and traditions. In the words of a former trainee Chinese Communist Party propagandist, to be a modern-day Chinese nationalist is 'to become a de facto Han supremacist'.[18]

This majority cultural dominance is fused with, and enforced by, an authoritarian – and increasingly totalitarian – one-party state. Power over all areas of life ultimately rests with the Chinese Communist Party (CCP), the world's largest organisation, with about 89 million members and a pledge that puts Party first. This holds true even when such control is relaxed, notably with the freedom to pursue wealth and material wellbeing

*As commander-in-chief of the PLA, Chinese president Xi Jinping
increasingly appears in military uniform*

that has so characterised China since the 'reform era' began at the end of the
1970s. In the end, all power rests with the Party: even the military, the People's Liberation Army, is ultimately tasked with obeying and defending the
Party rather than the nation. In the words of paramount leader Xi Jinping:
'The Party exercises overall leadership over all areas of endeavour in every
part of the country.'[19]

The peoples of China have endured a tragic history involving mass suffering, deprivation, humiliation, oppression and chaos, wrought by foreign
powers and their own power-driven rulers alike. Against this grim background, today's leadership of the Communist Party promises a 'China
Dream' of 'national rejuvenation'. As outlined in a three-and-a-half-hour
speech by Xi Jinping in 2017, this combines security, social harmony, material
prosperity and not just pride but national greatness.[20] The way this greatness
is articulated – or sometimes merely alluded to – reveals a tension between
universally laudable goals like education, health, technological innovation

and environmental sustainability on the one hand, and on the other an obsession with political control. According to the official rhetoric, what is good for China will be good for the world. But only the Communist Party decides what is good for China, and that is what is good for the Party. And only the Party can deliver. There is a deal, of sorts. The Chinese people have exchanged political freedom and democratic choice for those other goods, or at least whatever combination of them may be available at the time.

But what is the ultimate priority? Does the Party hold power in order to raise the living standards of the people, or is the point of raising living standards to keep the Party in power?[21] This circular logic distorts China's foreign policy in destabilising ways.

From the end of the civil war in 1949 through to the death of Mao, various admixtures of revolutionary fervour, intimidation, ideology and security, plus the basics of national, material and human development (such as improved literacy and life expectancy), held things together. That was, except at the times they did not – notably the Cultural Revolution – and terror held sway. In the reform era, the unwritten contract became more pleasant: much more about economic benefit – the chance, at last, to build a better material standard of living with all its attendant human dignity, after cruel decades of extreme poverty. That alone was conceivably a potent incentive for obedience and social harmony. But 1980s economic growth was accompanied by rising expectations of political freedom. These were smashed by PLA tanks and guns in Tiananmen Square on 4 June 1989. Wealth or fear alone, or even combined, were no longer enough to ensure the Party's grip. An overpowering inculcation of nationalism became a renewed source of the regime's legitimacy. A new 'master narrative' of Chinese history and 'patriotic education' was scripted from above, indoctrinating new generations.[22] After many years of mutual tolerance, this narrative re-demonised Japan, America and the West. It fostered a populist nationalism that in turn risks spinning out of the Party's control.[23]

From the 1990s onwards, twin pillars of prosperity and patriotism have supported the party-state. If one falters, the other is relied on all the more. Without question, the enterprise and effort of the Chinese people have brought a historic accomplishment: since 1979, hundreds of millions have achieved wealthier, healthier, happier lives. This was not a gift from the regime. Once it lifted the more bizarre and counterproductive controls of collectivisation and central planning, and eased a three-decade reign of terror, the Party under Deng Xiaoping 'unleashed the pent-up economic energy of the Chinese people', allowing them finally to deliver economic benefits to themselves.[24] By way of public order and state capitalism, the regime has done much to enable such prosperity, just as before 1979 it prevented it. Thus if the people's material gain were to diminish, the Party would fear for its legitimacy. So it is no coincidence that as economic growth has slowed, the cultivation of Party rule and nationalism has further intensified. Paranoia and a sense of perpetual struggle are infusing and warping many areas of policy.

And that binds the fate of the regime with China's actions and destiny abroad. It may prove a hazardous compact, and not only for China.

For many years the default assumption among foreign analysts – taking China's leaders at their word – was that China's top foreign and defence priority was to ensure a stable international environment, thus allowing economic growth and development at home.[25] After all, China claimed a record of never having invaded other countries, even if this was open to debate depending on the definition of words like invasion and country. In any case, the view that Beijing was not interested in projecting power abroad may have held true when China was rising, less so now that it seems to consider itself risen. In his 2017 speech to the Party Congress, Xi called China a great or strong power twenty-six times.[26] Former leader Deng Xiaoping's popular guidance for foreign policy, 'tao guang yang hui', or 'hide one's capabilities and bide one's time', was consigned to history.[27]

So what happens when, within the one government, a nationalist compulsion to upset the regional order clashes with a lingering economic need to maintain some of its benefits? Over the past decade, the Chinese leadership has chosen to confront Japan in the East China Sea, Vietnam and the Philippines in the South China Sea, India on the disputed border and the United States across the global board, from the western Pacific to cyberspace. Hopes have diminished that differences with Taiwan would eventually and peacefully wither. Within Hong Kong, Tibet and Xinjiang, tension and repression have worsened, and international concern has mounted. Confidence and sometimes recklessness abroad have coincided with insecurity at home, a hardening of authoritarian rule, surveillance and punishment of dissent, an extreme degree of control now termed 'net-worked totalitarianism', where 'political control is at the heart of things'.[28]

Many foreign voices that once advocated engagement with China have thought twice, arguing that it is China, not they, that has changed. Some prominent Chinese thinkers acknowledge this.[29] Since 2009, the CCP has more starkly defined the nation's core interests – those over which China was prepared to go to war – as including not only national integrity and unification but also the contested South China Sea. Other countries that for whatever reason see danger in Chinese power are guilty of 'Cold War think-ing'. In 2019, the definition of China's existential interests went further still: amid trade conflict with the United States, even the nature of China's 'fun-damental economic system' and support for Party-backed or state-owned corporations became defined as 'economic sovereignty' and thus another 'core interest'.[30]

The Chinese leadership has also linked its own credibility and legiti-macy with advancing China's interests across the wider region: the Eurasian footprint of the Silk Road Economic Belt, but particularly the Maritime Silk Road, China's Indo-Pacific. The Belt and Road is Xi Jinping's iconic initia-tive, not only because he has declared it so, but presumably because he sees a direct link between China's ability to protect its distant interests and polit-ical stability at home. This sets China apart. Alone among the great powers, China's Indo-Pacific strategy connects directly with the survival of the domestic political system and the vested interests of the leadership. Perhaps it did not need to be this way, if China's rulers had made different choices, and accepted the prospect of an opening economy leading to reduced Party control. But as things stand, in the words of respected China-watcher Rich-ard McGregor, 'China's domestic insecurity feeds rather than restrains its desire to assert itself overseas.'[31]

It can be debated whether China can in the long run lessen its dependence on the Indian Ocean lifelines of energy and trade – for instance, through overland pipelines and transport routes or, with global warming, the long-term opening of an Arctic sea lane to the Atlantic. China's now accounts for more than a fifth of global energy consumption, and in 2017 China overtook the United States as the world's largest importer of oil, a vulnerability that will endure as China's domestic oil production continues to decline. Car ownership has increased rapidly: in 2018 China had more than 300 million motor vehicles. Fuel security has become a major concern for the public, not just the government. More than half of China's oil imports are from the Middle East and Africa, although this proportion has fallen with a doubling of supply from Russia since 2014. Energy remains one of the main reasons China has emphatically turned to the sea. But it is not the only one.

The Chinese leadership now links naval modernisation to the protection of far-flung interests.[32] This is clear in the new official concepts of 'global reach and deterrence' and extended 'frontier defence' that underpin China's rapid development of expeditionary forces such as aircraft carriers, nuclear-powered attack submarines and a marine corps tripling in size to reach 30,000 deployable personnel by 2020.[33] The Gulf of Aden deployments, the Djibouti base, submarine forays to the Indian Ocean, the PLA's evacuations of Chinese nationals from Yemen: are these hints of stronger measures when China deems its interests abroad more vitally threatened?

Some observers suggest that a straightforward way for China and other strong states to keep the peace is essentially to keep out of each other's way. Thus the United States could make space for China in East Asia, and in turn China could accept the Indian Ocean as India's sphere of influence.[34] Such geopolitical politeness sounds nice and sensible, but even if it was ever realistic, now it is too late. The spheres of influence argument faces the awkward reality that one reason America is in Asia is to protect Asian partners such as Japan and Taiwan, whose own choices and interests China shows little sign of accommodating. The argument also overlooks the fundamental redefinition of China's national security that has been wrought by the extension of China's geoeconomic interests across South Asia and through the sea lanes to Africa and the Middle East. By its own admission, affirmed in a 2019 defence strategy, China seeks to use its military 'to safeguard overseas interests'.[35] China has growing interests at stake in the Indian Ocean, some legitimate, some questionable, and indicates no intention of recognising this zone as India's backyard or sphere of influence. China will no more readily abandon its interests along the Maritime Silk Road than will America suddenly withdraw east to Hawaii.

One compelling explanation as to why Xi's China is so intent on the Belt and Road – and securing diplomatic and security advantages to match – is that time is palpably not on China's side.[36] This is contrary to the popular perceptions of China's unstoppable rise that Beijing cultivates. There is a strong case that Xi's agenda – from tightening control at home to extending influence abroad – is a high-risk strategy propelled by intense insecurity. Xi is trying to lock in relative gains in global influence now, in a window of perhaps no more than a generation, before a perfect storm of national difficulties begins to strike. These include a slowing economy, mountainous debt, people's frustrated aspirations, inequality worse than India's, environmental stresses, international tensions, and the demographic cliff of an ageing population, which by 2050 will include more than 329 million people over the age of sixty-five.[37] A popular assumption is that China is the master of long-term planning; that its decision-makers are constantly outwitting more short-sighted nations by playing a game measured in decades and centuries. That jars with the epic – and intimately tragic – myopia of the one-child policy, introduced in 1979 at the start of the reform era, and rescinded only in recent years. The formal end of the one-child policy has not yet motivated couples to have children. China's population will begin to decline within years; already more people retire each year than join the workforce. This challenge compounds with other problems, such as the prospect that a shift to hard authoritarianism and the Party's destruction of China's nascent institutions of governance – such as the legal system set up during the reform era of the 1980s to the 2000s – will bring political and economic stagnation. This could combine with risks of international conflict heightened by a reliance on hardline nationalism to sustain Party legitimacy.[38]

Perhaps these readings are wrong and the system will adapt, even flourish. Such straight-line projections assume the Chinese people will tolerate yet more repression in exchange for stability, as if they have an infinite appetite for the control-for-prosperity bargain the Party imposes. Surveillance technologies will pre-empt and erase dissent. China will innovate and keep mastering the commanding sciences of the age – next-generation telecommunications, artificial intelligence, quantum computing, robotics, renewable energy. And the region will learn to obey, or at least stand aside in silence.

More likely, though, the future will be very messy. The stunning protests in Hong Kong for much of 2019 sometimes reached 2 million people at a time, one of the largest per-capita popular mobilisations anywhere in history. These are a reminder that people power still matters, certainly in 'greater China' and potentially in the People's Republic itself. If China truly had its own house sufficiently in order that it could impose its will upon the region and the world, it would not be spending anywhere near as much on domestic security as it does on the People's Liberation Army, let alone more.[39]

The Chinese government likes to dismiss criticism by referring to the sheer scale of China's population and some collective sense of 'the feelings of the Chinese people'. Plainly the Communist Party governs with the consent, however induced, of most of the population. Polling data, for what it is worth in an authoritarian setting and when occasionally it is available, suggests a large majority support the leadership, its anti-corruption purges and its nationalistic and anti-American stance.[40] But the number of Chinese people who can be counted as potentially at odds with a Han-centric Communist worldview is impressive in its own right. Add together something like 6 million Tibetans, 7 million Hong Kongers, 24 million Taiwanese, 11 million Muslim Uighurs in Xinjiang, 10 million other Muslims, 31 million Christians and 70 million former members of the banned Falun Gong spiritual movement.[41] Already that is 159 million people. These are very approximate figures and of course the notion of all these communities somehow mobilising at once seems far-fetched – though the 2019 Hong Kong crisis has emboldened many of them to do so in protests overseas. But were it a country, this non-CCP greater China would have the eighth-largest population in the world, bigger than that of Bangladesh, Japan or Russia. No wonder the CCP persecutes activists for Taiwan, Tibet, Xinjiang, Falun Gong and democracy as 'the five poisons'.[42] Potential discontents also include former members of democracy and human rights movements, the many Chinese who struggle with basic employment or living conditions, especially transient labourers from the countryside without residential rights in the cities where they work, or those in the middle classes whose support for the party-state is more conditional on standards of living than on ideology or fear. Nor does it include those millions among the diverse global Chinese diaspora who do not accept the CCP line. We should not assume that the current relative silence of anti-government voices on the Chinese internet equals support for the nation's new 'superpower ideology'.[43] Even those who have succeeded in the PRC evince only guarded confidence in their own system: in no other great power in history have the elites been so eager to park their money and their children abroad. Presumably they are hedging on the basis that while the China Dream may make progress, the system underlying it is brittle, and if it fails it will do so spectacularly.

Dissent is one thing, but an excess of patriotic zeal could bring its own problems for the regime. On the security front, sooner or later China will face public expectations to deploy its military in combat to protect self-proclaimed interests far from home. Popular culture has come to reflect disturbingly inflated assumptions about what the PLA can and will do in China's name, with jingoistic Rambo-style movies such as *Operation Red Sea* and *Wolf Warrior 2*.[44] Perhaps in an effort to wind back such adventurist expectations, further such patriotic military films, notably a planned *Wolf Warrior 3*, have reportedly been cancelled at the government's behest.[45] The PLA's fast modernisation does not mean it will be ready for all contingencies, and presumably the government is beginning to recognise the danger of the public imagining that it is.

The question is not whether China claims, or even perceives, its actions to be principally defensive in nature. For all the rapid modernisation of its military, China has mostly shown remarkable restraint in using armed force. That means, incidentally, that this is a military with no combat experience. It has not fought a war since the stalemate with Vietnam in 1979; it has barely fired a shot in anger since the late 1980s, when the targets were Vietnamese troops stranded on a disputed reef and Chinese citizens in the heart of Beijing. Xi regularly reassures the world that China does not seek 'hegemony'. But it certainly seeks disruptive changes that multiple other powers do not want. The shorthand for this is revisionism, a determination to undo the status quo. The United States now goes so far as to call this out bluntly as a Chinese goal of 'Indo-Pacific regional hegemony in the near-term' and 'global pre-eminence in the long-term'.[46]

Even if Beijing's strategic interests and objectives are not so black-and-white or maximalist, Xi has set a very high bar for success: China will only meet its strategic goals if it can compel other countries to do its bidding. For all those others, even the United States, the bar is correspondingly lowered: they will prevail if only they succeed in resisting.

Plainly China has never found itself trusting the United States, regardless of Beijing's insistence that 'trust' form the basis for international affairs. Even as the dominant view in Washington was that economic globalisation would erode security tensions, China's security planners were struggling to see a silver lining to the US-led alliance system and military presence in Asia.[47] Critics suggest President Obama should have tried harder to engage China. The response is that he tried, at least with as much sincerity (or naivety) as he and his distracted administration could muster. But for as long as the United States was committed to encouraging democracy inside other states, or to upholding a status quo that protected Taiwan, or Japan and other allies, the Chinese Communist Party's existential paranoia would trump cooperation. There are of course phases when US–China relations have been marked by direct armed conflict – the Korean War – or American coercion in the name of protecting Taiwan: the crises of 1954 and the mid-1990s. The United States military has kept hedging against future

Chinese power, not least to reassure allies. Yet today's Chinese strategists seem to overlook that America, more than any other nation, assisted China's rise for decades: entirely at odds with a zero-sum realist worldview, let alone a Cold War mentality.

An insightful variant of international relations realism contends that even defensive measures by states can heighten instability: a 'security dilemma' in which defence looks like offence, each state reacts to the other and mistrust spirals into confrontation.[48] This relates to the famous 'prisoner's dilemma' of game theory, which suggests that under conditions of anything less than perfect trust, two rational and well-intentioned people will fail to cooperate. With the security dilemma, it gets even worse, because, in a multipolar world, third parties get anxious too. Thus country B's defensive response to country A – by building up its military – does not just threaten country A but country C as well, which arms in turn. Even accepting the Chinese claim that, as country B, its militarisation is in significant part a response to the power of country A (America), that leaves not just some imaginary country C but a veritable alphabet of real nations in the Indo-Pacific feeling threatened by China's new might. The largest is India.

India

India would seem to have much in common with China and its grand problems. To maintain political stability and live up to its promise as a nation, it must address the needs of a mega-population – in 2019 something like 1.37 billion people and growing – providing them material welfare, security and self-respect. In some ways, the task for India is even harder than for China. Like China, India has a history of oppression by colonial powers, along with plenty of internal strife. It is still at a relatively early stage along the uneven journey of building a developed and cohesive nation. Unlike China, though, India has truly bewildering cultural diversity: a historic multiculturalism of twenty-two major languages, along with many ethnicities and religions.

And entirely unlike China, India has chosen to manage itself as a democracy: sometimes deeply flawed, but a government of the people nonetheless.

With a national government, twenty-nine states, seven territories and hundreds of thousands of elected village and municipal councils or 'panchayats', India is the ultimate many-layered democracy. For better or worse, it has more elected politicians than the rest of the world combined. Academic George Perkovich has memorably hinted at the challenge of governing one country that is 'more populous and diverse than the United States, Canada, Mexico, Central America, South America, France, Germany, and the United Kingdom combined'.[49] He could have added a piece of the Middle East: India has close to 200 million Muslim citizens, making this Hindu-majority state the world's third-largest Muslim population after Indonesia and Pakistan.

So what does India want and need? The nation's national interests are extensive and growing, along with its horizon of risk.[50] As with China, development, rapid economic growth and stability at home have long been paramount, and these require peaceful external relations.[51] But India must also factor in national pride and national insecurity on a vast scale. Yet unlike China, India's projection of power abroad is not an existential question; the credibility of any particular leader or ruling party is not crucial to the very survival of its model of government. Democracy offers a safety valve; when government fails to satisfy the people, it can be punished at the ballot box, but the system will endure. Even so, the stakes for India and its leaders are high. And under a Modi government exceedingly confident in its second term, the continuing erosion of some aspects of India's tolerant, secular and democratic model – such as freedom of the press and the rights of minorities – is cause for concern.[52] This is not only for intrinsic reasons of civil rights but also because the institutions of liberal democracy are a source of India's long-term resilience.

India is projected to become one of the world's three largest economies, along with the United States and China. In recent years, annual growth has been around 7 per cent, exceeding China's, although this seems to be slowing to 6 per cent or lower over the next few years. India's leaders nonetheless anticipate a $5 trillion economy during the next decade. But this will be no easy journey. It means meeting needs for business confidence, investment, vastly improved infrastructure, and reliable and expanding supplies of energy, demand for which will at least double by 2040. Economic reform remains a priority: despite some progress, India still favours political and security concerns over fully fledged free trade, typified in late 2019 by its eleventh-hour decision not to sign a regional trade agreement due to concerns over worsening its trade deficit with China. It also struggles to find its competitive edge. Automation in manufacturing and Trumpian protectionism are coinciding with the moment when India and its gigantic workforce should be replacing a more developed China in global production chains. So as labour-intensive farming jobs diminish, there is no ready substitute. Despite its reputation for computer skills, India is generally at a technology disadvantage. Vying with Saudi Arabia for the dubious title of world's largest arms importer, it relies on a formidable but unwieldy mix of military systems from Russia, America, Israel and Europe.[53]

Meanwhile, food and water security remain pressing concerns. All of this is to support what will soon be the world's largest national population, which could become the source of great national strength and prosperity, or of dissatisfaction and relative deprivation on an unprecedented scale. Living standards in India are rising: an estimated 271 million Indians were brought out of poverty between 2006 and 2017, a remarkable and historic achievement.[54] Still, there remained in 2015 something like 175 million Indians in poverty, as defined by the World Bank.[55] Average income and human development indicators – such as life expectancy and literacy – remain behind those of China. There are still a multitude of people in India with far more immediate concerns than sovereignty and international power games.

Indians are also overwhelmingly young. Estimates suggest that India has more than 600 million people under the age of twenty-five, the world's largest youth population. This adds a massive need for education and employment to the general requirement of economic dynamism. Young Indians often reflect optimism, but in the internet age they also have instant awareness of what they are yet to have. Within a generation, Indian telecommunications connectivity has exploded from about 5 million telephone landlines in 1991 to about 1.2 billion mobile phones in 2019. A hyper-commercialised mass media and rampant social media reinforces the challenge for India's government as it inherits China's mantle for history's greatest experiment in mass expectation management.

Yet even for a nation with as much human need as India, economic growth cannot be the whole solution. For one thing, there is the ecological price. As with China, population pressures and economic growth involve horrendous strain on the natural environment, with corresponding resource insecurities, particularly over water. Air pollution levels are among the world's worst, due not only to runaway expansion in industry and transport but also to aspects of economic underdevelopment, such as the burning of wood and biomass for cooking and warmth.

India's energy mix is changing, with growth in renewables and nuclear power, but most of its electricity derives from fossil fuels, including coal. Meanwhile, motor vehicle use is rising dramatically – although, unlike in China, the real explosion in car ownership lies ahead, with projections of an eightfold increase to perhaps 175 million by 2040. Like China, India has an acute reliance on imported oil: in 2019, a record 84 per cent of its total consumption.[56] The proportion of imports continues to rise, despite official aspirations to the contrary. And that oil is overwhelmingly from the Middle East and Africa: transported across the very sea lanes that China too is seeking to secure. It's a shorter route, but India's energy dependence on Indian Ocean sea lanes helps explain that country's own substantial naval modernisation, and entangles it in other nations' Indo-Pacific dilemmas.

In India's national priorities there is also a fundamental tension between stability and sovereignty. To hold together such a gargantuan and unwieldly nation-building project as India's, the political and bureaucratic leadership cannot fundamentally compromise a national identity that was built on overcoming internal differences in order to win independence from foreign oppression and humiliation. Indian pride and mobilisation are potent because of diversity, not in spite of it – which is why the emboldening of Hindu nationalism could hinder India's interests in the long run.

India lives in a dangerous neighbourhood with two nuclear-armed neighbours, Pakistan and China, with which it has fought wars and has unresolved border disputes. Indian public opinion perceives Pakistan, and the long reality of cross-border terrorism, as a priority threat.[57] At the same time, the public, but even more so the policy establishment, see China as India's long-term rival – or, as one Indian diplomat more politely puts it, 'the power that has the most direct impact on India's strategic space'.[58] There is thus a need for Indian governments to demonstrate resolve, deterrence and a willingness to retaliate against coercion from those countries that involves the shadow – or use – of force. And increasingly India's security leaders think that, to protect their country from coercion, they may need to tolerate instability – or occasionally even exacerbate it. Signalling risk is becoming a way to keep India safe. It's a perilous paradox.

For instance, in recent years the Modi government has repeatedly used or threatened small-scale force to warn that India will stand up for its interests. In response to continuing terrorism from inside Pakistani-controlled territory, Indian forces have launched commando raids and even airstrikes, raising international fears that conflict could escalate with another nuclear-armed state. In the disputed Himalayan Doklam area in 2017, Indian troops blocked Chinese roadbuilding, bringing on months of confrontation. Such actions have been criticised for breaking with Indian traditions of 'strategic restraint' and raising the spectre of war, but that is part of their point: to end the old perception that India is a passive giant uncomfortable with power, and that other nations can assert their interests against it with impunity.[59] Sometimes pride and assertiveness will distract India from the big strategic challenge of China: for instance, in 2019 the Modi government went out of its way to threaten mutually harmful economic repercussions against Malaysia and Turkey for their criticism of Delhi's actions against Kashmiri autonomy.[60]

Or are India's displays of toughness mainly about winning elections?[61] A simple view of Indian foreign policy, perpetuated since at least the 1998 nuclear tests, is that all this sabre-rattling occurs mainly because it plays well with voters, especially the Hindu nationalist base of Modi's Bharatiya Janata Party. National security was one of the reasons for Modi's resounding electoral victory in 2019, securing a second five-year term.

But the lazy assumption that India is on some catastrophic path of populist warmongering discounts deeper threads of restraint and diplomacy.

An extraordinary feature of independent India is not how much conflict it has been involved in, but how little. India has avoided major war since it fought Pakistan to liberate Bangladesh in 1971. The 1999 conflict with Pakistan in the mountainous Kargil district was contained; India refrained from sending its air force into disputed airspace, and thus accepted hundreds of infantry casualties, to allay fears of escalation.[62] India would have felt justified in attacking Pakistan after major terrorist attacks in 2001, 2002 and, mostly horrifically, in Mumbai in 2008, but ultimately chose peace. Nuclear fears played their part, but so did the Indian state's under-appreciated ability to manage the anger within its massive democracy – to tone down the war-talk when it got too dangerous.

And while perceptions of China as adversary have long been rife within India's defence circles, the government has proven adept at moderating nationalist sentiment when the two great powers collide. During the 2017 Doklam crisis, Indian leaders and officials doused any warlike rhetoric, and both government and opposition parliamentarians refrained from seeking political advantage over the issue.[63] India's resolve achieved a temporary Chinese backdown, but Delhi wisely chose not to proclaim victory too loudly, allowing a mutual saving of face. India was willing to criticise China and 'tolerate risks of conflict' while trying to cut a deal in the background, and in the long term to improve its deterrent forces for likely future clashes.[64] India's widely respected foreign secretary during that critical time, Subrahmanyam Jaishankar, was in 2019 appointed external affairs minister, suggesting the re-elected Modi government is determined to place foreign relations in skilled and steady hands. In candid public remarks shortly before taking on that role, Jaishankar described India's need for pragmatism and 'issues-based alignments' to optimise its relations with all major powers: 'cultivating America, steadying Russia, managing China, enthusing Japan and attending to Europe', while still prioritising the immediate neighbourhood and developing a more extended definition of the region.[65]

'Whatever you can rightly say about India, the opposite is also true,' said the Cambridge economist Joan Robinson, many years ago.[66] Her point then was about the nation's perplexing economy and society, but can apply today also to India's worldview and external policies. This makes it hard to frame a consistent picture of what a fast-changing India wants in a changing region. India wants peace, but is prepared to risk conflict to get it. In Jaishankar's words, 'Playing safe may end up as an opportunity denial exercise which will finally add to our risks rather than mitigate them.'[67] India wants and needs strategic partners in technology, commerce and security, yet its prospective partners do not all trust one another – they include America and Russia, for a start. And in the end, Delhi still covets its 'strategic autonomy' and will commit to be nobody's ally. However ambitious Indian leaders become on the world stage, they cannot escape problems at home – including political unrest, militancy and terrorism in the state of Jammu and Kashmir. The Kashmir issue is exploited by Pakistan and external jihadists, but India must also face up to its own glaring governance failures in winning the consent of new generations of Kashmiris. The sudden removal of Kashmir's semi-autonomous status in mid-2019 dealt a damaging blow to India's image as a multicultural state respectful of local sensitivities and indeed of Islam.[68] India wants to project as a confident, modern and cohesive state, yet also faces internal conflict from separatist movements in its remote northeastern states, the remnants of Maoist or 'Naxalite' movements, and surges of oppressive Hindu extremism assisted by online propaganda and social media.

In engaging the world outside, a rising India is still less than the sum of its parts. Delhi has no choice but to invest seriously in the tools of statecraft, yet its diplomatic service remains tiny, barely a thousand officials by some counts.[69] As a democracy, India could do much more to harness the private sector and its diaspora in promoting its interests and outlook, but its undersized foreign affairs bureaucracy has long resisted this, jealously guarding its control of the way the nation engages with the world.[70] India is hardpressed to meet rising expectations about providing security for its massive diaspora, helping non-resident Indians who find themselves in trouble spots abroad, from the Middle East to Southeast Asia and the South Pacific.

The Modi government is serious in its intent to Act East, expand economic horizons, modernise the navy and sustain a kind of competitive coexistence with China and other powerful states in Southeast Asia and beyond. Yet India's attention is constantly being diverted inward, and to a troubled neighbourhood of Pakistan, Afghanistan, Bangladesh, Sri Lanka, Nepal, Bhutan, Myanmar and the Indian Ocean. India's policy elite want to look beyond the sterile struggle with Pakistan to focus on China as tomorrow's strategic competitor, but cannot escape the fact that China and Pakistan are now literally inseparable through the China–Pakistan Economic Corridor and the presence of many Chinese nationals there.

As Indian decision-makers grapple with all these fissiparous policy imperatives, China may provide a key. Competing – and coexisting – may push India closer to getting its own house in order. India no longer has options between coming to terms with China and taking a magnanimous lead in its own neighbourhood: it will need to do both. That is because China's arrival there is compelling India to improve its relations with smaller states – especially the Indian Ocean islands – that it had previously tended to neglect or bully.

In theory, India and China have overriding interests in common: a stable region for their economic development; energy, resource and environmental security; and maintaining stability, cohesion and management of expectations in societies with billion-plus populations. In reality, mistrust has worsened over the past decade. Existing differences over the border dispute and China's military and nuclear assistance to Pakistan have been compounded by new frictions, including over China's growing interests and naval presence in the Indian Ocean and India's security ties with the United States, Japan and others. India's determination to set firm and principled boundaries to its association with China's Belt and Road Initiative, along with China's obstruction of Indian membership of global 'top tables', from the United Nations Security Council to the Nuclear Suppliers Group, are clear markers that competition is likely to keep trouncing cooperation in India–China relations.[71]

Indian threat perceptions of China relate ultimately to China's aspiration to be the pre-eminent power in Asia and, at a global level, a peer only to the United States. New Delhi sees Beijing as determined to keep India as permanently a second-tier power, restricted to South Asia and the Indian Ocean, and potentially not even able to shape the strategic environment in this neighbourhood. India sees China's cultivation of Pakistan as intended to secure not only Chinese energy supply routes but also Chinese influence and access in the Indian Ocean generally. In particular, India sees the accentuation of a long Chinese policy of using nuclear-armed Pakistan to keep India off-balance, deterred and caged in a South Asian strategic system, limiting India's ability to challenge or constrain China in the Indo-Pacific and globally.

Ultimately, India fears China's superior economic and strategic weight, and the fact that China, with greater military and nuclear capabilities, could coerce India in a crisis. The upside is that this sets for Delhi an achievable goal: India can give priority to resisting, rather than imposing its will. India may not have crossed that threshold of great-power status whereby it can compel others, but perhaps it does not need to, for at least it can resist them.[72] For now, in the face of Chinese strength, some of India's more prudent security practitioners, such as Admiral Sureesh Mehta, have recognised that their country should not compete with China directly, and that instead India's best protection in extremis is some form of 'asymmetric deterrence': an ability to inflict unacceptable harm on a stronger foe.[73] It is analogous to the strategy of denial and deterrence that China has long adopted against the United States, but now may be moving beyond. Thus India focuses on its ability to patrol and interrupt the sea lanes of the Indian Ocean, while strengthening its small arsenal of nuclear weapons, aiming to make them invulnerable on submarines.

India is also tilting away from its habit of strategic autonomy. It is working with a wide range of nations on sensitive security issues, such as maritime surveillance and anti-submarine warfare. Beyond working with traditional defence technology partners Russia and Israel, India is getting serious about cooperating with Indo-Pacific democracies to slow and moderate China's expansion in the Indian Ocean. This explains surprising progress in collaboration – such as military logistics agreements – with Japan, Australia and France. But foremost among India's security partners is the United States.

The United States

Expert opinion is divided over the future of the United States in the Indo-Pacific. Will America remain committed? And what will this mean – crisis, conflict and economic woe, or deterrence, stability and riches? Some claim that withdrawal is inevitable; others that America is back; others still that it never left. But two key questions are often overlooked. First, if America is indeed now locked in a long-term struggle with China for global influence, can it possibly succeed *without* maintaining or reaffirming its presence in the Indo-Pacific? It is difficult to see how it can. Second, does the United States need to be *dominant* in the Indo-Pacific in order to protect its interests and thwart what it sees as the China challenge? Much current American rhetoric, after all, is about empowering other states to protect their sovereignty. Does that mean America can serve its interests sufficiently by playing a supporting role? The answers to these questions are vital to understanding the region's future.

Until the shock onset of the Trump presidency, it seemed fairly straightforward to explain America's interests in Asia. The United States had vital strategic stakes in the region, and would not, as American policy scholar Michael J. Green put it:

> tolerate any other power establishing exclusive hegemonic control over Asia and the Pacific ... for over two centuries, the national interest of the United States has been identified by key leaders as ensuring that the Pacific Ocean remains a conduit for American ideas and goods to flow westward, and not for threats to flow eastward toward the homeland.[74]

Asia was the home of key alliances, an accidental and informal empire, which Washington had developed in such a way as to control the security environment: to ensure that it remained the dominant and indispensable partner to all, and that allies and potential adversaries alike were not tempted to disrupt the status quo.[75] American credibility globally depended on its ongoing support for allies, notably Japan and South Korea, hence a need to help them manage risks from China and North Korea. In the military and diplomatic sense, America needed to balance China while engaging it as an economic partner and a stakeholder in global order. Given Asia's centrality to the future global economy, here was the region where America's interests in free trade, flows of investment, and the promotion of rules and increasingly democratic civil society were becoming most acute. The addition of India as a strategic partner would help the United States in a changing global balance of forces. In total, Washington's stakes in Asia were critical to an expansive sense of national interests entwined with nothing less than a US-led 'world order' based on liberal-democratic values.[76]

Academics occasionally aired ideas of the United States reducing its presence in Asia (and indeed the Middle East and Europe too). These tended not towards total isolation but to 'restraint' or 'offshore balancing' in which American forces would somehow preserve 'command of the commons' from afar, maintaining 'access to the rest of the world' and standing poised to return if critical threats arose.[77] Such thinking tended to underestimate China's strength, determination and maritime ambitions ('at most an Asian land power') or how hard it would be for America to regain its military advantage in Asia after withdrawing its forces.[78] But at least it recognised the potential of regional middle players to protect themselves from China and complicate its ambitions.

Recent trends and developments have shaken the picture, accentuating the contradictions between different explanations of what America wants in the region – and whether or why it may stay. Much of the confusion is within the Trump administration's own regional security posture. On the one hand, there is the tenor of the president's wild pronouncements, typically via Twitter: ungrateful and ungracious comments about allies, along with calls for them to spend more on defence. Allies are unsettled by the seeming randomness of Trump's dealings with China and North Korea: talk of grand bargains one day and confrontation the next. All the while, they endure the unravelling of the tapestry of free trade arrangements, notably the Trans-Pacific Partnership, which they had worked so hard with previous US administrations to weave.

On the other hand, official strategic documents and the efforts of the Washington policy establishment – supported by Congress – have focused more on the Indo-Pacific than under Obama. They connect America's regional interests with a worldwide struggle against Chinese influence. The US National Security Strategy of late 2017, along with many statements and speeches since, has identified the Indo-Pacific as the frontline of this contest, touching all elements of national power, from military to media, technology to trade, intelligence to infrastructure.[79] This will be a long and comprehensive strategic competition, with security, diplomatic, economic, ideological and domestic political dimensions. Much of the American public – 54 per cent, according to a 2019 poll – see China's power and influence as a major threat to American interests.[80]

The North Korean nuclear weapons threat alone gives the United States a profound reason to remain strategically engaged across the Pacific. More broadly, the Pentagon has designated the Indo-Pacific as the principal geographic theatre for the full-spectrum rivalry with China, the front line of potential future conflict. There is great contention as to whether America's military, diplomatic and developmental role here is anywhere near adequately resourced, let alone properly coordinated. Flashes of intense attention back to the Middle East, like the 2019 Iran crisis, hardly help. Further doubts about American commitment have arisen with revelations that President Trump delayed the construction of military facilities on Guam – essential for deterring China and North Korea – to fund his contentious border wall.[81]

Yet the Congressional outrage this decision provoked suggests it is premature to conclude the United States has somehow given up on the Indo-Pacific. Indeed, the opposite may be true. Admittedly, among the many confusions of the Trump era, it remains unclear whether America is serious about primacy in Asia – as opposed to a sufficiency approach of working with others (allies, partners, Taiwan) in holding the line. But even that may prove enough to forestall the possibility of Chinese dominance. Advocates of a policy of American supremacy may settle for a balance of power that disadvantages China, or at least does not further embolden it.[82]

American staying power in Asia has often been underestimated before, notably in the post-Vietnam and post–Cold War moments. It is important to unpack precisely what interests America continues to have in the region – actual stakes, not merely intentions, good or otherwise. These are more extensive than often imagined. In economics, America remains the region's largest investor by far: at US$1.3 trillion, its foreign direct investment in Asia is more than that of China, Japan and South Korea combined.[83] In security, America's foremost Indo-Pacific alliances – Japan, South Korea and Australia – are not optional extras but mainstays of its global strategic position. Were they to collapse, owing to American failure to honour its defence commitments, then the United States' credibility and ability to harness its dozens of other allies worldwide would wither.

But most crucially – and here the current era connects to the logic that saw America through two world wars, the Cold War and the past few decades – American policy has long concluded that no one power (or consortium of powers) should be allowed to master the whole of Eurasia, the 'world island', as early geopolitical thinker Halford Mackinder so grandly called it.[84] Even a more restrained interpretation of American strategic interests sees such an outcome as unacceptable.[85] Yet that is the kind of ambition that China and Russia together wish to give the impression they harbour today.[86] In theory, such a power or powers could in time isolate or threaten even the continental United States. In old-fashioned geopolitics, this could have included the economic exclusion of America from much of the world's markets (as if, some might wryly note, the Trump administration is not finding its way to such a harmful outcome unaided). In principle, and in past American (and earlier British) practice, the antidote to such danger is a combination of sea power, alliance building, maintaining a forward military presence, and a commitment to a global order based on free trade and international law. A hypothetical Chinese or Sino–Russian strategy of comprehensively excluding the United States from global supply chains, investment patterns and financial flows – a Eurasia-centric 'world without America' – is exceptionally hard to imagine as succeeding.

Distance obviously makes it difficult for America to sustain sole pre-ponderance in Asia, but also lends certain advantages. There are some major drivers of Indo-Pacific strategy that China, India and Japan possess yet America is lucky to lack. It is not trapped by geography: China and India have each turned to the sea to break out of the Asian continental enclosure, however vast, and can never wish away their direct dependence on Indo-Pacific sea lanes or their proximity to troublesome neighbours. Crucially, the United States no longer relies on the sea lanes for its energy or resource security – though this makes it more likely to withdraw from the Middle East than from the Indo-Pacific. Nor does American nationalism revolve around unfinished nation-building or unresolved regional rivalries in the way that India's or China's do. Yet competition with China has rapidly become a galvanising issue in America politics, on both sides.[87] In that sense, nationalism is becoming another factor in America's Indo-Pacific compulsions.

A faint silver lining to the Trump era is a realisation among allies just how much they benefited from previous American leadership. And US political institutions will no doubt struggle as the country comes to terms with social fragmentation and a tougher economic trajectory. Yet overall, American power is more likely to adapt than decay. And even a United States that manifests 'America First' in rhetoric and trade practices is seek-ing to renew and adapt its alliances, not reject them. The 2019 Indo-Pacific strategy is an evolution, not a repudiation, of the Obama-era pivot to Asia: both initiatives relied on networks of allies and partners. In turn, those allies are judging that by doing more for themselves, as well as with each other, they stand a better chance of persuading America that it is worth staying in the Indo-Pacific – or of coping, at least temporarily, if it eases back. In other words, a 'balancing' strategy makes sense for allies no matter what. That is certainly the reasoning in the nations that have been described as the northern and southern anchors of the US alliance system: Japan and Australia.

CHAPTER 6

MANY PLAYERS

Not so long ago, the idea of 'multipolarity' – a many-sided world with no nation especially in charge – had little appeal to America and its allies. For all its terrible risks, the bipolarity of the Cold War had at least been relatively stable and predictable. And from the fall of the Soviet Union in 1991 to the global financial crisis of 2008, the globe seemed to experience a unipolar moment, where the United States was indisputably on top. During this time, multipolarity was often enlisted as code by Russia and China for their aspirations to end US dominance.

Now the wheel has turned. China may not yet be on top, nor America anywhere near the bottom. But suddenly multipolarity is music to the ears of myriad countries, including those that long valued American leadership. From US allies to emerging powers that prize their autonomy, the complex and many-sided vastness of the Indo-Pacific provides space to discover their own power, forge new partnerships and absorb or deflect China's influence. Academic observers have long been divided about whether multipolarity makes the world more stable. Some say that more stakeholders with more complex webs of interdependence encourage moderation; others argue that in the long run only bipolarity can bring a true balance of power to prevent potential aggression.[1] In any case, in the new era of the Indo-Pacific, multipolarity is becoming a fact: the notion of a strategic order that fails to acknowledge the rights and agency of many players has become a non-starter. It is difficult to see how it could be less stable than the kind of US–China bipolarity defined by Trump and Xi, or less respectful to the interests, identity and dignity of other nations than unipolar worldview centred on Beijing.

Japan

A decade ago, Japan was in a state of geopolitical melancholy, like the protagonist at the start of a Haruki Murakami novel: sophisticatedly self-aware, mindful of its disappointments and deterioration, yet little motivated to act. The country seemed dormant as a strategic player, barely willing to engage in power politics to protect and advance its interests. That has changed. In recent years, Japan has proved the most active and diplomatically adventurous nation – other than China – in pursuing the relationships it needs to secure its future in the Indo-Pacific.

Foreign visitors to Tokyo can leave with a pervasive sense of stability and comfort, of an advanced society resigned to gentle decline in the power hierarchy of the world. Whatever its history – indeed because of it – this is not a nation in search of trouble. Yet the past decade has proven it would be a mistake to assume this is a country living in a post-modern bubble. Instead, one of Japan's most basic national interests has not changed since it first industrialised in the second half of the 19th century: to guard its economic vulnerabilities as a resource-poor island nation. Today's Japan is also serious about protecting what it can of a rules-based international system, due somewhat less to professed ideals than to a pragmatic recognition that liberal democracy has been overwhelmingly good for Japan's wellbeing and sovereignty since 1945. That said, self-determination and human rights have become declared guiding principles for Japanese diplomacy, linked in rhetoric at least to the idea of a Free and Open Indo-Pacific.[2]

Japan retains its share of national pride, coupled with a more than regular share of security worries. North Korea threatens Japan as much as, or even more than, it does South Korea (estranged family) and America (strong and far away). Japan, by contrast, is close by, the historic enemy, easily vilified yet militarily self-restrained – a convenient combination. Thus North Korea often tests its missiles over Japanese territory. In living memory, it has kidnapped Japanese citizens from their beaches. In 2001, an alleged North Korean spy ship fought the Japanese coast guard. Meanwhile, Japan and Russia have never resolved ownership of northern islands occupied by Soviet forces at the end of the Second World War, and the Japanese air force continues to scramble hundreds of times a year to fend off Russian incursions into contested airspace.

Yet by far the main source of Japan's resurgent strategic anxiety is China. This is despite a remarkable economic relationship. For many years China has been Japan's largest trading partner (though America is a close second), and from 1979 to 2006 was the largest recipient of Japanese aid, partly a kind of belated war reparation and bolstering China's rapid economic development.[3] Today China–Japan differences are not confined to bilateral rivalry or the fact that China has so quickly eclipsed Japan's economy or defence budget, and is challenging its technological edge. These problems coincide with the Chinese Communist Party's revival of past wrongs to depict Japan as a contemporary menace, and the rekindling of disputes over islands, waters and airspace.

Japan focuses on two threats: China's bid to dominate not only East Asia but a broader maritime region; and Japan's persistent vulnerability to seaborne strangulation of its lines of supply, especially energy and food.[4] Keeping the seas free and open has a very literal meaning for Japan's national survival. Japan's dependence on imports of oil, natural gas and coal was profound well before the Fukushima triple disaster of 2011 – earthquake, tsunami and nuclear – and increased after that crisis shook public confidence in nuclear energy. Even as some of the closed reactors come back online, reliance on imported fossil fuels remains acute. The Middle East, Southeast Asia and Australia remain vital sources for Japan's energy and resources, and it all travels by sea. Oil is Japan's largest import, of which probably more than 80 per cent comes from the Persian Gulf and around 90 per cent passes through the South China Sea.[5] Japan is the world's largest importer of LNG, and again most of it comes from the south. Japan thus has a compelling need to prevent Chinese control of the South China Sea and the waters around Taiwan, and would have reason to support Taiwan and the United States against forced 'reunification'.[6]

Yet for all its proclaimed confidence under Abe, Japan no longer seeks sole leadership of its region. Even a more limited contest for the economic loyalty of Southeast Asia is no longer just between Beijing and Tokyo.

Instead, Japan is seeking to limit Chinese power – or North Korean belligerence – by building a web of partnerships with many others. Tokyo is no
longer placing all its hopes on Washington: hence its Indo-Pacific strategy
of cultivating friends from India to Europe to Southeast Asia and Australia.
Not without symbolism did Prime Minister Abe seat the leaders of his fellow 'quadrilateral' countries – India, Australia and America – opposite Xi
Jinping at the June 2019 G20 summit in Osaka. Japan is mindful, though,
that not all its priorities align with America's, especially under Trump.
Tokyo's pursuit of free trade and a rules-based global order runs counter to
the protectionism of the Trump administration.

Moreover, Japan is pragmatic about its economic relations with China.
Japanese investment is gradually shifting from China to other, more strategically like-minded countries such as India and Vietnam, building on an
accumulation of quality infrastructure investment in Southeast Asia that
continues to outvalue China's more recent and trumpeted ventures.[7] Nonetheless, Japan's attitude to the Belt and Road now falls under a rubric of
'cooperate and compete': Japanese businesses will sometimes work with
China on joint infrastructure projects in third countries, provided Japanese
standards of transparency and economic viability are met.[8] In parallel,
Japanese development assistance is focused on coordination with the
United States and Australia in offering alternatives to the BRI, or in building
up smaller countries' ability to monitor and protect their maritime
resources, presumably from China.

For its ultimate security Tokyo still puts a premium on keeping the
United States as military ally, deeply engaged in Asia – whatever humiliation from Donald Trump this entails. After all, the US 7th Fleet, based
in Yokosuka near Tokyo, could be a critical force in future conflict. Japan
also counts on America's willingness and ability to send reinforcements
across the Pacific. And America's policy of extended deterrence – where it
essentially promises to protect Japan, even with nuclear weapons if need
be – keeps at bay the possibility of Japan building its own such arsenal.
For Japan and America's other allies, the choices made in Washington
remain critical to their Indo-Pacific future. Nonetheless, a big part of Abe's

signature Free and Open Indo-Pacific strategy has been to hedge and buttress by making the most of multipolarity, from India to Europe to Southeast Asia. India is a priority, as affirmed in that Modi–Abe train ride. Indeed, Abe's recently retired adviser, Kanehara, has gone so far as to say: 'Only with India on our side can we guarantee a strategic balance on the global scale with China.'[9] Yet only one country is privately referred to by some Japanese officials as a 'quasi-ally': Australia.[10] Despite Canberra's rejection in 2016 of an audacious proposal for Japan to provide a new submarine fleet and thus bind the two countries' navies, this relationship has not been fundamentally dented. The advent of Trump and the acceleration of Xi's strategic ambitions have only deepened the trust and coordination between America's two key Indo-Pacific allies.

Australia

'The Indo-Pacific is where we live,' said Australian prime minister Scott Morrison in a foreign policy speech in Sydney in June 2019. 'It is the region that will continue to shape our prosperity, security and destiny.' This puts plainly how much is at stake for Australia. The interplay of geography, history, resources and population has left the country with unique circumstances. It has a relatively small population of about 25 million, yet a huge territorial footprint, including responsibility for some of the world's largest maritime zones. It also has a complex neighbourhood. Australia is a developed democracy but its region includes diverse levels of development and regime types, from small and fragile Pacific island states to populous powers, authoritarian, democratic and shades in between. As an island continent, Australia is distinctly dependent on lifelines to the world: flows of trade, energy, finance, people, knowledge. Despite tremendous natural resources, the country also relies heavily on imports: critically, it imports essentially all its refined transport fuels, of which it retains irresponsibly frugal stocks (in breach of international standards), and is thus economically vulnerable to disruption or blockade in the waterways of Southeast Asia.[11] As a middle player in a connected world, Australia has extensive national interests. And Australian governments – and the expectations of the Australian public – have tended to define those interests in ever-expanding ways over recent decades.

The very fact of exceptional economic success – the only major developed economy to have avoided recession for a generation – translates into high public expectations that a government will preserve the conditions for prosperity, making economics a matter of security and stability, not just material welfare. Moreover, Australians are accustomed to their country 'punching above its weight' to support both global order and the wellbeing of weaker countries close by, such as Pacific island states. As a middle power, unable to command security through force or weight, Australia is deeply invested in a rules-based international order, even though some prominent conservative voices – such as Prime Minister Morrison in 2019 – like to suggest that some rules are better than others.[12] Its policy elites have sought to link its domestic values (and national identity) as a multicultural and liberal democracy with pragmatic national interests in an Indo-Pacific order based on mutual respect and the sovereign equality of nations:

> Australia does not define its national identity by race or religion, but by shared values, including political, economic and religious freedom, liberal democracy, the rule of law, racial and gender equality and mutual respect. Our adherence to the rule of law extends beyond our borders. We advocate and seek to protect an international order in which relations between states are governed by international law and other rules and norms.[13]

Foreign minister Marise Payne has sought to take this further, declaring that 'principles' of democracy and individual rights 'produce stronger relations between countries', and that Australia should lead by example, 'not standing idly by when other countries are coerced'.[14]

It is a valiant logic, but reinforces that Australia's interests are simply too extensive for it to protect and advance on its own. In an interdependent world, every nation's interests outweigh its capabilities, but this problem is particularly acute for Australia. Here is a country that has always relied on a great and powerful friend – first Britain, then after 1942 America – with a corresponding 'fear of abandonment', in the words of eminent foreign policy expert Allan Gyngell.[15] Today Canberra's foreign policy unabashedly accentuates partnerships, including with fellow middle players stuck between Washington and Beijing, such as India, Japan and Indonesia.[16] This view is embraced across the political aisle: as shadow foreign minister Penny Wong declared in Jakarta in 2019, Australia 'can only realise our objectives through a multipolar region'.[17] Australia has taken a lead in crafting creative new 'small groups' for trusted security talks, and in building a multilayered diplomacy combining these 'minilaterals' with big bilateral partnerships and the inclusive regional organisations that Australia has done so much to propel.

But in military heft there remains no substitute for the US alliance. Here lies the rub. Australian policy is confused over whether to treat the alliance as an instrument for protecting Australian interests or as an interest in itself. Prime ministerial rhetoric uncritically describing the alliance as 'our past, our present and our future' only clouds the picture further.[18] Australia relies acutely on American defence equipment, intelligence and, in the ultimate crisis, the expectation under the ANZUS Treaty that overwhelming US force would come to its aid. Australian and American forces have become 'interoperable', seamlessly training and fighting together. Even with the vicissitudes of Trump and his attitude to allies, the Australian public recognises the alliance as essential: in a 2019 opinion poll by the Lowy Institute, 73 per cent believed the US would come to Australia's defence if the nation were under threat. At the same time, 69 per cent felt the alliance made it more likely Australia would be drawn into a war in Asia that would not be in their nation's interests.[19]

What, then, are Australia's main objectives in charting a way through a contested Indo-Pacific era ahead? Like all nations, it wants prosperity and peace, security and sovereignty. But tensions are arising within and between these neat-sounding goals. For instance, in a contested region, adherence to rules should be a net benefit for the sovereignty of a small or medium power. Yet if all the emphasis is on sovereignty, then acceptance of the rules becomes selective, eroding the edifice of a rules-based order. Another tension within Australian foreign policy in the Indo-Pacific is this: Australia wants Chinese regional dominance prevented, but not in ways that bring war or economic breakdown.

Australia's spectacular volume of trade with China is world famous: a third of its merchandise exports go there, with iron ore the dominant commodity.[20] However, this does not convert to the overwhelming economic vulnerability many imagine. Australia's trade dependence on China is cushioned by China's own dependence on Australian iron ore (for which there is no ready substitute) and the fact that Australia's economy is not overly reliant on exports to begin with, compared with some countries in Asia or Europe.[21]

Still, a solid trade relationship with Beijing is a high priority for any Australian government, mindful that voters are heavily motivated by the state of the economy. As China rises, some observers thus draw a stark choice for Canberra, between its foremost economic partner and its security ally. This makes for easy and alarmist headlines. But it is not merely a simplification; it is plain inaccurate. The People's Republic of China is indeed Australia's top trade partner, but as an investor in Australia's economy it lags in ninth place, behind even such small countries as Singapore, the Netherlands and Luxembourg.[22] If Hong Kong investments were added to China's, the total would still rank in just fifth place, behind America, Britain, Belgium and Japan. The United States is consistently Australia's leading investor: in 2018, it accounted for almost 27 per cent of the total stock of accumulated foreign investment, compared with 1.8 per cent for China – and the gap has widened in recent years.[23]

So if security competition in the Indo-Pacific is pressuring Australia to choose, then that choice is far more nuanced than simply a preference between prosperity and security. Trade is about transaction, while investment is about trust. It is so far demonstrably untrue that large trade ties with China are leading to reduced security links with America. In fact America's closest allies, Australia and Japan, have more important trade relations with China than those Southeast Asian countries over which

Beijing has more effectively expanded political influence. Thus trade relations are *not* determining strategic choices, and a US alliance does not reduce a nation's strategic autonomy in choosing with whom to trade.[24] Moreover, other leading foreign investors in Australia – such as Japan – have their own security differences with China, and see Australia as a place to safeguard their own resource futures. This explains, for example, Japan's development of Australian gas fields. Like many middle powers, Australia is not only a player in the many-sided game; it is a coveted part of the gameboard.

Economics can be a tool of diplomatic pressure, but only if the signals are conveyed via politics. The intersection of politics, domestic interests and public perception is where a country is most able to use economic links to exert influence over another on security issues, thus compromising an irreducible aspect of sovereignty – independent decision-making.[25] Australia has been at the centre of global controversy in recent years over reports of Chinese Communist Party interference in its politics and society, such as the use of political donations to influence foreign policy and the intimidation of dissenting voices within Australia's diverse Chinese communities.[26] Pushback has included strengthened laws against covert influence and espionage, with a ban on financial donations to political parties from foreign governments. The debate has opened fissures on issues such as national allegiance and democratic values, including within Australia's diverse Chinese-origin communities. Part of the challenge ahead is for the Australian government to reassure the nation's 1.2 million people of Chinese heritage that its national security laws are intended to protect them from foreign government interference, rather than to accuse them of disloyalty. Australia is being described as an early example, the 'canary in the coalmine', when it comes to detecting and discouraging Chinese state interference in sovereign affairs.[27]

Any notion that Canberra's security decisions have been at America's behest is a misreading; on these issues, Australia has been more leader than follower, a middle power acting independently, with all the risk and responsibility this carries.[28] Thus the Turnbull government's resistance to Chinese party-state interference began well before the United States took a similar path. Australia's prominent decisions to block Chinese investment in critical infrastructure – such as blocking telecommunications giant Huawei from building a national 5G network – preceded America's own restrictions on Chinese enterprises. Critics of Australia's US alliance have often understandably called for a more independent foreign policy. Certainly it is a poignant counterfactual to imagine what would have come of Australia (and perhaps Britain) declining to join the folly of invading Iraq in 2003. But independence does not mean swapping deference to Washington for deference to Beijing.

The Australian experience points to a likely pattern for many middle players seeking to preserve their interests, values and identity amid US–China strategic competition. Links between foreign policy, security, economics and domestic resilience will complicate the management of tensions in any of these sectors. The new normal will require acceptance of constant friction. It will be impossible even to separate Australia's relations with its smallest neighbours, the Pacific island states, from the China factor. Since 2018, Canberra has invested in a major 'step-up' of aid, diplomacy, education and security presence across Melanesia. Publicly, the government insists this is largely about doing the right thing as Pacific 'family'. It is true that, despite phases of neglect and mutual frustration, Australia has historically sought to strengthen its fragile neighbours. But of course Australia is also acting in its fundamental self-interest. China's presence in the South Pacific has rapidly expanded, to include naval visits, critical infrastructure projects and bids at political influence, both open and opaque. Despite its seemingly out-of-the-way location, the South Pacific has since 2015 been officially declared by China as a branch line of the Belt and Road.[29] For the first time since 1942, Australia is countenancing the prospect of a potentially unfriendly major power building military bases on its eastern flank, and seems determined to stop that possibility.[30]

Thus, within years of declaring a broadly Indo-Pacific policy, and recognising the need to protect its interests across the expanse of the Indian Ocean as well as the old Asia-Pacific, Australia is suddenly discovering strategic risks close to home. Its limited capabilities – defence and diplomatic – will not allow it to cover all fronts. Little wonder Canberra is also looking to disparate partners, beyond the US alliance. Thus India in the Indian Ocean; Japan and France across the Indo-Pacific; and in the waters of Southeast Asia, a new significance for a complicated neighbour, Indonesia.

Indonesia

Like India and China, the great archipelagic nation of Indonesia seeks a stable region to allow sorely needed economic development. Indonesia has been called the improbable nation, its unity imposed on more than 270 million people across several hundred ethnic and language groups. There is a 'veneer of shared history' but unsurprisingly little common culture, given that this nation is scattered across thousands of islands.[31] Thus its sheer existence as a united, independent and – since 1998 – fully democratic state is a bewildering accomplishment.

But new tests lie ahead. Indonesia has long aspired to 'free and active' diplomacy, claiming to lead not only Southeast Asia but much of the non-aligned world. But this has often amounted to a kind of statecraft akin to the nation's celebrated art of *wayang kulit*, or shadow puppetry: audiences, from the populace to foreign powers, are diverted by a semblance of action while the reality may be insubstantial. A mixture of nationalist rhetoric and talk-heavy ASEAN diplomacy has often substituted for strategic direction, leadership or the building of national strength. Yet now Indonesia is on a path to overtake Japan as the world's fourth-largest economy by 2050. In a more contested region, Jakarta will need to do more to bridge promise and reality, to develop and utilise the power and capabilities required to protect its sprawling interests.

Unlike China or even India, Indonesia struggles to qualify as a major power – as a country that can defend itself, let alone impose its will on others. Its military has long been more for maintaining order within the nation than facing external foes. That is not surprising, for domestic instability, Islamist ideology and terrorism are enduring challenges in a disparate and still maturing democracy. Like India, Indonesia's power is less than the sum of its parts. And the nation's ability to organise and mobilise remains in doubt. Much internal dysfunction remains, including a politics at risk of veering to populism or Islamism. The military remains a political vested interest, with potential to regress further from reforms intended to ensure democratic and civilian authority.[32]

So here is a shining anomaly. Indonesia is a sea-soaked nation: its maritime exclusive economic zone (EEZ) is four times the size of its land and it has the second-longest coastline in the world. Yet it has a large army and a weak navy. Indonesia's leaders know this is not a tenable posture in a contested region. President Joko Widodo ('Jokowi') has acknowledged his country's central Indo-Pacific geography, recasting the nation as a 'global maritime fulcrum' (*Poros Maritim Dunia*). In his first-term inauguration speech in 2014, he emphasised national aspirations as a sea power connecting two oceans:

> We have to work hard to return Indonesia's status as a maritime nation. Oceans, seas, straits, and gulfs are the future of our civilization. We have been showing our backs too long to these seas, to these oceans, to these straits, and gulfs … *Jalesveva Jayamahe*, it is at the sea we are glorious …[33]

It's a bold and logical vision, recognising that the sea brings Indonesia mixed blessings: opportunity and vulnerability, identity and obligation. Much of Indonesia's resources – fisheries, oil and gas – are offshore. The nation's strategic importance to almost every other country derives from its location: their commerce and military forces traverse its internal waters and airspace, but Indonesia draws scant economic return from such traffic. Indonesian diplomat-scholars have led the world in devising law to define sovereignty over waters within an archipelago. Yet their nation has struggled to manage or even monitor the blue territory thus won, with internal seas plagued by illegal fishing, smuggling and piracy.[34] For Indonesia truly to fulfil its promise as a nation – cohesive within and credible to outsiders – it will need to govern the space between its islands, at a time when the central location of those waters makes them so strategically important to the Indo-Pacific rivalries of others.

Indonesian president Joko Widodo proclaims his country's
maritime destiny in his 2014 inauguration speech

The challenge remains formidable. Progress on the fulcrum agenda has
been modest. A patchwork maritime bureaucracy is being sewn together.
Indonesia has long been known for some of Asia's worst port infrastructure
but this is improving, with Japanese rather than Chinese funding.[35] The
navy is growing. Indonesia is building the fast patrol vessels it needs for
policing its scattered maze of waters, but its forces remain much weaker
than those of more developed neighbours Australia and Singapore – let
alone China's – when it comes to ocean-going, intelligence-gathering, warfare or deterrence. This matters, because China is pushing its claims in the
disputed South China Sea, brushing up against Indonesia's Natuna Islands.
Strictly speaking, neither side calls it a territorial dispute: the clash so far is
over fish. Indonesian leaders have taken a firm stance against illegal fishing – boats from many countries have been burned, shots fired. But
Indonesian civilian forces have backed down when larger Chinese coast
guard ships intervene, even in Indonesian waters. Subsequently, Jakarta has
deployed its navy to protect fishing grounds.[36] Ugly tests of resolve are a
matter of time.

Diplomatically, Jakarta can claim credit for leading the other nine ASEAN countries to acknowledge the new regional challenges, by reaching a hard-won consensus on an 'Indo-Pacific outlook' document in mid-2019. This reflects Southeast Asia's collective will to sign up neither to a China-centric order nor to a US-led strategic confrontation with China, and signals the desire for a third way of managing differences through rules, non-coercion and regional diplomatic institutions centred on ASEAN. Indonesian officials can thus claim credit for persuading the region to accept that its future is indeed Indo-Pacific – with the likes of India and Australia as integral players. But that is about framing the problem, and may prove to be setting up ASEAN diplomacy to face tensions it cannot handle. It is about Indonesia playing a weak hand well, rather than changing the power realities.[37]

So observers still wonder whether Indonesia will get beyond the shadow play and become a truly consequential power. Games may hold a clue. To prepare for uncertainty, governments, militaries and think tanks are reviving a mid-20th-century fashion of 'wargaming' the future. Such strategic simulations typically play out US–China relations many years into the future, but sometimes factor in third powers. In games of the author's experience, Indonesia is the dark horse: underestimated yet positioned to exploit great powers through flexible plays of diplomatic balancing or bandwagoning, while quietly amassing its own economic growth and transmuting that into future military strength.

That is where game and reality diverge. Predictions of continuous economic growth are not self-fulfilling. Indonesia's creditable advocacy of free trade runs up against traditions of growth-impeding protectionism. Infrastructure gaps remain large. The Indonesian government is by no means averse to the potential material benefits of China's Belt and Road – after all, Xi Jinping was permitted to announce the Maritime Silk Road in Jakarta. But headlines about Indonesia asking China for a 'special fund' miss the fine print.[38] Indonesian authorities want Chinese money only on their own terms and are striving to hedge: allowing China to fund railways, but offering more strategically critical port projects to Japan and India. The energy sector, meanwhile, remains a muddle: foreign investment is discouraged by old-fashioned nationalisation, and Indonesia's own oil production is slowing.[39]

Indonesia is at a crossroads in more ways than one. It is yet to reconcile its post-colonial fixation on sovereignty with the need to do all it can to protect its expanding interests. Sometimes this will mean mobilisation of its own resources, sometimes a more creative approach to partnerships, and sometimes a willingness to take a stand. These conundrums are not uniquely Indonesian.

Sea of many flags

Jakarta's foreign policy anxieties reflect and refract across Southeast Asia. It is easy to generalise about the ten ASEAN countries: prioritising development and social cohesion, caught between the United States and China, determined to preserve their autonomy, wedded to their ponderous ways of consensus diplomacy, weaker than they ought to be given that together than have a population of 650 million and a US$3 trillion economy. It is equally simple to magnify divisions, especially between those that are supposedly pro-China – such as Cambodia and Laos – and those that hew a more independent path.

But Southeast Asia can be a subtle place, and the most meaningful differences and similarities among its states are complex and cross-cutting. Contradiction is commonplace. Thus at times the most pro-Beijing voice is the nationalist leader of a democracy allied to the United States (Duterte in the Philippines). Meanwhile, Vietnam's communist regime actively seeks to resist China through a defence partnership with its one-time mortal enemy America, while also strengthening its own military as it secures equipment and training from Russia and India. After Indonesia, Vietnam has the most potential to be a serious regional power and no one's tributary. Malaysia's leader decries Chinese colonialism one year then praises its telecommunications technology the next. Singapore's president warns of the dangers from America stepping up its military and economic competition with China, while the island city-state accommodates visiting American aircraft carriers and robustly counters Chinese political interference.

The interests and postures of the ASEAN states are not in absolute contrast but vary by degrees: all want the economic benefits of China's continued growth and engagement, but all – even including little Laos – fear Chinese dominance. Cambodia may seem a China client state, but the perception that current elites have sold the national interest to Beijing is stoking public anger and long-term strife. To varying degrees, all ASEAN nations are willing to foster a multipolar region, where the United States, Japan, India and others remain engaged to balance China. All now recognise that the Indo-Pacific is a geopolitical reality, and that it is better for ASEAN to recognise this through its institutions rather than reject it. All Southeast Asian states also cherish ASEAN unity and agency, even if this is sometimes more idea than reality. The classic example is their persistence in seeking to negotiate with China a code of conduct to manage differences in the South China Sea. This glacial diplomatic process has endured since 2002, during which time China's militarised island-building has remade the disputed waterscape such that any future code will be more about protecting than preventing China's illegal gains. The aspiration to use inclusive diplomatic forums to address the region's hard problems may seem noble, but also can defer confrontation while the strategic balance shifts in dangerous ways.

Such is the case on the Korean Peninsula. The Republic of Korea, or South Korea, has profound interests across the wider Indo-Pacific. Its dependence on Indian Ocean sea lanes for energy is more acute even than that of China or Japan, not only for its own oil needs but for the petroleum it refines and exports. It is a US ally, a developed democracy, and the world's fifth-largest exporter, with shipbuilding among its major industries. It has the world's sixth-busiest cargo ports, vast commercial and fishing fleets, and a powerful ocean-going navy. Its big trade and investment relationship with China is coloured by a growing mistrust following Beijing's punishment of Korean companies over Seoul's willingness to host American anti-missile defences. Yet despite its wider regional integration, South Korea has long been transfixed by problems close to home. Its relations with

Japan – a country with which it should have much common cause – are distorted by the legacy of Japanese colonisation and wartime oppression. The failure to fully come to terms with this is a pointless blind spot in Tokyo's mostly enlightened diplomacy. Largely, though, Seoul's diplomacy and military remains focused on the troubled relationship with its dangerous and desperate northern neighbour.

There are signs of South Korea becoming a more ambitious regional player: for instance, through long-range naval exercises, security and intelligence talks with Southeast Asian countries, and even the role of its special forces in the Middle East. In 2019 President Moon Jae-in promoted a 'New Southern Policy' to engage more with ASEAN – which could give the Southeast Asian nations a new alternative to Chinese investment, and expand South Korea's diplomatic room to manoeuvre beyond the constricting diamond of China, Japan, Russia and the United States.[40] Seoul and New Delhi have discovered each other, with collaboration in the steel industry and car making – Hyundai has a fifth of the fast-growing Indian motor vehicle market – being augmented in 2019 with naval logistics, defence technology and Samsung mobile phone production (shifted out of China).[41] It is not clear whether Korean officials will voice the Indo-Pacific terminology so embraced by America and Japan.[42] But actions matter more. Just as Japan's rivalry with China has propelled Tokyo's activism across the Indo-Pacific, so too South Korea's struggle to assert itself against both those large neighbours is driving Seoul to larger horizons, and benefitting new partners along the way.

For an impoverished nation of 25 million, North Korea has a vastly outsized impact on regional and global security, thanks to its nuclear weapons program and propensity to threaten war. It is not entirely cut off from wider Indo-Pacific strategic dynamics. Pyongyang has used the sea lanes for smuggling, including to support its missile and nuclear programs. The North Korea–Pakistan axis was part of a covert bazaar in nuclear and missile technology for many years. And North Korea's constant assaults on international law – from nuclear and missile tests to cyber attacks and assassination – give regional institutions something to unite against. Crisis on the Korean Peninsula – with the possibility of all-out war – is one of the key potential flashpoints that could throw the regional and global future off course in fundamental ways. This would affect many powers – not only China, the United States, Japan and South Korea, but also Russia.

The status of Russia as an Indo-Pacific power is quite debatable. Russia has long been in part a Pacific power, but its fleet at Vladivostok atrophied after the fall of the Soviet Union. Putin has been pushing a 'turn to the east' since at least 2013. This has involved fostering energy exports to China and Japan, or renewed arms sales to China, Vietnam, India and Indonesia, particularly as Russia's own aggressive actions in Europe undermined its chances of a cooperative and prosperous future there. Russia's interests in the Indo-Pacific are entangled with three imperatives: wider strategic competition with the United States and other democracies; the need to manage relations with a powerful China; and Russia's residual pretensions as a global power. Yet these bring limits too. The contest with America and the 'West' will still play out primarily on a European and North Atlantic stage. With Beijing, for all the appearances of a model strategic partnership, it is ultimately a marriage of convenience, in which Moscow fears being treated permanently as junior partner.[43] Of course, the Russia–China affair bears close watching, especially if Russia follows through on claims made by President Putin in October 2019 that it will help China with technology to detect US missile launches.[44]

But even analysts warning that the Russia–China condominium will shut other powers out of Eurasia note that China still sees itself as accommodating Russian needs and fears merely in a 'transitional phase' – in other words, before China becomes truly dominant.[45] In any case, Russia's really substantial relations with China are less in the maritime Indo-Pacific and more on the Eurasian landmass, supporting both economic connectivity and illiberal Central Asian regimes, while countering what both powers deem terrorism.

So, while Moscow would be comfortable seeing US power diminished in the Indo-Pacific, it will let China take the lead. It is highly questionable whether Russia would entangle its own vital interests in a US–China confrontation: would Russia truly be willing to let China drag it into war with the United States?[46] On the other hand, China will be wary of Russian recklessness engaging it in a crisis not of Beijing's own devising.[47] The PLA would not have been grateful when a Russian plane on a joint patrol blundered into South Korean airspace, provoking a furious fusillade of warning shots, in July 2019. Moreover, Russia is a strange kind of friend to China when it sells advanced armaments to India and Vietnam. In any case, no amount of rebalance to the Indo-Pacific will prevent Russia's long-term decline. Russia retains a massive nuclear arsenal and is an intimidating force in dark arts like cyber and intelligence. Its navy and air force are making their presence felt, from Japan to Southeast Asia, and even occasionally in the South Pacific. But it remains a lopsided power with a vulnerable economy and poor demographics. In exchange rate terms, the Russian economy is smaller than Canada's.[48] Dependence on energy exports, coupled with a weak oil price, does not help. Its population is in long-term decline, compounded by poor health and life-expectancy statistics.[49] In the Indo-Pacific over the coming decades Russia could be a major and disruptive player, but is unlikely to be a decisive one.

The global region

Like Russia, Europe has plenty else to worry about. Strikingly, however, even as the European 'holiday from history' has come to an end, and security, economic and political problems have amassed close to home, some key European countries and the EU more generally have begun to take the Indo-Pacific seriously, for the first time in many years. Europe has long been focused on Asia, especially China, as a place of commercial opportunity, and many European countries initially welcomed the Belt and Road solely through that prism. Meanwhile, European corporations are established arms suppliers to the region. But a more nuanced and risk-conscious European engagement with the Indo-Pacific is emerging. This is driven by a recognition of economic interest in the sea lanes, the geoeconomic subtext to the Belt and Road, the global nature of China's cyber and intelligence activities, and the overall risk to the liberal international system from resurgent great-power tensions.

Paris has led the shift, wholeheartedly endorsing the Indo-Pacific concept as being at the heart of its global strategy.[50] France can claim to be a genuine Indo-Pacific power, given its many island territories in the Pacific and Indian oceans, which give it enduring command over the largest exclusive economic zone of any nation. France has 1.5 million citizens, 8000 troops and a small naval fleet permanently stationed in those territories, augmented by long-range ship visits such as the aircraft carrier *Charles de Gaulle* in 2019.[51] It is strengthening security ties in particular with India, Australia and Japan. India and Australia are among France's foremost arms customers. Amid strains on the rules-based global order – coming from China, Russia and America – President Macron has spoken up for liberal-democratic principles in the Indo-Pacific, talking openly of the need to discourage Chinese 'hegemony'.[52]

French and British warships have transited contentious waterways – the South China Sea and the Taiwan Strait – to reinforce the normality of law-based freedoms to use the sea. Germany is contemplating doing the same. But entirely reasonable questions can be asked about the seriousness of this European commitment to Asia. Would a distant country like France really put its forces and economy at risk in a maritime confrontation with China? While dealing with the consequences of Brexit, how much diplomatic capital will Britain really invest in, say, the rights of Hong Kongers or Uighurs? Britain is notably reinvesting in its diplomacy east of Suez – opening more posts, deploying more staff – but the overall strategy remains uncertain. Consumed with Brexit, British policy-makers were still debating in 2019 whether to formally recraft British regional engagement as an Indo-Pacific rather than Asia-Pacific policy.[53] Nonetheless, European powers, the EU collectively, and Britain are now looking at the Indo-Pacific through more than a commercial lens.

For somewhat 'external' players like Europe or Russia, it is unclear how much is truly at stake in the Indo-Pacific. But for the many nations resident in the region, there is no question: they have everything to gain – or lose.

Small islands states in both oceans are finding themselves terrain for the rivalries of large powers. This could be leveraged for much-needed development – indeed, it may seem enviable to have China and many of its competitors suddenly vying to deliver aid, infrastructure and training. But no nation wants to be another's battlefield, even if only figuratively, especially if the price of all this attention is an erosion of sovereignty, of the independent ability to make choices about foreign policy or resource use or infrastructure without constant pressure from stronger countries.

This is an obvious problem in the South Pacific and the Indian Ocean, where the power disparity is so stark between big nations like China and India on the one hand and microstates like Vanuatu and Maldives on the other. In Africa, too, there are signs of a great-power scramble for influence, with Japan, India, America and the Europeans looking to balance China, and countries such as Zimbabwe and Zambia having second thoughts about the impact of Chinese wealth on national freedom of decision and action.[54] Moreover, it is local communities in countries of the Indo-Pacific littoral that bear the brunt of pressures on the regional commons. Here the strategic rivalry among nations is intersecting with commercial exploitation of natural resources, exacerbated by climate-induced pressures on local populations and ecosystems. What happens, for instance, when industrial-scale fishing in the Indian Ocean – increasingly dominated by China's subsidised fishing fleets of long-range vessels – coincides with the impacts of climate change, such as rising sea levels and worsening storms?[55] Any one of these factors would threaten the livelihoods of coastal communities in many small nations; together they could be devastating. Small islands states will be deeply affected by great-power tensions, even though they understandably have their own more immediate security priorities related to climate change, resource pressures, crime and social order.[56]

Substantial South Asian countries like Bangladesh and Sri Lanka are also feeling the tension, with India and Japan openly competing with China in infrastructure and influence. The outcomes are far from forgone conclusions. Bangladesh, for instance, is not the passive or permanently impoverished backwater it was once assumed to be, but is accumulating its own power (with an economy growing at a rapid clip of 8 per cent a year). Dhaka is setting conditions to play off diversified donors and allow itself significant autonomy.[57] For instance, China's port-building plans in Chittagong have been kept at bay, with a nearby Japanese project welcomed instead. However, Beijing's offer to give the Bangladeshi navy submarines and a base for them on the Bay of Bengal warrant scrutiny, given the obvious possibility of Chinese naval access as an eventual quid pro quo.[58]

Even in Pakistan, where Indian influence is entirely absent and America's increasingly unwelcome, there are signs that China's presence is no longer seen as an unmitigated blessing. Pakistan is now host to a comprehensive overlay of Chinese infrastructure: an 'economic corridor' of ports, rail, road, energy, industry and agriculture, along with military cooperation and rapidly growing communities of resident Chinese nationals. The aims, for Islamabad, include achieving material development, national security, legitimacy for the quasi-democratic civil-military regime, and stability in restive provinces. But the pace and scale of China's ambitions, perceptions of a neo-colonial agenda (such as purchasing farms to prioritise food exports to China) and the resentments among some local populations raise the prospect that the China factor could end up worsening, not reducing, Pakistani domestic unrest and India–Pakistan hostility.[59]

In Africa, meanwhile, there has been little sign so far of governments taking an active role in wider Indo-Pacific diplomacy: they have focused instead on inviting and, where possible, managing the opportunities of investment from China and its competitors. In August 2019, African leaders 'noted' rather than 'supported' Japan's Free and Open Indo-Pacific strategy, three years after its launch in Nairobi. Individual African leaders are becoming more forthright in trying to set the terms of engagement, notably with Chinese Belt and Road projects: for instance, in June 2019 Tanzanian president John Magufuli suspended a Chinese port development, criticising the financing for its 'tough conditions that can only be accepted by mad people'.[60] As Africa's economic and demographic weight grows in the decades ahead, it is likely that African governments will more actively manoeuvre between China, Japan, India, the United States and Europe, seeking a say in the future of their wider region, including the Indian Ocean. After all, by 2050 the population of Africa is expected to cross the 2.5 billion mark, and go on to surpass the combined populations of China and India.[61]

Seen from the oil-exporting states of the Gulf, the Indo-Pacific great game remains more about supply than demand. Along with the constants of Middle East political violence and instability, the Arab states and Iran have seen a bedrock shift in the vital oil trade: their main customers are no longer American and European but the powers of Indo-Pacific Asia – China, Japan, South Korea, India.[62] Those oil-importing Asian countries in turn have been slow to accept that such energy dependence could require them to follow in America's footsteps and take on commensurate security responsibilities in and around the Persian Gulf or the Strait of Hormuz. India has shown interest in sending its navy into the Gulf, but China and Japan seem more intent on securing assurances from Iran that their ships will not be targeted in its confrontations with America and Europe.[63]

At the same time, the governments of the Gulf countries seem in no rush to take the initiative in defining what their relations with the competing Indo-Pacific powers will look like. An exception is Iran's state of near-conflict with America; however, that seems as much a choice made in Trump's Washington as in Tehran. That said, dramatic media reports in 2019 of a deep-seated Iran–China security partnership, complete with plans for 5000 Chinese soldiers to guard future oil and gas infrastructure investments inside Iran, are unverified and implausible, with China proving cautious about defying US-led sanctions and Iran unwilling to host foreign forces.[64] For the most part, the oil-exporting nations of the Middle East seem driven by near-term economic opportunism rather than long-term strategic purpose in shaping their relations with China, India and Japan. More generally, Muslim countries are yet to come to terms with the systematic state persecution of co-religionists in China. From Turkey to Saudi Arabia to the populous Indian Ocean states of Bangladesh and Pakistan, governments have callously downplayed the mass human rights abuses in Xinjiang.[65] This is nonetheless an issue that may in time open fissures between China and the Islamic world.[66]

Islam is one of many transnational communities in this connected region. The Indo-Pacific may be principally a region of nations, but non-state networks – of multinational business, religion and civil society – continue to operate across borders. These networks reflect their own sense of what matters, of a regional and international interest as opposed to narrowly national interests. What is less certain is how much impact they can have as states large and small reassert economic boundaries and insist that their citizens prioritise loyalty above national interests. Also poorly understood is whether civil society networks – such as non-government organisations with environmental or human rights concerns – can have much impact across borders in a region where countries have never relaxed or pooled their independence in the EU manner. Few nations in the region are tolerant of transnational entities – whether global social movements or the United Nations bureaucracy – having a decisive say in their domestic affairs. Still, the instant cross-border impact of online information flows, especially from social media, means that the political effect of mass mobilisation cannot be quarantined within national boundaries. A recent example has been the international citizens' movement in support of the Hong Kong democracy protests. For its part, China is seeking absolute censorship and surveillance – and a capacity to quash dissent across borders.

The Indo-Pacific is truly the global region. Most every nation with a stake in trade, the international balance of power, and the maritime commons has interests at play. Rather than the straightforward binary of a US–China power game, the Indo-Pacific is a puzzle, a tangle of interests overlapping, aligning, converging, diverging and conflicting. Not only does it have a multipolarity of players; the contest also has a complexity of many levels – security, economics, diplomacy and more.

CHAPTER 7

COVERING THE WATERFRONT

ndo-Pacific nations engage and contend across the waterfront, in both senses. The contest spans a wide spectrum of issues: not just military defence, but commerce, diplomacy and the manipulation of knowledge. And much of the action is at sea or in the ports and harbours – where the land meets the water, the belt meets the road. To get a glimpse of this, I embarked as a guest of the Royal Australian Navy.

Watching the sea

Around us is another humid dawn in the equatorial calm of the Java Sea. But today is a special moment for Australia's navy – a warm welcome to Jakarta. This is the capital of Australia's largest neighbour and a country that once upon a time was seen less as friend and more as prospective foe. Much has changed. Indonesia is now one of Australia's more promising security partners. Its growing economy and creative diplomacy are bumping it closer to the core of a dynamic region. Indonesia matters. It is no wonder that China's leader chose Jakarta as the place to proclaim the Maritime Silk Road.

The Australian navy's flagship is the 27,000-tonne HMAS *Canberra*. Technically, it is called a 'landing helicopter dock', though it looks like an aircraft carrier, with a huge flat deck. The bridge of the ship is vivid with high-tech navigation consoles but also provides the more old-fashioned and exhilarating option of sweeping views, and from here we see the water traffic thicken again, for first time since we left the congested Singapore Strait two days ago. Cargo carriers, chemical tankers, huge vessels transporting natural gas within distinctive white domes, passenger ferries, trawlers, tugboats, a Chinese civilian ship that has intriguingly matched our speed and route, and now an Indonesian naval escort.

The aptly named 'Indo-Pacific Endeavour' task force – ships, helicopters, an army detachment – is close to the home leg of its marathon mission. For three months, 'IPE19' has flown the Australian flag across the most vital sea lanes for the island continent, from the Indian Ocean to the South China Sea. It proves that Canberra is walking its talk of the Indo-Pacific. Australian forces have trained with counterparts in India, Sri Lanka, Thailand, Malaysia, Singapore and Vietnam. There's been plenty of goodwill and public relations, as well as less diplomatic moments – such as when potentially blinding lasers were pointed at the Australian helicopter pilots from Chinese fishing vessels.[1]

Now we enter Jakarta's port, Tanjung Priok, Indonesia's largest. In recent years, it has begun shedding its reputation for inefficiency, but to the untrained eye it still seems like organised chaos. This is merely the thirtieth-busiest port in the world. Our warship – the largest Australia has ever commissioned – is soon just another visitor engulfed by canyons and forests of containers and cranes. Back home in Australia, it is election day, 18 May 2019. But no one here seems much bothered by that. The art of steering the ship of state suddenly looks amateurish compared with the patient teamwork of berthing a billion-dollar warship in a narrow and unfamiliar dock. At last it's done, and there's a ceremonial welcome, salutes and admirals and Balinese dancers.

The real spectacle, though, is all around. This Indo-Pacific waterfront is the buzzing backroom of a rising economy: ships, cranes, containers, trucks, a global bazaar of names like Maersk, Meratus, COSCO, CMA CGM, Wan Hai, Temas Line, Evergreen, Hamburg Süd, SITC. In the distance is the haze of the city, with notorious traffic and a population of 10.6 million and growing. In weird juxtaposition are a few silvery warships transplanted into the midst of it all. Business and security often seem like distant worlds but suddenly they are side by side.

Nothing matches going to sea to see. To observe up close the highways and crossroads of the Indo-Pacific is to witness the inner workings of the

The Australian navy flagship HMAS Canberra *enters Tanjung Priok, Jakarta's commercial port, in 2019, during the 'Indo-Pacific Endeavour' deployment*

world. That is especially so for the straits of Malacca and Singapore, where a traffic separation system allows hundreds of ships to pass each day. Billions of people today – half of living humanity – belong to a global middle class of relative comfort, choice and dignity.[2] Yet few glimpse behind the veil of peace and plenty to see the constant vast engine that sustains this astonishing achievement across the seas. In reality, it is two distinct machines: the shabbily technicolour spectacle of giant cargo ships bearing the barely imaginable burden of global commerce, and the smaller and sleeker grey hulls designed to prevent war by being ready to wage it.

Superficially, these are different worlds, insulated and parallel, literally ships passing in the night. Commercial shipping resembles a global system where we long lulled ourselves into imagining that borders barely rate. One vessel carries a cargo assembled in many places to many places more. Their national flags of registration are often of convenience – that is, to minimise legal liabilities – and have no relation to the ship's ownership, multinational crew, or port of origin or destination. For many years, few nations have tried to muster or manage a 'merchant navy' they can call their own, though China is leading the way in changing that.

Meanwhile, military fleets – true navies – remain floating bastions of sovereignty, defence and force. The evolution of naval technology, towards smaller vessels with clean lines and few obvious weapons, belies a discreet capacity for surveillance and destruction. These qualities are accentuated in the world's submarine fleets, increasingly concentrated in the Indo-Pacific. Modern frigates and destroyers, the workhorses of surface warfare, look miniature alongside giant container ships reaching almost 200,000 tonnes; it is clear which fares worse in a collision.

But there are hidden cross-currents to the interaction of economics and security in the Indo-Pacific sea lanes. Wealth and power politics are intersecting, not bypassing. Thus navies are not only for warfighting: much of their time they are practising other arts, from flag-flying diplomacy to high-seas policing to evacuations and disaster relief. They are useful for cooperation between states as well as for competition – and a typical deployment involves both.

The route of HMAS *Canberra* in early 2019 was one thread in a filigree of hundreds, a tracery of intensifying naval activity criss-crossing the map. A Chinese Indo-Pacific task group of three ships and some 700 sailors visited Australia's Sydney Harbour en route to the South Pacific after counter-piracy operations in the Indian Ocean. For its part, China had earlier hosted a dozen foreign navies for a massive fleet review off Qingdao. The flagship of the Marine Nationale, aircraft carrier *Charles de Gaulle*, led a French task group from Djibouti to Southeast Asia, conducting exercises in various combinations with India, Japan, the United States, Australia, Singapore and Vietnam. The Indian navy reached a rapid tempo of exercises, training almost simultaneously with the Americans in the Indian Ocean, with Australia, France and Japan in the Bay of Bengal, the South Koreans off Busan and the navies of Vietnam, Singapore, the Philippines and America in the South China Sea. French and Canadian warships exercised their right to transit the international waters of the Taiwan Strait, as the British amphibious assault ship HMS *Albion* had done in the South China Sea months earlier. For its part, Japan sent one of its largest ships, the flat-deck 'helicopter-carrier destroyer' JS *Izumo*, to the Bay of Bengal and the South China Sea, where it trained with many foreign forces, including the American aircraft carrier USS *Ronald Reagan*. Soon after, Japan sent another helicopter carrier and destroyer to join the huge US–Australia Talisman Sabre exercise off the coast of Queensland.[3]

On the civilian front, the mega-commerce of the ocean highways is not simply a stateless saga of win-win prosperity, a rising tide lifting all boats. Perhaps it never was, but in any case states are reasserting themselves, once again seeking to rule the waves. Control of ports and ownership of shipping companies are becoming elements in a 'weaponisation' of international supply chains. Some analysts point to Chinese state ownership and control of a fast-expanding international network of submarine cables, shipping lines and commercial ports (many of which double as hubs for Chinese digital and data giants).[4] It is claimed, for instance, that a global consortium dominated by Chinese state-owned shipping group COSCO, involving foreign private lines including Marseille-based CMA CGM, may secure privileged access to tonnage and ports for China in the event of a trade conflict.

More broadly, the argument is that the economic power of Chinese national control of supply chains and ports could be turned towards strategic purposes such as intelligence gathering and economic sabotage or simply shutting out competitors' commerce. COSCO, for example, is also a major logistics contractor to the Chinese navy, and has already equipped some civilian vessels to refuel and resupply warships at sea. This may sound paranoid and could in any case prove innocuous if a rules-based system of global cooperation endures. But it could form a critical part of the great game if interstate competition escalates to confrontation or worse. And of course if crisis strikes, just as civilian economic connections may suddenly become security assets or liabilities, so too will navies suddenly put aside their apparent indifference to the realm of civilian shipping. After all, they are trained not just to escort but, in the last resort, to track, interdict and sink.

Trade winds turn

'The great object of the political economy of every country,' wrote Adam Smith in 1776, 'is to increase the riches and power of that country.'[5] Riches *and power*: this observation from the founding theorist of market economics was often overlooked in the spree of globalisation over the past few decades. For many governments, the guiding view was that the widest possible extension of open markets and economic interdependence would invariably benefit all nations. Any consequent changes in the balance of power among them would be a manageable cost of the endless cornucopia of cheapness and plenty. On its own terms, there's no gainsaying the positive-sum logic of free trade. The immense achievement of global economic growth since the aftermath of the Second World War, and more sharply since the end of the Cold War, speaks for itself.

This dynamic has been pervasive in the Indo-Pacific – or, more accurately, until recently, the Asia-Pacific. Billions of people have improved their standard of living, with the economic growth initially of Japan and the East

Asian 'tigers', then of China, Southeast Asia and India, and increasingly now of other Indian Ocean littoral states and much of Africa. It is an epochal tale of human endeavour and wellbeing. Many governments are trying to sustain this spirit in their efforts to secure free trade agreements, whether bilaterally or region-wide, notably the Regional Comprehensive Economic Partnership centred on ASEAN. But much of the wind has dropped from the free trade sails.

The era of what may come to be seen as high globalisation, the 1990s and 2000s, was marked by trade flows with strong global, Asia-Pacific and East Asian dimensions. The flourishing commerce among China, Japan, Europe and the United States was dominant, masking multinational value-chains of the many-stage production of 'made in the world' manufactures, typified by smartphones and computers.[6] Many manufactures also involved Southeast Asia, South Korea and Taiwan, the latter an island of dominance in semiconductors. An Indo-Pacific overlay also accrued, with Asia-Europe commerce being carried overwhelmingly by sea, China–Africa trade suddenly arising, and India growing to be another sizeable trading partner for many, especially the United States and China. Crucially, the resource base for global and Asia-Pacific trade became increasingly Indo-Pacific, with rapidly rising demand from China and other East Asian manufacturing centres for energy, minerals and food from Australia, Africa and Latin America. In value as well as weight, the overwhelming portion of trade was and continues to be seaborne: in 2018, according to the World Trade Organization, almost two-thirds by value of China's exports and imports were transported by sea, with most of the rest by air, and the water's share can only have been even greater for India, Japan, Southeast Asia, Australia and others.[7]

But free trade was never the whole picture. Throughout this time, some governments remained more conscious than others about Adam Smith's warning of the inherent tension between economic logic and the power contest among nations. China stands out, not only for the scale of its vulnerability to interruptions in external resource supply, but for its determined and systematic effort to employ the power of the state to build and protect those lifelines. National survival – regime survival – is not being left to the market. The underlying logic is a far cry from the windy win-win rhetoric of the Belt and Road and its 'community of common destiny'.

Now, all nations get it. The past few years have brought a sudden popularisation of the concept of 'geoeconomics', coined in 1990 by American strategist Edward Luttwak, in an immediate post–Cold War recognition that 'the methods of commerce are displacing military methods' in the quest for national advantage.[8] National frontiers and sovereignty still matter, but nations are now competing for advantages through economics rather than, or, more precisely, in addition to, military force. Between 2008 and 2018, the United States finally turned Luttwak's prescient observations into policy, and came to view economics and security as convergent instruments of power relations.[9] No longer is 'economic, financial and technological interdependence an end in itself': nations now recognise that it gives them both leverage over and vulnerability to their rivals.[10] Another way of defining matters is 'weaponised interdependence'.[11] In the words of one academic, this is about the 'securitisation of economic policy and the economisation of strategic policy … across a chessboard of geographic advantage and vulnerability'.[12]

Yes and no. Like a lot of catchy labels in world affairs, the term geoeconomics is not entirely accurate. Often geography does indeed matter: for instance, the scramble for privileged peacetime access to ports or particular sources of raw materials such as oil or the rare-earth minerals essential to so many electronic devices. Even cyber security has surprisingly strong connections with geography. The submarine cables and satellites needed to transmit via the internet are linked to terrestrial reality. Data centres can be material chokepoints. But cyber attacks also leapfrog geography, instantly crossing borders. In cyber competition and the use of law for strategic advantage, geoeconomics becomes less about geography and more about simply wielding, guarding or gaining national strength.

Beyond geography, the global geoeconomic contest involves a race for advantage in the defining technologies of the future. In simpler, earlier times, these were often warfighting and deterrence technologies: ballistic missiles, nuclear fission and fusion, jet engines, stealth materials, sensors, precision targeting. Now the most sensitive scientific battleground is around 'dual use': seemingly innocent civilian research that can have game-changing effects in national security. Under its 'Made in China 2025' strategy, China has explicitly declared the ambition – perhaps providing the world with more warning than intended – to dominate these technology frontiers. It includes artificial intelligence, advanced computing, quantum technologies, robotics, autonomous systems, commercial space technologies, additive manufacturing and the Internet of Things, along with new generations (5G and beyond) of the mobile telecommunications that will connect it.

It is not as if all earlier scientific struggle was narrowly military: the 'space race' of the 1950s and 1960s was also about strategic advantage and intimidation. But today the civil–military lines are almost impossibly blurred. The contest is primarily between the United States and China, but also brings in Europe, Australia, Japan, India and others. This is not merely about America and China vying to generate, protect or steal new secrets. It combines with fronts of diplomacy, economics, inducements and threats, to compel other countries to take sides. It brings an overlay of interstate tension and confrontation, of espionage, infiltration, paranoia and denial, to the laboratories of supposedly innocent and independent universities, to the boardrooms of corporations, to the self-interest of consumers and the moral choices of citizens. It would be nice to believe a sense of business as usual will return. It won't.

The prolonged standoff over China's giant telecommunications corporation Huawei is a prominent example. Huawei is credibly accused of an inextricable connection with the Chinese state and the Communist Party, which wields power within the enterprise, as it does within all large Chinese companies.[13] This compromises the trustworthiness of Huawei investments in core telecommunications and cyber infrastructure in other countries, a risk flagged when the Australian government refused Huawei involvement in its national broadband network in 2012, and then rejected Huawei again for 5G in 2018. The United States, Japan and New Zealand have followed Australia's 5G example, with America adopting an especially tough stance, and others including India, Canada, the United Kingdom and many European countries are tightening their restrictions to varying degrees. For its part, Canada in late 2018 detained a senior Huawei executive – the company founder's daughter Meng Wanzhou, no less – for extradition to the United States on charges related to fraud and sanctions busting. China retaliated with a grotesque act of hostage 'diplomacy'. It arrested two Canadians – a businessman and an analyst from the globally respected International Crisis Group non-government organisation – and eventually charged them with espionage when it was clear that the Canadian authorities would not release Meng. Their fates and hers had been cruelly tied.[14]

Another feature of the 'geoeconomic' competition that transcends simple geography is the use of economic interdependence for outright coercion: to punish behaviour in other domains, such as security or politics. Whatever we call it – geoeconomics, economic leverage, weaponised interdependence – the idea of subduing without bloodshed is as old as statecraft. The greater and more asymmetric the interdependence, the stronger the weapon. China is far from the only belligerent: Japan and South Korea have notably rekindled old disputes over nationalism and history, using import–export prohibitions as a form of economic punishment in recent times. Of course, the United States is a past master in economic pressure, from its ill-fated embargo on oil to Japan prior to Pearl Harbour through to its recent use of financial and trade sanctions against Russia, North Korea and Iran. Even India has begun to throw its weight around. But China is using economic coercion on a habitual basis: from blocking Norwegian salmon over a Nobel Prize given to dissident intellectual Liu Xiaobo, to ejecting South Korea's Lotte department stores over the deployment of American anti-missile defences.[15] Threats are made against airlines over the way they imply Taiwanese autonomy in naming flight destinations, or against sporting teams and leagues over individual officials' support for the protests in Hong Kong.

Some governments and many corporations cower at the thought of Chinese economic punishment for political resistance, but the results of such coercion are mixed. Economic leverage tends to be a one-shot armament: once struck, a nation tends to strengthen its defences and look to diversify its vulnerabilities by finding more reliable suppliers or markets – thus Japan sought new sources of rare-earth elements after Chinese punishment over a maritime incident in 2010. Commercial coercion tends to occur in areas that are not critical to China's own economic health: thus Australia may be threatened over tourism and wine, even coal, but not the vital iron ore for which it is China's principal source.

The headlines are wrong when they suggest that 'Trump's trade war' was the origin of the contemporary geoeconomic struggle. It is much more than a trade war, and America was joining a contest already well advanced. The recklessness and unpredictability of President Trump in using tariffs as a blunt instrument against China – and most everyone else – has been widely condemned; if it escalates without limit, a battle of tariff for tariff will make the whole world poorer. However, the notion of a 'trade war' obscures the fact that through a wide range of other means, such as systematic theft of design and manufacturing secrets, China had for some years already been waging a comprehensive geoeconomic campaign against the United States and others.

For instance, a US grand jury has heard that Huawei allegedly had in place a bonus program to reward employees for stealing sensitive technical information from competitors, and Chinese law obliged Chinese companies to support state intelligence gathering. The realities were affirmed in December 2018 when multiple countries announced that hackers working for the Chinese Ministry of State Security had penetrated internet managed service providers to systematically steal 'intellectual property and sensitive commercial data in Europe, Asia and the US'.[16] All nations spy, but this was of a different kind and magnitude – and in breach of an agreement to eschew economic espionage, reached between Xi and Obama in 2015.

Pushback from Japan, America, India and Australia has prompted some prudent adjustments of China's ambitions and methods. But the contest is far from done. The scene is set for a continuing drama of vulnerability and control, move and counter-move. And it links to a wider frontage of competition involving security, diplomacy and the battle for hearts and minds.

Fuelling tension

The economic story of the modern Indo-Pacific began with energy. As Asian economies grew, they quickly outstripped any self-sufficiency in fuel. They turned to the Middle East and Africa, where much of the world's hydrocarbon reserves are concentrated. Today this energy drives the Indo-Pacific as the world's workshop: 'crude from the Middle East supports the entire supply chain of Asian manufacturers'.[17] China, Japan, South Korea, Taiwan, Southeast Asia, Australia and India all rely acutely on the Indian Ocean sea lanes for their lifeblood of fuel – and in turn for their prosperity, political stability and security. China's top oil sources include Saudi Arabia, Angola, Oman, Iraq and Iran. Japan's include Saudi and the United Arab Emirates; South Korea's Kuwait, Iraq, Qatar and the UAE. India's are Saudi, Iraq and Nigeria.

This energy reliance of Asian economies upon the Indo-Pacific sea lanes is now old news. Yet most have moved slowly to take full responsibility for protecting those energy supplies. Even in 2019, as Iran's confrontations with America and Britain threatened to disrupt global oil supply, many Indo-Pacific powers were cautious about sending military force to keep the Strait of Hormuz open. That does not mean they are indifferent to their energy vulnerabilities, as the multinational counter-piracy operations in and near the Gulf of Aden have shown. With a permanent naval presence in the Gulf of Aden, a base at Djibouti and the prospect of more bases near Gwadar and elsewhere, China will be increasingly capable of mounting military interventions if necessary, including if it perceives the risk to its oil coming not from Iran, but from America and friends. Iran has demonstrated a willingness to intercept oil tankers in practice. American strategic analysts openly consider it in theory.[18] Stopping just one tanker a day could eventually shake China's economy.

The pursuit of energy security in the Indo-Pacific is not just about navies escorting oil tankers. China, India and Japan, in particular, have long sought national advantage through energy investments abroad. China and India have competed to buy equity in oil and natural gas fields from stakes from Africa to the Middle East to Central Asia. But energy security in the sense of ensuring an uninterrupted supply at acceptable prices is not automatically assured through ownership of foreign assets. Typically, agreements with the host country require much of the oil produced to be sold to the local market.[19] Still, this has not stopped China and India waging outright bidding wars, from Nigeria to Iran to Kazakhstan, where China's deeper pockets, determined state mobilisation and appetite for risk have usually prevailed.[20]

Not that everything is going China's way. The energy security contest is also playing out in waters close to China. The jostling for oil and gas reserves may not be the primary motive for territorial rivalries in the South China Sea, but it is part of that constant geopolitical turbulence. Vietnam, in particular, is resisting China's incursions into waters close to its shore, conducting its own energy searches, selling blocks to foreign and commercial partners and encouraging them to drill away, among them state-owned or -aligned companies from India and Russia.[21] While Delhi may be wisely wary of trouble in the South China Sea, Moscow may be uniquely emboldened: China needs Russia to support its ambitions in Eurasia and its rivalry with the United States.

China's response to its energy predicament has many parts. It is seeking to be a superpower in renewable energy: for instance, as the world's largest producer of solar panels, wind turbines and electric vehicles.[22] China's economic growth was overwhelmingly coal-powered, and the nation initially resisted global expectations to cap and eventually reduce its carbon emissions. Today, China seeks to portray itself as a champion in combating climate change, even though it remains the world's largest coal consumer, currently burning more of this fossil fuel than the rest of the world combined.[23] For the time being China is still profoundly dependent on imported oil, gas and petrochemicals, for everything from road transport to mining, agriculture and manufacturing. An energy emergency would affect not only the economy, but people's confidence in the regime.

Thus, in addition to its security presence in the Indian Ocean, Beijing presses claims on potentially energy-rich waters in East Asia. China is also purchasing stakes in much more distant hydrocarbon deposits. It invests in ports, refineries and overland pipelines, while rapidly building a state-owned or at least state-directed fleet of tanker ships and, unlike most countries, flying them with the national flag, which among other things sets a legal basis for protecting them with force. As a further hedge, China is cultivating special diplomatic ties with supplier nations regardless of regime type, indeed favouring the authoritarian and corruptible. And, to top it off, China is creating a strategic petroleum reserve on its territory, to help it hold out for 100 days.[24]

Even in combination, these actions wouldn't guarantee China normal levels of energy supply in a crisis. The rapid building of pipelines will not even keep pace with China's increasing oil needs. Pipelines through Pakistan or Myanmar would themselves be vulnerable to sabotage or interruption, and in any case would merely shorten sea voyages, not replace them.[25] America's relative energy independence, with its rapid growth in shale oil production in recent years, would provide an advantage in a military standoff with China. Even so, the downsides and dangers of an American-led blockade strategy would be many, not least the global economic impact, the alienation of many third countries, and the difficulty of enforcing it without having, at a minimum, India and Japan – and ideally others, even Russia – on board.[26]

In any case, China's response to its energy security dilemma has become part of a much more expansive strategy to protect interests by projecting influence: the Belt and Road, and its accompanying military and diplomatic initiatives. This leads to the second stage of the geoeconomic contest: Beijing's bid to exert control, not only of energy paths but of wider supply chains and sources of raw materials across the Indo-Pacific, Africa and Eurasia. And almost immediately after, the third and fourth stages: the backlash and China's recalibration.

Many belts, many roads

Refusal may offend. By declining to join China's lavish international cele-
bration of the Belt and Road in May 2017, India became the ghost at the
feast: a reminder to the world of the unanswered questions behind Xi Jinping's grand project. The polite wording of the Indian government's
explanation may have seemed innocuous, but it had diplomatic consequences: an exposure of the self-serving, China-centric nature of the whole
Belt and Road show. The Indian statement combined an in-principle willingness to cooperate with China alongside a list of the many preconditions
for such 'connectivity initiatives', which:

> must be based on universally recognized international norms, good gov-
> ernance, rule of law, openness, transparency and equality. Connectivity
> initiatives must follow principles of financial responsibility to avoid
> projects that would create unsustainable debt burden for communities;
> balanced ecological and environmental protection and preservation
> standards; transparent assessment of project costs; and skill and technol-
> ogy transfer to help long term running and maintenance of the assets
> created by local communities. Connectivity projects must be pursued in
> a manner that respects sovereignty and territorial integrity. [27]

These would seem perfectly reasonable features of any 21st-century
project. A citizen in a well-governed society would expect no less from their
own government in assessing any local development application: a road, a
mine, a dam, a tourist resort. Admittedly, India has had far from a clean
record of applying such standards in its own territory. And a major reason
for its resistance, as we have seen, was China's affront to Indian sovereignty
by building its 'economic corridor' through Pakistani-occupied Kashmir,
territory claimed by India.

But India's stance called out the many other governments forgoing
the chance to set quality controls on their own collaboration with China.
Only two months earlier, New Zealand had handed the Chinese Communist Party the diplomatic equivalent of a blank cheque, signing a

Chinese-drafted memorandum that gave a stamp of approval to any activity conducted anywhere under the Belt and Road provided it was vaguely in line with 'international good practice, market orientation and professional principles'.[28] To be fair, Wellington was in abundant company: many nations across Asia, Africa and Eastern Europe were signing similar scripts, and the government of the Australian state of Victoria even undercut the national interest by doing the same without forewarning Canberra. For each signatory, it perhaps seemed a small and non-binding price to pay for remaining in good odour in Beijing. But together, such agreements were propagandist manna for Xi: pieces of paper he could brandish to tell the Chinese people that the world welcomed a new order on China's terms. They were also internationally irresponsible, making it harder for developing nations to influence the terms on which Chinese government banks were indebting them.

Still, India was not alone in its reluctance: France, Japan, Australia and America were all pressing the brakes. But Xi's claim to speak for Asia rang especially hollow with a rebuff from the world's largest democracy. India had drawn on its own proud anti-colonial traditions to declare a boycott of what it saw as the new imperial 'durbar', a reference to the gatherings of disempowered Indian princes forced to show loyalty to the British Raj.[29] India's stance marked a turning point.

Since 2017, the reaction has intensified. Debate has risen within many countries about the nature and impact of BRI projects, especially their nexus of debt, corruption and strategic advantage for China. Such nations as Sri Lanka, Myanmar, Malaysia and even Pakistan have applied fresh scepticism and scrutiny. This will continue even as official attitudes to China shift back and forth at each election, such as with another change of government in Sri Lanka at the end of 2019 (this time led by Gotabaya Rajapaksa, brother of the pro-China former president). The BRI and its co-option of elites is now an enduringly divisive issue among the people of many countries. The Indian Ocean nation of Maldives, population around 500,000, has become a test case, affirming that no country is too small to defend its interests.[30] From 2013 to 2018, under its increasingly dictatorial president Abdulla Yameen, Maldives accepted several major Chinese projects, including an airport and a 'friendship bridge' between two islands. It ended up with debt between US$1.6 billion and somewhere approaching the size of its entire $US3.6 billion economy. In early 2018, amid mounting criticism of Chinese deals and corruption, Yameen launched a 'self-coup', suspending parliament and imprisoning the chief justice. It was to no avail: within months, he was defeated in a presidential poll, and new president Ibrahim Mohamed Solih subsequently secured an overwhelming majority in parliamentary elections, giving him a mandate to investigate corruption and end the tilt to China.

Europe has become divided, with Germany and France sounding the alert, and the European Union becoming increasingly wary, recognising China not only as a partner of sorts but also as 'an economic competitor in the pursuit of technological leadership and a systemic rival promoting alternative models of governance'.[31] An expert report in early 2018 called out a European drift to 'pre-emptive obedience' of China, warning that 'from the perspective of liberal democracies, all areas of interaction with China are potentially problematic'.[32] Italy nonetheless went on to embrace the Belt and Road, the first G7 country to sign one of the notorious rubber-stamp agreements, before almost immediately feeling buyer's remorse, adding the caveat that any such cooperation would need to meet EU standards.[33] Britain, meanwhile, has put itself in an awkward bind. The uncertainties of Brexit have fostered a desperation for new 'global' economic opportunities: in April 2019, Chancellor of the Exchequer (treasurer) Philip Hammond called the BRI a 'vision', and revived talk of a 'golden era' in UK–China relations.[34] At the same time, a parliamentary committee was warning of China's increasing challenges to British interests and values, and of London's 'unwillingness to face this reality':

> The UK approach risks prioritising economic considerations over other interests, values and national security ... China's Belt and Road Initiative (BRI), in the form it is currently being pursued, raises concerns regarding UK interests. We encourage the Government to employ a

strictly case-by-case approach to assessing BRI projects, and to continue to refrain from signing a Memorandum of Understanding endorsing the BRI.[35]

An even clearer warning sign of the pitfalls of the BRI has come from Australia, which since India's stand has found it easier to withstand the pressure from China and domestic business lobbies to simply 'sign on'. Canberra's guarded approach to the BRI coincided with growing resistance to Chinese influence on national political decision-making. For Australia's leaders, it has become clearer that offering blanket endorsement for China's whole program does not automatically bring material paradise, nor does withholding it mean economic purgatory. The Australia–China iron ore trade continued its staggering growth even as both sides of politics in Canberra stuck to a rigorous 'case-by-case' policy of ignoring, opposing or occasionally accepting BRI-related projects. One of the smartest responses has come from Japan: allowing, even encouraging, businesses to collaborate with China on particular infrastructure projects that make commercial sense, adhere to good governance standards, showcase Japanese quality and limit Chinese control. It is the BRI on Japanese terms, with no need to applaud Xi's every dream.

Under its Free and Open Indo-Pacific strategy, Japan has played a leading part in a multi-nation geoeconomic pushback that could just as well be labelled 'many belts, many roads'. Even on its own, Japan is the largest infrastructure investor in Southeast Asia: in 2019, it had projects underway there worth US$367 billion, as opposed to China's $255 billion.[36] With Delhi, Tokyo is pursuing specific projects to ensure that no one country can dominate the ports from Malacca to Hormuz: notably, Japan and India are jointly developing a new container terminal at the port of Colombo.[37] With the United States and Australia, Japan has formed a 'trilateral infrastructure partnership' to coordinate their efforts. Their so-called Blue Dot Network, established in late 2019, is a partnership among governments, industry and civil society to provide trusted standards for quality infrastructure: an international seal of approval for nations or communities wondering whether a project from China (or anywhere) is as good as promised. As for the reliability of alternative infrastructure to the Belt and Road, their much-trumpeted joint offer of electricity generation and internet connectivity to Papua New Guinea will be a test case for the Washington–Tokyo–Canberra consortium. Australia and America are also each pursuing their own efforts. Australia's 'Pacific Step-up' involves development financing, an undersea telecommunications cable (in lieu of a Chinese project said to pose security risks) and a focus on training of local governments. This emphasis on education makes sense. Australia and other developed democracies cannot hope to outbid or outdo China in quantities of steel and concrete, or the pace, scale and short-term cost. But by providing training on governance and transparency, they are well placed to help those nations decide whether to accept China's seeming largesse, and how to negotiate a deal that is in their long-term national interest.

The merits of pushback are becoming clearer. If all had blindly taken China at its word and joined uncritically in the BRI chorus, the people of many Indo-Pacific nations would have lost two great benefits. First, other countries would have been less motivated to improve their efforts to end the region's appalling infrastructure deficit. The perceived threat from China has mobilised development projects by others: Japan, America, Australia, India, Europe. From Sri Lanka to the Solomon Islands, Bangladesh to Vanuatu, the less developed nations suddenly find wealthier countries competing to finance the infrastructure they need. Even China's most mesmerising promises of trillions of dollars in BRI lending will meet only a fraction of the region's requirements. Now the spectre of strategic competition has prompted rival projects, and there is no reason why, in many cases, the target countries cannot end up choosing both. Perhaps there is win-win after all: recipients win with more choice of suitors willing to finance their development. And some degree of governance standards – transparency, accountability, prudence, choice – may be preserved.

The second reward for resistance is that China is pausing and adjusting. It is recalibrating the BRI to try to limit the damage done to China's image and to restore international confidence. The second grand durbar of the

BRI, in April 2019, was more circumspect, not exactly humble but a little less hubristic. Xi offered 'extensive consultation, joint contribution and shared benefits', in development that was 'open, clean and green', adopting 'widely accepted rules and standards'.[38] On the surface, Chinese officials will of course take the ideological line and reject any criticism of the BRI as Cold War thinking. But that does not mean that they don't listen, or that privately they don't worry. After all, Xi has faced gathering domestic discomfort about the BRI as well: why is China lending the nation's wealth abroad when there is so much need at home?

It is no longer controversial to challenge the motives and impact of the Belt and Road. This can now be called what it is: a new kind of colonialism. At one level it may be about connectivity and development, with elements of commercial logic and Chinese state banks out to make a profit. But it stretches credulity to claim this is overwhelmingly a 'market-based' scheme, devoid of ideology.[39] Principally this is about China First, an epic strategy combining economics with geopolitics. Its multiple objectives reinforce each other to China's advantage: the export of excess capacity and overproduction in steel and coal; the consolidation and securing of supply lines of energy, resources and food; the control of China's restive western Xinjiang region; the global dominance of economic value-chains and production standards, creating advantages for Chinese corporates and technologies; and the extension of diplomatic leverage and influence, subordinating many nations to China's preferences and interests.[40] The BRI may have begun as Xi's audacious gamble to knit together many policies China was pursuing anyway – economic, diplomatic, military. But it is accurately classed as a grand strategy, mobilising all levers of power for a common purpose: to make China dominant in the Indo-Pacific and Eurasia, and a global power at least on par with the United States, perhaps even at the centre of a new world order.[41]

In all of this, critics should overstate neither China's strategic genius nor malign intent. The result may be partly Trojan horse – a strategic infiltration disguised as a gift – but it is also partly Frankenstein's monster: a bit of everything, an improvisation with a life of its own. The use of debt to give China control over assets and leverage over foreign governments appears more occasional and opportunistic than the systematic 'debt-trap diplomacy' and 'predatory economics' that is now widely alleged.[42] Most often, China has renegotiated debt with the many nations struggling to pay, deferring trouble (and further ensuring their indebtedness long term) but refraining from forcing them to surrender assets. A possible new pattern, based on a 2019 precedent in the case of Congo, will be for the International Monetary Fund to step in and bail out indebted countries on the condition that unsustainable debt burdens are renegotiated.[43]

Nonetheless, the debt-for-equity solution is gravely consequential when it does occur, notably in Sri Lanka, when China gained possession of the port of Hambantota, a potential future military base at the heart of the Indian Ocean sea lanes. Even such isolated incidents have been enough to chasten nations en masse about the risk of BRI temptation leading to geopolitical indenture. There are alarming risks in borrowing from a lender which has strategic reasons to want the asset used to the secure the loan.[44] Djibouti, where China already has a military base and a stake in the Doraleh civilian port, has an acute debt problem with China. This tiny but strategically positioned nation has been projected to take on public debt worth somewhere between 88 and 104 per cent of its modest overall gross domestic product. The US administration warns that Djibouti faces the prospect of handing further assets to China, including the Doraleh container terminal itself.[45]

In the South Pacific, Australia and the United States hold concerns about unsustainable debt burdens from Chinese lending to tiny island nations, and Beijing's quest to control of resources and ports. In mid-2019, the prime minister of Papua New Guinea, James Marape, briefly flagged the possibility of asking China to refinance his country's entire multi-billion-dollar public debt, equal to a third of the nation's economy.[46] This raised the prospect of China seeking collateral in major assets such as mines or ports. Within twenty-four hours, Marape's office had withdrawn the announcement, saying it had been made in error, acknowledging the rest of the government had not been consulted, and reflecting that PNG had many choices of countries to deal with in its development.[47] The warnings of debt-trap diplomacy, it seems, are beginning to hit home.

Nearby in the Solomon Islands, it is constantly game-on. In late 2019, as this small nation ended its diplomatic recognition of Taiwan at China's behest, media reports emerged of two major projects: a Chinese-funded attempt to lease an entire island, complete with deep-water harbour, and another apparently commercial bid to redevelop a gold mine, with Chinese state-owned enterprises to build major road, rail and port facilities.[48] Media scrutiny prompted the Solomon Islands government to halt the island-leasing plan, but this is just one of many locations where China seems interested in securing a harbour that could have military as well as civilian uses.

Debate continues about whether the Belt and Road is really about weaponising debt. In the South Pacific, for instance, the evidence so far is that indebting small nations is an occasional consequence and not a direct aim.[49] But another connection is at work: the role of infrastructure ambitions as a transmission belt for a more blunt and old-fashioned instrument of statecraft: force of arms. China has long insisted that the Belt and Road has nothing to do with martial might. Then, in July 2019, Chinese state media reported that state councillor and defence minister Wei Fenghe had told a gathering of defence officials from the South Pacific and the Caribbean that China stood ready to deepen military cooperation with their countries 'under the framework of the Belt and Road Initiative'.[50] It may have seemed a harmless point – he referred mainly to areas of common ground like counter-terrorism, peacekeeping and disaster relief. But China was no longer pretending that the BRI was a purely civilian endeavour. Here was an admission of reality: that, all along, the flag was following trade: a footprint of security, with attendant imperial risks of becoming mired in conflict and strife.

The Maritime Silk Road is part of a broad waterfront of strategic competition, reaching from commerce to infrastructure to propaganda and military power. China has recognised those linkages all along. Now other countries are waking up to the integrated and many-layered nature of the contest. This awareness will be crucial to asserting their own interests and setting boundaries to help manage risks of coercion and conflict in the long run.

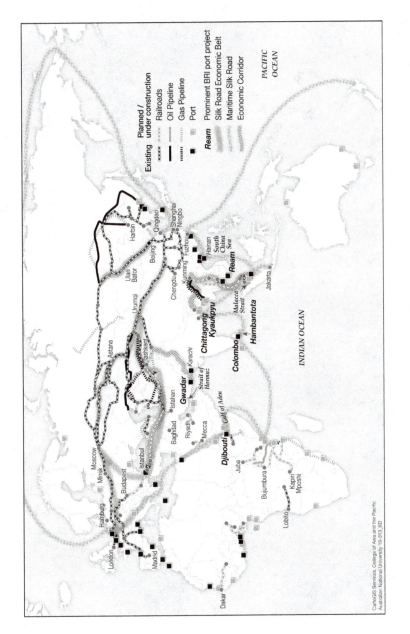

The Belt and Road

CHAPTER 8

FAR-FLUNG BATTLE LINES

Unsettlingly at ease in military uniform, Xi Jinping strode into a five-storey building on the northwestern outskirts of Beijing. It was the façade to the Chinese military's new Battle Command Centre, which includes a complex of caves within the hillsides of solid karst, a natural nuclear bunker. As paramount leader, Xi holds the titles of President of China and, more importantly, General Secretary of the Communist Party. Today, though, he was here as Chairman of the Central Military Commission: commander-in-chief of the People's Liberation Army, 2.5 million strong. Images broadcast across the nation on China Central Television (with its exquisite acronym CCTV) showed him in the pixelated camouflage uniform of the PLA's new 'digital battledress', addressing row upon row of warfare planners applauding or diligently taking notes. It was a far cry from the understated civilian style of Xi's predecessors. There was little hiding and biding here.

China's Indo-Pacific military map

It was not Xi's first televised visit to the headquarters. This time, in November 2017, he used it not just to inspect the troops but to demonstrate the new China's expectations of its military. The highlight was a videolink with the recently opened base in Djibouti. Xi addressed the arrayed garrison from afar, commending their mission to protect 'international peace and stability'. He ordered the whole PLA to 'strengthen the senses of crisis and war' and 'spare no efforts to improve combat readiness'. The troops needed to be prepared to face emergencies from all directions, he said. As if to illustrate

The opening ceremony at China's military base in Djibouti, 2017

the scale and reach of those ambitions, the main planning room was dominated by a colossal map, not just of China, not even of the South China Sea,
but of the expanse from Japan to the horn of Africa: the Eurasian continent
and the Indo-Pacific; the Belt and Road; the geopolitical *Yin* and *Yang* of
China's region of strategic interest. If China's sphere of influence was limited
to East Asia, nobody had told the PLA. Xi is not concealing the fact that
China is involved in military competition far from its shores, and is preparing for a theatre of armed operations spanning the Indo-Pacific, from
Tianjin to Djibouti.[1]

The scale and pace of China's military modernisation is astonishing. In
1990, by some credible estimates, China's defence budget was around US$10
billion – less than a third that of, for instance, the United Kingdom or
France. Three decades later, China's military spending has increased more
than twentyfold: its official 2019 budget of about US$177 billion does not
account for purchasing new capabilities like warships, or for research and
development, much of which is mixed up with the civilian sector. Experts
say that including these would push the spending about one-third higher.[2]
Less well understood than the numbers is China's fast-spreading military
reach and ambition, across the oceans and the world. A central question of

global geopolitics in the 21st century is how much military power Beijing can project and sustain across vast distances.[3]

A large part of China's massive armed forces will always be tied up with territorial defence, since China's borders touch fourteen other nations, more than any other country in the world. Even as many of these frontiers become manageable through Belt and Road diplomacy with Russia and the Central Asian states, others will bear watching: Chinese forces are on guard, for instance, against turmoil on the Korean Peninsula. More forces yet, including the 1.5-million-strong People's Armed Police, are devoted to maintaining internal security. The PLA is, after all, the army of the Communist Party, not strictly the army of the nation, and its foremost mission is to keep the Party in power no matter what. Much of the PLA is also dedicated to missions along China's maritime eastern periphery. Above all, there is the permanent threat to invade Taiwan: a hair-trigger promise of war that the CCP has bound itself with through the Anti-Secession Law of 2005. This undertakes that China will use 'non-peaceful' means to 'reunify' if Taiwan ever declares independence. In other words, the PRC has chosen to make an unfinished civil war from the first half of the 20th century a guiding motif of its legitimacy and a major reason for its military rise. The eastward mission of the PLA also involves rivalry with Japan, and the assertion of control over the disputed South China Sea.

But increasingly, Beijing is preparing its forces for missions, expeditions and even garrisons much further afield. The navy has become truly an ocean-going or 'blue water' force, with more than 300 ships, including eighty-three substantial warfighting vessels or 'principal surface combatants' and sixty-two submarines.[4] This is supplemented by a highly militarised coast guard, with some ships larger than the warships of many navies.

The navy's operations will be structured increasingly around aircraft carriers, probably up to six of them by the 2030s. The bizarre origin of this program provides clues to the extreme determination – and deception – behind China's military rise. China's first aircraft carrier was built around the shell of one of the last ships designed by the Soviet Union. The half-finished ship was purchased by a Hong Kong–based Chinese businessman for the tiny price of US$30 million from an economically desperate Ukraine in 1998 under the poker-faced cover story that it would be used as a floating hotel and casino.[5] There followed a tortuous two-year journey from 2000 to 2002, with the hulk being towed at a sea slug's pace from the Black Sea to the Atlantic, round the Cape of Good Hope, then, like the tsar's less lucky armada of 1905, through the Indian Ocean and the South China Sea. The bluff paid off. The truth was clear to all by 2012: the real end user was the People's Liberation Army, and the drastically refitted and renamed *Liaoning* was launched from the Dalian shipyards.

By 2016 this imposing ship was deemed combat ready, with twenty-four attack aircraft and an enormous morale-boosting role for China's prestige as a great power, although some experts call it more of an experimental ship, a 'university for training pilots' and testing technology rather than a front-line battle platform.[6] But now the PLA knows full well how to build, improve and reverse-engineer these most demanding of surface vessels. A second, more advanced and Chinese-built carrier has been launched and a third is under construction, the design improving each time. These will sail in American-style 'battle groups', with protective envelopes of destroyers, drones, jets, helicopters and submarines.

Chinese military documents characterise these carrier groups as a 'strategic fist' for long-distance operations, although it is important not to overstate their strength.[7] They are smaller than their American counterparts, and their crews and pilots have little experience in the life-and-death intricacies of naval aviation, which the US Navy has been perfecting through almost a century of lethal trial and error.[8] Chinese doctrine seems to consider that aircraft carriers remain irreplaceable as mobile platforms for establishing air control over distant seas and even foreign territory. Ground bases can't be shifted about at whim, and air-to-air refuelling has its own limitations. Yet given the growing danger from submarines and missiles, and likely continued disadvantages against American power, China may see its aircraft carriers as less than ideal for full-scale wars close to its coast. Instead, they will be especially suited for voyaging afar to deter and intimidate weaker players, missions of protection and coercion in the South

China Sea and the Indian Ocean – perhaps occasionally the South Pacific too. One analyst crisply explains that China's carrier-centred navy is 'not designed so much to challenge US maritime supremacy as to inherit it'.[9]

For the time being, China can be expected to deploy only a modest proportion of its great military heft to the Indian Ocean, Africa and the South Pacific, as guardians of Beijing's resources, interests, nationals and prestige along the Maritime Silk Road. Much of this unpleasant work may fall to China's private military companies, mercenary units staffed by former PLA soldiers, much as ex-US and allied troops fill the ranks of Western security contractors. Such forces have already found themselves in tense situations in South Sudan and Iraq. In Pakistan, Chinese nationals are under repeated attack – twelve times in 2018 alone – from local militant groups such as Baluchi separatists, resentful of China's resource exploitation and occupation of their homeland. Protection at this stage is provided by 15,000 Pakistani troops dedicated to guarding Chinese Belt and Road projects throughout the country. If and when the hired guns or local troops themselves get into strife they cannot handle – or exacerbate it – then pressures will increase on the real Chinese military to step in.[10]

What could Chinese military presence across the Indo-Pacific look like? Aircraft carriers, warships and submarines will be joined by special forces and elements of the Chinese marine corps – expected to grow to somewhere between 30,000 and 100,000 troops. Only a small number of the 2700 planes in China's air force are likely to range far, although experiments have begun in long-range air deployments and exercises, as distant as Turkey or deep into the Pacific. Taken together, this will still only be a small proportion of China's overall military, much of which will retain principal missions on or close to Chinese soil.

Yet even by sallying forth with a fraction of its might, China will greatly raise strategic anxieties among the resident nations of the Indian Ocean, South Pacific and Southeast Asia, as well as those others – notably Japan and Taiwan – dependent on the sea lanes. A small part of the Chinese military could make a big difference against local forces, most of which are not used to encountering technologically advanced and potentially hostile militaries close to their territory. Like a latter-day evocation of the 'treasure ships' of Zheng He, the very appearance on the horizon of a Chinese carrier battle group could be enough to compel submission by a smaller country, especially one without a reliable ally. Chinese submarines will give pause to India, Japan, Australia or other nations reliant on the Indian Ocean during times of tension. A single amphibious assault vessel with a battalion of marines could be enough to impose order or protect Chinese nationals in a small island state or civil conflict zone. From the late 2020s, China will deploy a new kind of guided missile submarine – an underwater arsenal ship, with nuclear propulsion, able to hide offshore and launch salvos of highly accurate missiles at land targets, whether terrorist groups or military adversaries, much as America and Russia have done in the Middle East.[11] These will be ideal instruments for the gunboat diplomacy of a 21st-century Chinese empire in the Indo-Pacific.

And in any case, Chinese security planners no longer appear to treat these distant regions as separate or secondary. Rather, as the map in Xi's Battle Command Centre so boldly suggests, and as leading military Sinologist Andrew S. Erickson has noted, this is formally recognised in the science of Chinese military strategy as one 'single arc-shaped strategic zone' for China's 'forward edge defence'.[12] It will become normal practice for China to pivot its military power from one part of the Indo-Pacific to another, much as the United States has done for decades. The sturdy roads of imperial Rome were engineered as much for fast-marching legions as for commerce. The Maritime Silk Road will double as a military highway. And it will have vital strategic waypoints: not just rest stops and supply depots, but watchtowers and forts.

Base race

The South China Sea is not merely a neighbouring territory for China to dominate, or a playground for nationalism and resources, but a vital stepping stone to military presence further afield. As explained by one of the world's pre-eminent experts on the PLA, University of Macau professor You Ji:

... the PLA's land reclamation in the Spratlys was meant to serve the tactical and even strategic purposes to establish forward deployment on route to the Indian Ocean ... battlefield construction crucial for controlling the choke points in the South China Sea and beyond, that is, to secure the Malacca Strait for Chinese oil shipments ... the PLA's South China sea and SLOC [sea lane of communication] operations are thus integrated and the emergence of a Chinese Indo-Pacific doctrine appears inevitable.[13]

This theory is supported by growing evidence of preparations for a Chinese base in Cambodia, at Ream on the Gulf of Thailand, from which bombers, fighter jets and warships can more easily reach most of Southeast Asia, the vital chokepoints like the Strait of Malacca, and into the Indian Ocean.[14] A base in Cambodia could form part of a growing chain of 'strategic strong points' (*zhanlue zhidian*) for China's Indo-Pacific presence: civilian deep-water port facilities with the potential for military use. These include Djibouti and potentially Gwadar, Pakistan, in the west; Hambantota and perhaps Colombo in Sri Lanka at the heart of the Indian Ocean; Kyaukpyu in Myanmar and several locations such as Chittagong or Cox's Bazar in Bangladesh, on the Bay of Bengal between the Indian Ocean and the Strait of Malacca; and East Timor, Vanuatu, the Solomon Islands or elsewhere in the region's southeast. This is in addition to the existing home port for much of the PLA Navy on Hainan Island, with submarine dens built into coastal caves, and the sprawl of militarised and artificial islands in the South China Sea.[15]

Much of the analysis of China's port and base projects available in the public domain remains fairly speculative, though concerns being aired by various governments are presumably informed by sensitive intelligence and diplomatic reports. Some media commentary understandably questions whether there is truly a Chinese agenda of regional domination at work, or whether Beijing's plans are essentially defensive. *The Economist*, for instance, has pointed out that key dual-use facilities on the Belt and Road map are ideally located to defend China's oil and raw material imports from future blockades.[16] But this follows precisely the pattern of empires past: the right real estate for extended defence doubles as stepping stones for power projection, and would be ideal for denying resources to others, such as Japan.

China is determinedly joining a base race that, to be fair, it didn't start. Beyond Indo-Pacific Command headquarters at Pearl Harbor in Hawaii, America has long had formal bases from Japan to South Korea to Guam and (at times) the Philippines, and west to Djibouti and Diego Garcia, alongside trusted visit arrangements in Singapore and Australia. Japan is present in Djibouti too, and its warships are showing up increasingly in Southeast Asia, the Indian Ocean and Australia. India is pursuing special access to Indian Ocean island states such as the Seychelles, Gulf states Oman and the United Arab Emirates, and Southeast Asian countries, notably Vietnam, while maintaining its own naval command in its Andaman and Nicobar islands.[17] Australia has its own strategic outposts in the Indian Ocean, the Cocos and Christmas islands, flies surveillance patrols out of Malaysia's Butterworth base, and is looking to reopen for naval purposes an originally Second World War–era facility on Papua New Guinea's Manus Island. France retains a small but effective military presence on a strategic string of islands across the Indian Ocean and the South Pacific, all technically French metropolitan territory, such as Réunion and New Caledonia. Britain has Diego Garcia, and has reportedly considered re-establishing a small military presence in Southeast Asia, possibly in Brunei.[18]

Chinese strategists have long thought of the western Pacific as American-controlled 'island chains' that constrain China's naval freedom to move (or to pressure its neighbours). They are now seeing the wider Indo-Pacific as comprising an even larger zone of contest, where each side is seeking to outflank the other with strings of bases and friends, or at least neutral spaces. And other nations quietly see the potential to extend the concept of island chains into the Indian Ocean.[19] This helps explain the base race. Alongside networks of trade, investment and infrastructure, a 21st-century patchwork of military facilities is consolidating, even if these are less mighty bastions of territorial dominance and more lightly fortified lily pads, combining surveillance perches with contemporary versions of 19th-century coaling stations, caches for resupply and refuelling, jumping-off points for expeditions and patrols. But all would help rivals project power. And were war to come, all would be early targets.

Strategic theatre and reality

Governments like to play up the many missions to which their forces are put other than war. On any day, most any military is engaged in the full range of non-combat tasks, from humanitarian assistance and disaster relief to countering crime at sea, detecting and fighting terrorism, search and rescue, peacekeeping, and evacuations from trouble spots. Military forces, especially navies, are deployed for diplomatic duties: goodwill visits, flag flying, exercises and drills with foreign counterparts, or imparting knowledge and skills through 'capacity building' as a currency of building trust with new partners. Militaries join civilian envoys in dialogue with friends and prospective adversaries alike, to share information or discuss protocols to manage conflict, through so-called risk reduction and confidence-building measures. It all looks very reassuring, even though much of it doubles as cover for building an advanced intelligence picture.

But in the end, nations invest multi-billion-dollar sums in high-technology and classified military equipment because war remains conceivable. That may be a supreme tragedy and anachronism in an era of global interdependence and the overwhelming collective challenge of climate change. But it is a reality. Even under the nuclear shadow of mutually assured destruction, and the cyber cloud of mutually assured disruption, almost every government still heeds the old Roman dictum: *si vis pacem, para bellum* – if you want peace, prepare for war. If China, mindful of Sun Tzu, wants to win without fighting, then it needs to give the impression of being in deadly earnest. And that is precisely what has occurred with its military modernisation. In this, China is not alone.

The Indo-Pacific includes the nations with many of the world's largest defence budgets: America, China, India, Russia, Japan, South Korea. This makes it the world's weapons bazaar: defence technology companies from Europe and Israel have joined Russia, America and China in a lucrative spree of arming up. The region includes the world's largest militaries by man-power: China, India, America, Russia, the two Koreas and Pakistan. Most of the world leaders in the hidden hand of cyber war are here: America, China, North Korea, Russia, Australia, Japan, South Korea, Singapore. And it is where nations are most actively projecting power over distance, competing in military technologies and professing cooperation in defence diplomacy. Naval modernisation is concentrated here: not just the fast build-up of the Chinese fleet, but the steady improvement in the capabilities of India, Japan, Russia, Australia, South Korea and the Southeast Asian countries.

So the military competition in the Indo-Pacific is daunting, but not unlimited. It is not technically a full-blown arms race. That term is often thrown about loosely, but specifically refers to such factors as nations spending an unsustainably large proportion of their wealth on weapons, or frenziedly competing in the number and destructiveness of the armaments they target at each other. Military spending worldwide is indeed at its high-est level since the Cold War.[20] But people forget the much greater degree of rivalry during the Cold War: at its height, the Soviet Union was spending around 20 per cent of its GDP on the military, with even the much richer United States sometimes spending more than 10 per cent.[21]

By comparison, most nations today devote a fraction of that to defence, with the global average at 2.1 per cent of GDP.[22] North Korea is a perverse outlier, spending up to a quarter of its national wealth on the military, which is as much about maintaining domestic control as it is about national defence, or threatening other nations.[23] Even considering that Beijing hides parts of its military spending as civilian research and development, it is unlikely that China's true defence expenditure goes far over 2 per cent. The PLA budget has grown massively, often by more than 10 per cent a year, but broadly in step with the rise of the Chinese economy. Under Xi, troop num-bers have actually been cut, to redeploy funds from wages and living costs to advanced weapons instead. This all suggests China could ramp up mili-tary spending further should tensions worsen – though with already meagre welfare spending, this would harm the Communist Party's ability to offer a social safety net for an ageing populace.

The problem is similar in a poorer India, where military spending has varied between 1.6 and 2.4 per cent. Japan can hardly be accused of the 'remilitarisation' China likes to allege: its defence spend is roughly 1 per cent of GDP, but slight annual increases are being invested in high-consequence capabilities like amphibious troops, defensive counter-missile batteries, submarines, advanced US combat aircraft, and modifying helicopter carriers to take fighter jets.[24] The United States, meanwhile, continues to be the world's largest military spender by far, at around 3.2 per cent of what remains the largest GDP. Its defence budget of more than US$700 billion seems staggering, but is nonetheless mismatched with the sheer ambition of the global strategic presence and missions America has accumulated over decades. This gulf grew with a 21 per cent decline in US defence spending from 2011 to 2018. Resumed growth in expenditure will be needed simply for upkeep of existing capabilities and to keep pace with the ever-growing sophistication and cost of technology.[25] American capabilities are spread globally, not concentrated in Asia, and serious concerns are growing that it is losing, or has already lost, its conventional – that is, non-nuclear – military advantage over China in the western Pacific.

This is not a region gripped by total war, or even yet the prospect of it. Military objectives are mostly limited. With the exception of the Korean Peninsula or China's threat to seize Taiwan, most countries are focused on missions and defensive strategies that fall far short of launching or resisting full-scale invasion. This is a far cry from the Cold War or the world wars, where the fears or reality of territorial aggression were the order of the day. In the maritime Indo-Pacific, beyond Taiwan, even the direst military contingencies are likely to work differently. The intent of armed force typically will be to exert or resist pressure, not to wage or counter conquest. The threat of war will be about politics and diplomacy by other means. But the complexity and uncertainty of those scenarios means that armed conflicts could gravely escalate.

None of this allows room for complacency. It is not business as usual in the military balance of the Indo-Pacific. Numbers are not the only measure; size is not everything. What will matter in future military confrontations is not just who has the most tanks or soldiers. But there is justified anxiety among security experts from America and its allies, notably Australia, that the United States has already allowed its long-time military advantages in the Indo-Pacific to erode, at least in the western Pacific. They argue that China is in a position to launch crippling missile strikes on American forward bases and to use the threat of anti-ship ballistic missiles to prevent America's navy intervening to stop possible future Chinese attacks on Taiwan, Japan or Southeast Asian countries, a strategy known as A2/AD, or anti-access and area denial.[26]

This does not mean that future conflict is a forgone conclusion. For a start, America and its allies are exploring new ways to counter China's military: move and counter-move in military investment, deployment and training. Advantage will lie in intricate combinations of factors: how real-time intelligence and surveillance can support speed and targeting; how distributed networks of allies and bases enable forces to be sustained at distance; how realistic training and long experience remain essential, no matter how new and expensive the 'platforms'; how the eerie new capabilities of drones and artificial intelligence will still need humans in the loop; how the whole can be much greater than the sum of its parts, with air, sea, land, space and cyber power joined together; and how calculations and miscalculations of risk could flip the table.

Traditional Western conceptions of war and military advantage – codified by the Napoleonic-era Prussian strategist Carl von Clausewitz – were about mass and weight, concentration of force, centres of gravity. But von Clausewitz also acknowledged that the outcomes of war are not predetermined by brute strength. Decision-making matters in penetrating the 'fog of war'. Thus, in 21st-century war – or in the calibrations of risk that could prevent it – decisive power may lie with information, speed and networks. The edge may be with who finds and fires first – or who inspires sufficient fear from being able to do so. There is a new fog about how wars begin or expand. Never has secrecy been so central to military advantage. What you cannot see can hurt you much more than what you can.

Beneath the waves

It was the oceanic equivalent of a close encounter with an alien spaceship: worlds almost collided in the South China Sea. In September 2019, little Vietnamese fishing boats – motors aside, the kind of humble wooden craft that has plied these waters for centuries – landed an 11,000-ton catch that made global news. Gliding past them on the surface was a behemoth of the deep: the massive metallic hull of no ordinary submarine. The ungainly acronym SSBN – ship submersible ballistic nuclear – lends a clue to what lurked behind the basalt grey carapace. Here was a vessel devised neither to be seen nor heard, but rather to carry enough weapons of mass destruction to obliterate whole cities suddenly and from beneath the waves. The Chinese ensign rippled red from the fin. One of the Vietnamese skippers caught photographs and footage showing in weird juxtaposition the nuclear-armed sea monster looming behind a little trawler. How exactly they came to cross paths in the disputed vicinity of the Paracel Islands is a mystery: the images show the submarine's casing to be entirely dry, contradicting rumours that it had surfaced after become tangled in fishing nets.[27] Perhaps this relatively new and advanced Chinese vessel was having mechanical problems (a thought hardly less troubling than if it was not). Whatever the reason, it is hard to imagine a starker intersection of the Indo-Pacific's seemingly separate layers of economic and military rivalry.

Beneath the Indo-Pacific waves, a contest is on to develop submarines, a 20th-century game-changer still valued for combat, surveillance and deterrence. The secrecy of submarines may be under challenge from seabed sonar arrays, other submarines and disruptive technologies such as autonomous undersea drone swarms and magnetic anomaly detection, enhanced by improved computing. Indeed, anti-submarine warfare is an area of significant renewed investment. But the oceans are becoming at best translucent, not transparent, and submarines will likely remain a strong investment for decades yet. China is developing new generations of submarines, seeking to diminish the exceptional American advantage in this field.

Japan remains a leader, its advanced twenty-two boats a daunting shield. Dozens of 'hunter-killer' or 'attack' submarines – with nuclear propulsion – quietly patrol the Indo-Pacific at any given time, gathering intelligence, learning the signatures of future targets, testing the waters and topography essential for their stealth, and practising for war. Australia is banking much of its strategic future on twelve of the world's largest diesel submarines, to be built with French technology, though it will have to cope with its current six ageing boats for many years yet. Indonesia is commissioning the first submarines to be constructed in Southeast Asia, built in a deal with South Korea, with more to come. China is supplying subs to Pakistan, Bangladesh, Myanmar and Thailand; Russia has built six for Vietnam. India is constructing submarines to a French design, while also building its own class of nuclear-powered vessels to carry nuclear ballistic missiles.

In theory, the nexus of submarines and nuclear weapons is one of the great stabilisers of security among nations in the Indo-Pacific. There is a dark two-part logic at work here. The first part is that nuclear weapons deter war from starting because they are so catastrophically destructive. The second part is that submarines, being almost impossible to find, are the best way to ensure that a nuclear attack cannot be stopped through a pre-emptive strike. Undersea nuclear weapons are thus supposedly the ultimate guarantor that nuclear war will not occur, because they would survive to devastatingly retaliate to a nuclear attack, making a first strike pointless to begin with.

No wonder a new nuclear arms race is gathering pace below the Pacific and Indian oceans: a multipolar replay of the famous Cold War contest between America and the Soviet Union beneath the Atlantic, the Pacific and the Arctic ice. America and Russia have for many years deployed nuclear warheads atop long-range ballistic missiles on nuclear-powered submarines – SSBNs, also known as 'boomers'. China and India too are joining this elite and costly game. China, in particular, is investing in at least five boomers, with new generations of missiles designed to reach the continental United States. A plausible theory for Beijing's determination to dominate the South China Sea is so that it can keep its SSBNs, the ultimate deterrent and equaliser with America, hidden in the deep waters.[28] For India, too, nuclear weapons are an existential issue, and Delhi is beginning to see its SSBN

China's first aircraft carrier, the Liaoning

program as its own equaliser with China. Indeed, as Indian and Chinese infantry faced off in the Himalayas in 2017, at the disputed Doklam plateau where Tibet and India meet Bhutan, there are unconfirmed reports that Prime Minister Modi explored sending India's sole boomer, the experimental *Arihant*, to sea, perhaps as a signal of India's preparedness and resolve. It may well be for the best that the vessel was out of action from an accident.[29]

Even Pakistan and North Korea have caught the nuclear-armed submarine craze, attempting a next-best option of putting nuclear arms aboard inferior diesel-electric submarines. In October 2019, North Korea launched a ballistic missile from a submerged platform, a stepping stone to a submarine-launched capability.[30] In the years ahead, no fewer than six nations may have the world's most dangerous weapons at large beneath the waves of this pivotal region.

That is even less reassuring than it sounds, for the logic that undersea nuclear weapons are the silent peacekeepers turns out to have some serious flaws in the new circumstances of the Indo-Pacific. In fact, it can take decades of risky experimentation for countries to perfect the technology, skills, psychology, doctrines and command systems required to make such weapons live up to their promise of peace and stability, the holy grail of what is called 'continuous at-sea deterrence'. In the meantime, the scope for horrendous mishap is real. If a nation sends its boomers to sea when a crisis begins, what kind of destabilising signal does that send the other side? In extremis, there is the possibility that, once conflict has begun, the commander of a nuclear-armed submarine that has been detected will choose to fire its devastating weapons before being sunk, in a dreadful choice of use it or lose it.[31] In the Indo-Pacific, only America's nuclear-armed submarine fleet is likely to maintain an advantageous combination of technology, experience and geography: US forces and their allies will stand a far greater chance of finding Chinese submarines, hemmed into the South China Sea, than China will of finding America's in the vast Pacific.[32]

Nuclear shadow

The SSBN contest is where so many of the dimensions of Indo-Pacific strategic competition intersect: great-power politics, maritime claims, naval strategy, technology advantage and the usually unspoken threats of dire escalation. The popular assumption that economic interdependence, above all, is what has kept a general peace among powerful nations since 1945 overlooks the grim reality that nuclear weapons have never gone away.

Again, the Indo-Pacific has become the vast ground zero for nuclear deterrence and risk: it is the epicentre of a 'second nuclear age'. It is also home to most of the world's nuclear-armed states: America, Russia, China, India, Pakistan, North Korea.[33] If there were a collapse of the US alliance system and its umbrella of extended deterrence – where allies abjure nukes of their own because of America's protection – then Japan, South Korea and possibly even Taiwan could be on the list of the world's new nuclear powers. Most of the time, the role of nuclear weapons in the contemporary Indo-Pacific is not as terrifyingly obvious as it was during the Cold War. China and America have generally been scrupulous in their overt diplomacy in not implying a nuclear threat to one another, though this has arguably had the counterproductive effect of reducing a sense of urgency in disarmament or arms control. The 2017 *Arihant* story aside, China and India are likewise careful not to publicly flaunt the reality that they have nuclear weapons aimed at each other. The India–Pakistan tensions, on the other hand, have several times involved blunt nuclear threats, though so far these have in the end helped lower the temperature of tension and allowed sanity to prevail. The unpredictability quotient may be higher in the North Korea–US relationship, where periodic phases of bluster and belligerence have worsened under Kim Jong-un, with Donald Trump frighteningly reciprocating.

Even for those experts who devote years to understanding this depressing subject, the choreography of nuclear deterrence in the Indo-Pacific remains uncertain. The good news is that there are fewer such weapons in the region or worldwide than at the height of the US–Soviet Cold War, and that China, India and America, in particular, do not openly brandish such catastrophic armaments as part of their coercive diplomacy. Russia, Pakistan and North Korea are more forthright about their willingness to use nuclear weapons first in a conflict, although technically America too holds such a doctrine, despite Obama's efforts to wind it back, and under Trump it has become more pronounced. The calculated madness of nuclear threats – or indeed nuclear use – would also be highly unlikely to feature early in most conceivable future security crises in the region. There are many likely levels of escalation between an initial incident – such as a skirmish over a contested sea boundary or land border – and the nuclear threshold.

Nonetheless, a nuclear shadow lies over the Indo-Pacific. China for many years built its nuclear arsenal at a restrained pace, keeping it relatively small (hundreds of warheads to America's and Russia's thousands) and, like India, preaching both 'no first use' and disarmament. But these signs are increasingly hollow. On 1 October 2019, in a parade to celebrate the seventieth anniversary of the founding of the PRC, China's leaders chose to make a grotesque performance of nuclear firepower. Instead of focusing on the nation's civilian achievements, there was the ultimate display of insecurity and Cold War thinking, a Soviet-style pageant of dozens of war rockets carried on huge trucks through the streets of Beijing.[34] These included the

DF-41 intercontinental missile (capable of reaching the American homeland), the JL-2 submarine-launched missile, and the DF-17, with a hypersonic 'glide vehicle' intended to dodge missile defences and with a 'medium' range suited for reaching China's neighbours and American bases.

This flaunting of doomsday weapons suggests that China is abandoning its tradition of nuclear restraint. It is likely that more nations will join Japan in fearing Chinese nuclear intimidation. Certainly Beijing has kept its options open to expand its arsenal. It has refused to join the United States, Russia, Britain and France in halting production of the fissile material – plutonium and highly enriched uranium – at the core of nuclear weapons, thus helping prevent a global treaty on this essential building block of disarmament. It has accelerated its nuclear program, not only with submarines but also with mobile and hidden land-based missiles that can hit targets like Japan, India, Russia and the United States. And there is much debate what 'no first use' actually means, even raising the question of whether a conventional attack on Chinese satellites or communications systems linked to the nuclear force would be sufficient provocation. Obama's idealistic effort in 2010 to engage China in global disarmament – with the intent of Beijing being the third mover, after Washington and Moscow reduced their forces – foundered tragically. And if China would not follow America and Russia in cutting its forces, then India would not follow China, and Pakistan would not follow India. Disturbingly, India has hinted that it may shift away from its own 'no first use' doctrine.[35]

The wicked tangle of nuclear deterrence remains. It is part of an even denser thicket of military capability and risk, including batteries of missile defences (do these stop nuclear missiles or encourage enemies to build more of them?), satellites and anti-satellite weapons, artificial intelligence, drones, submarines and anti-submarine warfare. Whether nuclear weapons bring peace or Armageddon depends heavily on theories of leadership psychology, generally untested in a full-blown crisis. Do they discourage risk-taking or embolden it?

A plausible security future for the Indo-Pacific is not nuclear confrontation, but a state of permanent coercion, dominated by what strategists call the 'stability–instability paradox'.[36] That is, the shadow of nuclear war does not discourage conflict, but instead exacerbates it at lower – but still dangerous – levels. The fear of great violence does not stop violence in relations between nations, but makes the world safe for lesser violence – which in turn sustains the risk that aggressive change will occur, or that miscalculation will lead violence to spiral out of control. This is especially so when one side is more risk-hungry – or determined to force change – than the other. The 'revisionist' has the advantage. Thus North Korea feels it can pinprick South Korea with lesser attacks – a ship sunk, an artillery barrage, a cyber onslaught. Or Pakistan can nurture terrorism against India. Or China can 'salami-slice' parts of the disputed South China Sea and East China Sea, knowing that smaller nations, or even their ally America, are unlikely to make a stand that would risk war. A crucial question is whether the paradox intensifies in China's relations with the rest of the region, or indeed whether other nations somehow begin to leverage it against China.

To be clear, strategic crisis in the Indo-Pacific will most likely occur well short of nuclear 'thresholds' – those moments when leaders feel they have no choice but to bring nuclear threats into play. But the nuclear dimension is the most extreme of the many plausible conflict scenarios where diplomacy could fail. To understand the region's perilous future, we need to contemplate the frailties of its diplomacy.

Strands of diplomacy

Diplomatic jargon is notoriously removed from material realities. In a desperate effort to explain their work in ways that make sense to the rest of us, diplomats use physical analogies like 'architecture' to describe the profusion of meetings and agreements that help keep relations between nations peaceful, predictable and productive. In the Indo-Pacific, it's a fairly feeble metaphor. The structures of diplomacy here are far flimsier than those of commerce – the material realities visible in the crowded sea lanes every day – and the truth is that nobody knows whether they are effective in keeping the peace or preventing aggression. Rather than ropes or chains constraining the choices of strong nations, diplomacy is more like an over-lay of Lilliputian strings, holding the giants in place while it suits them.

Of course talk is better than war, and diplomacy deserves a chance – and chances are that most nations woefully underinvest in it. A far cry from the popular stereotypes of endless air travel and cocktail parties, diplomacy is cheap. Compared with defence budgets, it's a downright bargain.

Self-styled security 'Realists' or anyone sensitive to double standards may scoff at the idea of a 'rules-based order', often called upon by medium and smaller powers – and previously, but less so under Trump, the United States – to explain the benefits of established international laws and norms. Of course, it has always been a rules- *and power*-based order. But the rules moderate the power, adding, at the very least, some predictability, restraint and boundaries into a competitive dynamic otherwise based on the ugly logic of 'might is right'. The benefits of modern diplomacy – channels of respectful communication and laws that regulate much of the complexity of international interdependence – are real and irreplaceable.

It is worth noting too that key parts of the 20th-century rules-based order against which China seems to chafe – such as the United Nations Convention on the Law of the Sea (UNCLOS) – involved a substantial Chinese role in their formulation. Indeed, UNCLOS is a truly global heritage: South American and newly independent African states championed its idea of the exclusive economic zone, and Indonesia pioneered archipelagic rights. Other rules disproportionately benefit China at the expense of other large Asian nations like India, Japan and Indonesia. Unlike them, China holds a permanent seat with veto power on the United Nations Security Council and is recognised as having a legal right to possess nuclear weapons under the Non-Proliferation Treaty. Meanwhile, in America, even as the Trump administration inflicts severe harm on many of the global rules that previous US leaders took a lead role in establishing, officials scramble to insist that their nation is not scoffing at the law. The retreat from agreements such as the 1987 Intermediate-Range Nuclear Forces Treaty, which limited American missile deployments, for example, has been justified on the basis that Russia walked away first, and China as a non-signatory is intimidating its neighbours with precisely the mid-range missiles the treaty bans, such as those brandished in the Beijing parade.

So, amid the worsening armed mistrust across the oceans, what place then for diplomacy, rules and respect? Some myths warrant busting.

First, diplomacy is not about the pursuit of friendly relations at any cost. Diplomacy has little meaning unless it somehow relates to a nation's interests. It may and should involve negotiation and compromise, but that is not the same as sacrificing fundamental national interests – and values – to keep the waters calm. Concessions to a powerful country without first attempting resistance will simply invite more pressure.

Second, diplomacy involves power. It cannot be merely a moral or legalistic appeal to a strong country's better nature. And it should not be seen as an alternative to other levers of national capability – such as military force, intelligence or geoeconomic weight – but as a complement and force multiplier. When trying to manage a great power, such as China, other nations will achieve little through diplomacy unless they can combine it with some kind of sanction or penalty and a willingness themselves to endure punishment. Even small countries need to consider ways to make life difficult for large ones, even if only through exposing bullying behaviour and seeking solidarity with one another. But better if the small and medium countries ultimately have some defensive – and even offensive – capacity, should diplomacy fail. Having a formidable American ally greatly helps. But the burgeoning new alignments and middle-power coalitions – such as among Australia, India, Japan, Indonesia and Vietnam – and the build-up of their own militaries are about adding backbone to their diplomacy, not giving up on it.

Lost in the noodle bowl

Third, diplomacy is not an alternative to competition among nations, but an arena for it – one far preferable to a literal battlefield. Newcomers to the bewildering alphabet soup – or, more aptly, noodle bowl – of Asian, Asia-Pacific and Indo-Pacific diplomatic institutions can begin to make sense of it by looking for the power relations within the acronyms. Much of what is grandly called architecture – implying solid and dependable structures – actually boils to down to who meets whom and what they talk about: power and meetings.

Thus the EAS is supposedly the region's premier forum but usually resembles an annual half-day get-together of national leaders where little happens. Much the same can be said, from a superficial look, of the APEC process, the ASEAN Regional Forum or the ASEAN Defence Ministers Plus Eight meeting. Karaoke is sometimes in the order of business, China uses proxies like Cambodia to veto agreement on strategic issues like the South China Sea, and human rights abuses within member states – against the Rohingya in Myanmar or the Uighurs in China, for example – go barely mentioned. Institutions in the Indian Ocean fare no better, with the Indian Ocean Rim Association (IORA) failing to deal with issues ranging from overfishing to tensions among China, India and Pakistan.

But this is reading regional multilateral diplomacy the wrong way. Multi-nation institutions are only as empowered as strong nations wish them to be. The model of Europe is often held up unrealistically as an aspiration for the Indo-Pacific. Yet the European Union became a reality through the fundamental reconciliation of French and German power and interests, after generations of devastating war. By contrast, the security differences and mistrust in the Indo-Pacific are essentially unresolved, and getting worse.

The effectiveness of multilateral diplomacy, then, works mostly at the margins: managing, moderating, forestalling conflict. A classic example is the ARF, conceived in the optimistic early 1990s with a three-part mission: dialogue, confidence building and, ultimately, conflict prevention. The model was the Cold War's Helsinki Accords, where the overhanging dread of nuclear annihilation, combined with multi-layered conversations ranging from human rights to the mechanics of arms control, helped to reduce – but not on its own eliminate – the risk of war. Twenty-five years on, and the ARF remains further than ever from a conflict-prevention or mediation role – especially between the big powers.

One of the more depressing failures of multilateral diplomacy has been the co-opting of ASEAN in the erosion of its member states' rights and interests in the South China Sea. Every year, there are bright headlines – or really the same ones recycled – proclaiming that the ten Southeast Asian states and China are getting closer to finalising a 'code of conduct'. This miracle document will somehow prevent conflict at sea and open the way to cooperation in contested waters, perhaps even shared exploitation of resources. What is less enthusiastically advertised is the fact that these negotiations began in 2002. In that year, concerted diplomatic effort from the Southeast Asians extracted from (a much weaker than now) China a nonbinding 'declaration' that it would show restraint, avoid force, respect freedom of navigation, not increase its habitation of contested islands, and begin preparing a binding code of conduct.[37] Not only has China breached these undertakings, but the glacial pace of its negotiations has created a perverse situation. As noted in Chapter 6, the future code will likely legitimise China's threat of force in repelling others from the new nautical territory it has illegally accumulated. It will be a triumph of passive aggression.[38]

Again, this is not to say diplomacy in its multilateral settings is a waste of time. Gatherings like the EAS or the ARF provide a stage for holding nations to account, for calling out unacceptable behaviour – if only leaders are willing to use them this way. Such meetings provide a platform to settle and declare collective responses to a crisis, perhaps a natural disaster or pandemic. The forums can be a rallying place in those rare instances where behaviour by one state is beyond the pale for all others – although even building consensus to criticise North Korea has proven difficult.

The big meetings also provide a perfect façade for the real diplomacy – the consequential intrigue and plotting on the sidelines, nations conferring in trusted twos or threes or small groups. The convening of minilateral groups – even the controversial US–India–Japan–Australia quadrilateral – typically occurs on the margins of the major forums. Old-fashioned bilateralism remains dominant, with stronger powers competing to shape agendas and win smaller nations to their side. But middle powers can play this game too: multilateralism remains a place where agility and activism by small countries can pay off, if they seize opportunities to lead coalitions on specific issues. Indeed, sometimes in these settings the smaller nations can set the agenda and influence the strong.

That's why membership matters. The East Asia Summit still holds promise because at least its composition reflects much of the Indo-Pacific: a room too big for China – or America – to dominate. And China gets that, which is why it seeks to wrangle sensitive issues directly with weaker nations one on one, or collectively with the Southeast Asians minus the likes of America, Japan, India or Australia. More pointedly, China is investing in new international organisations it can dominate, like the Conference on Interaction and Confidence-Building Measures in Asia, an 'Asia for the Asians' arrangement that excludes Japan, Indonesia, America and Australia, yet conveniently includes Russia.

Thus the theatrical multilateralism of great leadership gatherings is doing little to build genuine security cooperation or reduce the risk of conflict in the Indo-Pacific. Cooperation will occur more in small groups and bilaterally. And preserving the peace involves a mixture of deterrence – the diplomatic signalling of military power – and the painstaking work of negotiating and implementing so-called confidence-building measures (or CBMs).

These are the kind of protocols, communications channels and understandings that helped keep the peace in the Cold War for so long. A good example is an agreement on rules to prevent 'incidents at sea' during 'unalerted encounters', giving shared understandings of how close each side's ships or aircraft can get to the other's before there should be cause for alarm. Other CBMs involve providing prior notification of major military exercises, helping to avoid miscalculation by confirming that a drill is just a drill and not the start of a war. Dedicated 'hotlines' can help frontline military commanders, diplomats or leaders communicate urgently with their counterparts to handle differences in a crisis. Transparency measures can be put in place to share data on numbers of weapons, perhaps even allowing the other side to inspect and verify that agreements have not been broken. Rival nations can hold regular dialogues about doctrine, intent and clear signalling of 'red lines' – triggers for conflict. Following the Cuban missile crisis in

1962, the US–Soviet relationship developed a sophisticated architecture for such crisis management. It did not always work – war scares continued into the 1980s – but the alternative would have been infinitely worse.

Yet the confidence-building measures of the new Indo-Pacific era are frugal fare. A decade ago, China rejected formal risk-reduction talks with those nations its forces were pushing up against at sea – notably America, Japan and Vietnam – instead using its own perceived recklessness as a tool of influence. The logic was that others would be less likely to resist assertive claims if they could not anticipate the Chinese reaction. Then, as the island-building program advanced, risk management began to suit China's consolidation of control. Now America and its 'freedom of navigation' patrols could be portrayed as the intrusive disrupter of the peace. Moreover, an intrinsic weakness of CBMs is that they only work to reduce risks of accident or miscalculation. They are of little use if one side intends to risk conflict – or initiate it.

Still, there is something to work with. China decided in 2014 to join the Code for Unplanned Encounters at Sea – a region-wide set of protocols, long heeded by America and its allies.[39] In 2018, China and Japan finally established a hotline to defuse encounters between their forces in the East China Sea.[40] In the Indian Ocean, China and India have developed an occasional maritime affairs dialogue, anticipating the trouble likely to arise between their forces.[41] On land, in the wake of the Doklam standoff, China and India have tightened the CBMs for how their troops should manage future clashes to prevent border skirmishes leading to war. Notably, all of these improvements in keeping the peace occurred after phases of high tension, and may have followed a reflection within China's military that it could not be the master of infinite risk. If others had shown no resistance, China would have been less likely to see sense in these instruments of compromise: a showcase example of how diplomacy and force work together, not apart.

But if diplomacy is a strategic shaping activity – about stopping or limiting or terminating war – then what shapes diplomacy? Behind the scenes, a subtle but crucial dimension of the Indo-Pacific power contest involves some countries trying to influence others' foreign policy decisions. What better way to win without war than to make your potential adversaries confuse your point of view with their own, thus ensuring that the diplomatic outcomes are on your terms?

From a Chinese perspective it would be ideal, for example, if influential policy-makers in other countries were to hold and propagate the view that standing up to China was neither right nor worth it. China is investing vast sums in trying to shape the global narrative about the future. Even before the Belt and Road was well underway, some estimates put its budget for 'external propaganda' at US$10 billion a year – likely more than the public diplomacy spending of the rest of the world put together.[42]

Especially opaque are those organs of the state and the Communist Party tasked to wage 'political warfare'. This is about subjugating the enemy without fighting. Political warfare is based on the notion, originating in the Soviet Union and later adapted by Mao, that there is a constant state of undeclared war between nations. Democracies, on the other hand, think of war as beginning only when the first shot is fired.[43] All nations have intelligence services that gather information covertly to advantage their country. China sees its spies as fulfilling this role and more, deploying them also to affect foreign decision-making. These efforts are dominated by the Ministry of State Security or *Guoanbu*, the world's largest intelligence service, and supplemented by a uniquely Chinese instrument of influence, the so-called United Front Work Department.[44] Xi has revived and resourced its mission, dating back to the Chinese civil war of the 1930s and 1940s. This is all about isolating those seen as the Party's enemies by winning over the middle ground, whether through propaganda, inducement or intimidation. Beijing's message of influence boils down to a simple three-part story: China's rise is benign. The growth of China's power is unstoppable. And anyone who stands in the way will be punished.[45] Never mind the internal contradictions in the logic. It is proving a tough storyline to challenge.

Battle of the narratives: Australia at the front

'The Chinese integrity of its borders is a matter for China,' said the charismatic young Australian senator, standing against an imposing backdrop of Australian flags and behind a lectern bearing his country's kangaroo-and-emu coat of arms. It all looked supremely official. To unsuspecting ears, his words may have seemed a harmless statement of the obvious. However, the 'borders' in question were not China's but the entirety of the disputed South China Sea. The politician was Sam Dastyari, a rising star and powerbroker in the Australian Labor Party. He went on to say:

> The role that Australia should be playing as a friend is to know that we see several thousand years of history ... where it is and isn't our place to be involved. And as a supporter of China, and a friend of China, the Australian Labor Party is playing an important role in maintaining that relationship. And the best way of maintaining that relationship is knowing when it is and isn't our place to be involved.[46]

These were fateful words, uttered during the 2016 Australian federal election campaign, and just weeks before the long-awaited international court adjudication between the Philippines and China on the South China Sea. Standing beside Dastyari was billionaire property developer Huang Xiangmo, a major financial donor to both of Australia's major political parties, and a Chinese citizen with such close reported connections to the United Front that a few years later he was barred from returning to Australia.[47] Dastyari's remarks were entirely at odds with both Australian government policy and his own opposition party's policy. Once media reports shone light on his links with Huang, it was the beginning of the end of Dastyari's political career.[48]

It was also a wake-up call about foreign involvement in Australia's institutions. An elaborate tapestry of Chinese party-state influence had developed within Australia, including donations to political parties, control of Chinese-language media, the cultivation of some individuals and the intimidation of others, and the dominance of community and student organisations. Suddenly this was beginning to unravel, with global consequences that continue to reverberate. Australia is now seen globally as a place of early warning when it comes to such influence and interference: a case study both on the challenge and how democracies can push back.[49]

The CCP has at least four reasons to exert authoritarian 'sharp power' inside Australia.[50] First, China wants to see the Australia–United States security alliance weakened, or ideally broken: anything that will end Canberra's willingness to lend military, diplomatic or intelligence support to America and Japan in a confrontation. Second, Australia is seen as a place to gather intelligence on American and allied national security secrets and military technology. Third, there is an imperative for China to try to silence Australia's independent diplomatic voice in support of other countries and those international laws and norms inconvenient for Beijing – hence, for instance, Beijing's effort to freeze diplomatic relations in 2013 after then foreign minister Julie Bishop's outspoken criticism of China's bid to control airspace contested with Japan.

And, perhaps most chillingly, Australia is seen as a priority target for the suppression of independent political views among all people of Chinese origin. Such silencing of dissent can occur through harassment or threats to individuals or their families back in China; the detention in China of Chinese-heritage Australian citizens or permanent residents who have criticised the CCP has been seen as a warning to others.[51] Or interference can manifest through pressure on businesses, local governments or media outlets.[52] Australia is a sanctuary for views that bring existential discomfort to China's increasingly totalitarian leadership: free voices from Hong Kong, refugees from the Tiananmen crackdown, Taiwanese, Uighurs, Tibetans, supporters of the suppressed Falun Gong spiritual movement, and Communist Party members turned democracy activists.

Along with its diverse sympathisers, the Hong Kong community in Australia provided moral backing to the mass protests of 2019. In response to all this, the CCP seems to have concluded that if it can drown dissent in Australia, it can do so anywhere. A normally relaxed society that likes to imagine it is a world away from trouble has found itself thrust onto the frontline of strategic contest, involving spies, lies, blandishments and bullying. On the streets of Sydney, Melbourne and Brisbane, some anti-CCP protesters wear masks to avoid their families in China being victimised. For their part, some pro-CCP Chinese students have mobilised – with support or encouragement from Chinese officials – to take Beijing's cause to Australian city streets and university campuses.[53] The Hong Kong crisis has highlighted the use of Chinese-language social media such as Weibo and WeChat, as well as CCP-affiliated newspapers and radio within Australia, to distort the narrative in ways that favour Beijing's interests and worldview.

A cliched notion of Australia's relations with China has it that Canberra fears offending Beijing because of its huge trade dependence. But on foreign interference, the Australian government's firmness – particularly in 2017 under Prime Minister Malcolm Turnbull – surprised many. A climate of concern about Russian interference in US elections saw Australia determined to strengthen its own democratic resilience. Laws were passed to combat corrupt, collusive, covert and coercive activity by foreign powers and their agents. Intelligence agencies warned openly of an unprecedented espionage threat. Foreign political donations were banned. Chinese corporations Huawei and ZTE were shut out of critical national infrastructure – although unlike the later American approach, the government named neither corporation, preferring to take a principles-based stance that excluded all companies susceptible to 'directions' from a foreign power. Within a short time, other nations, initially baffled by Australia's seeming paranoia, began to appreciate some of its concerns, and take their own measures.

But the contest of influence, the narrative battle, has not been limited to Western countries. Singapore has notably had its own intense but discreet struggles, involving the expulsion in 2017 of a prominent academic accused of being an agent for a foreign power. Singapore has studied the Australian experience with a view to further strengthening its laws.[54] Taiwan is the most comprehensive theatre of information war: money, media organisations, social media and community infiltration are all being leveraged in a bid to replace the government with one friendlier to China's objectives of unification and control.[55] Across Southeast Asia and the smaller nations of the Indian Ocean and South Pacific, the struggle for geopolitical influence has become mired in confusion about alleged corruption, business deals, Belt and Road loans and the personal choices of certain leaders, from the Philippines' populist quasi-authoritarian Rodrigo Duterte and Cambodia's Hun Sen to the electorally defeated former leaders of Malaysia, Maldives and Sri Lanka, Najib Razak, Abdulla Yameen and Mahinda Rajapaksa.

The game of perception and propaganda may seem secondary, even trivial, alongside the wealth-or-poverty weight of geoeconomics and the life-and-death power of military force. Nothing could be further from the truth: the United Front has been hailed as a 'magic weapon' for ensuring the CCP's rule, along with armed force and Party organisation.[56] In the geopolitics of the Indo-Pacific, the many middle players between Beijing and Washington are watching each other's responses to Chinese strength and assertiveness. Thus appearances are shaping reality. The Indo-Pacific power struggle involves a contest to shape attitudes, narratives and acceptable discourse among populations, political decision-makers, media outlets and businesses. The 'soft power' of persuasion and attraction is a legitimate tool of diplomats everywhere. But Beijing specialises – in ways more subtle and calibrated than Russia's disruptive blunderbuss tactics – in the 'sharp power' of foreign political interference to neutralise opposition and change the Indo-Pacific gameboard in its favour. The apolitical priorities of private companies have not granted them immunity, attested by the slew of apologies solicited by China on issues ranging from the designation of Taiwan on airline schedules to support for the civil rights protests in Hong Kong.[57] Major American studios pre-emptively package China-friendly entertainment, such as the abominable decision to depict the nine-dash line as part of a normal map of China in a children's movie co-produced by DreamWorks and a Shanghai-based partner.[58] Even sport is not off-limits. An inflection point was reached when China pressured the US National Basketball Association to apologise for a team official's tweet in support of Hong Kong's freedom movement. The subsequent cycle of apology and outrage further polarised America and China over the principle of free expression, and raised the prospect of economic decoupling extending into sports and entertainment.[59]

The colossal marketing campaign of China's Belt and Road, with its doublespeak of defining a China-centric world with a 'community of common destiny for mankind', is one with this coordinated push of soft and sharp power.[60] Each Belt and Road document signed with an indifferent or pliant foreign government is an arrow in the quiver of influence – a message that China will map the future, so holdouts might as well get with the program. In response, democratic countries have begun to compete with China's message on the soft power front, but have so far been unwilling or unable to engage in outright political warfare. Japan is becoming more adept at leveraging its quality infrastructure, diplomatic reliability and non-threatening strategic character to build partnership – even trust – with a wide range of nations, from South to Southeast Asia, Africa and the Pacific. America is a past master in soft power – and during the Cold War waged its own variant of political warfare too. But under Trump America has lost its touch in appealing to democratic values, and is at risk of alienating friends in ASEAN. India may talk a good talk – Modi's 2018 Singapore speech is perhaps the finest encapsulation of the Indo-Pacific idea – but struggles to outdo the allure of Chinese money in smaller nations, and is doing itself a disservice by holding out on a regional free trade agreement. In addition to pushing back against CCP interference operations at home, Australia has sought to counter China's influence in small island states through its own Pacific Step-up, meant to combine soft power with development funding and security assistance. But Australia's ability to persuade the Pacific island peoples of its good intentions has run up against the conservative Morrison government's resistance to phasing out coalmining – a priority concern for Pacific island nations facing the impacts of the global climate emergency on weather, resources and sea levels.[61]

Much of the information battle is being waged not between governments but within civil society. For academics, journalists and politicians – vocations defined as much by ideas as material realities – it is now an unpleasant reality that their daily work cannot be quarantined from an international power struggle to shape information and perception. Academic debates on security, international relations and political culture are no longer purely academic. Seasoned China watchers know full well that Chinese think tanks, media organisations, universities and even corporations can be vessels of Communist Party influence and ideational struggle against what the Party defines as hostile foreign forces. Such entities can thus be highly advantaged when they wage the battle of ideas against their democratic 'counterparts'. Here they often find themselves up against little more than parochialism and naivety (wilful or genuine): parliamentarians with short-term horizons, scholars unaccustomed to having real-world impact, or corporates and university administrators focused on the money. The democratic side often does not even realise a contest is occurring, or that they are being treated either as an adversary or a target of influence. It is the nature of political warfare to delay as long as possible letting the other side realise there is even a conflict.[62]

Of all the citizens of liberal democracy, it is journalists with their stubborn antennae for lies and repression who are proving the most effective antibodies in the narrative battle. Australia's China reality check was catalysed by a dogged handful of investigative journalists – some are still battling defamation lawsuits as a result.[63] While the institution of a free media, the so-called fourth estate, is under pressure globally from dictators and digital disruption, the struggle against authoritarianism and foreign interference is also giving quality journalism new purpose and relevance. One of the most effective ways for middle-size democracies to protect their values and interests is to cherish and support free media at home and abroad: for instance, training journalists in small countries (such as in the South Pacific, where local media scrutiny is adding much-needed speed bumps of contestation and transparency to the Belt and Road).

Meanwhile, some of the most effective resistance to China's efforts to dominate perceptions has arisen not from other governments but from loosely coordinated groups of people, notably a self-styled 'global anti-totalitarianism' movement among the overseas diaspora communities of

Hong Kongers, Uighurs and the rest. Moral suasion by the people of little Hong Kong may seem no match for the power of the Chinese state and its extensive propaganda machine, yet the independence and ingenuity of this resistance movement have amounted to its own force multiplier. Youthful activists have merged old-school street demonstrations with creative use of digital technologies – to coordinate gatherings, warn of police movements, reach out to mainland Chinese visitors and expose state violence to the world. Regular civilian items – umbrellas, face masks, hard hats, laser pointers – have been repurposed for guerrilla protest tactics. However Hong Kong's year of living dangerously was going to end, the resistance had already put down the permanent soundtrack to this moment in history: a crowd-sourced anthem, 'Glory to Hong Kong', sung by spontaneous crowds in malls, stadiums and schools, and recorded by a full orchestra and choir of masked volunteers in a video that went viral worldwide.[64]

It was a stirring way to win sympathy. By contrast, the CCP's extension of the interstate geopolitical contest to the home front in many other countries could prove deeply counter-productive for China's image and interests. Worsening public attitudes to China within Australia (which in 2019 saw a 20 per cent drop in the proportion of people who trusted China) may be a sign of things to come elsewhere.[65] This pattern could be especially harmful for people of Chinese origin in those societies, or indeed for social cohesion and the health of multiculturalism.

For its part, the Australian government has been at pains to point out that its new campaign to counter foreign interference is 'country agnostic' – that is, not aimed at any particular ethnicity or nation. There is also a sound ethical case that it would be racist for Australia not to act against Beijing's coercion and control of Chinese Australians. To leave these citizens without the sovereign rights of protection from a foreign power, purely on the basis of their ethnicity, would be to treat them as second-class Australians. Even so, the intrusion of geopolitical rivalry into domestic affairs could do lasting damage. This is not just about US–China conflict. The Indo-Pacific is a region shaped by migration. A future China–India war, for instance, could reverberate inside multicultural nations like

Canada or Australia – where Indians are the fastest-growing migrant community. As a sign of what may come, a small group of Chinese students in Sydney led an anti-India motorcade, a jarring spectacle of luxury cars, red flags and threatening slogans, during the Doklam confrontation in 2017.[66] Having led the world in pushing back against Chinese sharp power, Australia now has a responsibility to show leadership in reassuring its diverse Chinese communities that this is in significant part about protecting their equal rights as citizens.

Full spectrum, full circle

Social media manipulation and the personal intricacies of diaspora politics may seem a world away from Xi Jinping's battle command centre or the silent vigil of nuclear submarines. However, there is no escaping the unsettling reality that the CCP defines China's future in stark terms of struggle, against adversaries domestic and foreign. In the Indo-Pacific and globally this takes the form of a contest between states for advantage, influence and security across the complete spectrum of issues – not just defence but also economics, diplomacy and the control of information.

On the bright side, contrary to some worst-case assessments, China may not have a master plan for strategic dominance of the region. But even if that's true, it may be where the good news ends. The sheer scale of growth in China's national interests and capabilities, the way they have extended across the region, the destabilising entanglement of the many dimensions of competition (geoeconomic, military, diplomatic and narrative), and the inevitability of pushback – concerted or otherwise – means misadventure lies ahead, with potentially grave consequences. The elimination of mistrust between states is not a realistic early goal. For the medium term at least, it will be enough to maintain coexistence.

FUTURE

CHAPTER 9

NAVIGATING MISTRUST

The black swan is a singularly Indo-Pacific creature, native to Australia and found especially near the continent's southwest and southeast coasts. The sight of this waterbird stunned Europeans when they first entered a river on the continent's western edge in 1697. European culture had previously deemed the black swan a metaphor for the impossible: swans, of course, were only white, even though for Australia's First Peoples, black swans had been reassuringly normal for tens of thousands of years. More recently, the celebrated scholar of randomness Nassim Nicholas Taleb has revived the bird's symbolism, lending it fresh and undeserved notoriety as a synonym for improbable and often catastrophic happenings, a silhouette for all that could possibly go wrong.[1] 'Black swan event' is now a popular label for a discontinuity that is hard to predict, huge in consequence, yet obvious in retrospect: the First World War, the 9/11 terrorist attacks, the global financial crisis.

Black swans and black elephants

On closer inspection, such strategic shocks better resemble another creature, an imagined hybrid that can be called a black elephant: a black swan crossed with the proverbial 'elephant in the room' – a problem so big and obvious nobody wants to talk about it. A black elephant is thus a known unknown, a likely event – and a bad one – that everyone sees looming, yet still comes as a shock. The term originated among the strategic forecasters of Singapore's sharp-minded intelligence community, led by former civil service head Peter Ho, a reminder that small nations surviving among giants are often the best at seeing over the horizon.[2]

As Indo-Pacific strategic risks accumulate, there are black elephants aplenty.

China invades Taiwan, or at least bombards and blockades it, and a chain of calamity shatters the peace of East Asia. As part of their response, America and its allies blockade China from afar, widening the conflict into the Indo-Pacific. A skirmish that begins for any number of reasons leads to a shooting war in the South China Sea. Conflict and chaos on the Korean Peninsula drag in not only the United States but China too. India and Pakistan return to war; Chinese troops or civilians inside Pakistan are caught up, and Beijing gets involved. There's a border clash between India and China, or jostling over islands between China and Japan, and the hostility extends to naval confrontation in the Indian Ocean. An American or Chinese spy plane or ship is seized by the other side after a collision, and confrontation ensues in an effort to recover personnel or secret equipment. As an Iran crisis deepens, several navies, including those of China and India, converge on the Persian Gulf to protect shipping. They stay, build bases and set the scene for their own future clash. The People's Liberation Army intervenes to protect Chinese nationals or interests somewhere along the Belt and Road – in Africa, the Indian Ocean, South Asia, Central Asia, the Middle East or the Pacific. But the plan goes awry when Chinese troops get mired in local conflict. Many of these scenarios reflect the accumulation of risks inherent in China's rapidly growing international security footprint.

And all around, environmental pressures and the effects of climate change are likely to exacerbate power struggles. A zero-sum approach to the use of natural resources – such as freshwater or fisheries – could raise the risk of confrontation among nations, notably between China and India, or between China and the smaller nations of Southeast Asia, whether downstream on the Mekong River or in the South China Sea. It is plausible that Beijing could be seeking access to foreign farmlands and fisheries partly as a food security strategy, based on the harm that climate change could bring to China's agricultural output. Even where climate concerns are not the cause of conflict, they will magnify the human toll from the failure of nations to find cooperative responses or manage their differences.[3] If strategic mistrust persists, how, for instance, will regional nations possibly reach an accord on the resettlement of increasingly large populations displaced from coastal areas by sea-level rises? According to the US National Intelligence Council:

> Population growth will continue to concentrate in areas vulnerable to sea-level rise, flooding, and storm surges. By 2035, roughly 50 per cent more people than in the year 2000 will live in low-elevation coastal zones worldwide, with the number in Asia increasing by more than 150 million and in Africa by 60 million. Many megacities, such as Bangkok, Ho Chi Minh City, Jakarta, and Manila, will continue to sink because of excessive groundwater extraction and natural geologic activity.[4]

Climate change is likely to displace very large numbers of people – 20 million or more in Bangladesh alone. Most of this displacement will probably be within national borders, not across them.[5] Nonetheless, the interplay of the long climate crisis with power rivalries among nations will be especially pronounced in the Indo-Pacific, with its combination of vulnerable populations, rival nations and extreme weather events – a calamitous triangle.

It's frighteningly easy to imagine plausible scenarios for confrontation in the Indo-Pacific – that moment when sufficient interests or uncertainties are in play that leaders may signal their willingness to risk conflict. And none of this litany of risk includes the real black swans – the unknown unknowns. In such a fertile habitat, a large and connected geopolitical space, these are prone to proliferate.

For example, what new foreign policy disruption can we expect from the Trump presidency, especially if in a second term it heightens both its confrontation with China and its disregard of allies? If America were truly to leave its own Indo-Pacific strategy unachieved, and fail to support its friends in Asia, what new patterns of coercion and conflict would be unleashed – and would these really all go China's way? Is it truly inconceivable that territorial aggression will be forever off the table? What if Japan and South Korea come to blows over disputed islands? How would a US–Russia conflict expand into the Indo-Pacific?

Will India by the mid 21st century still be the relatively restrained giant it was in the 20th century? What if China or India – or both – break with past practice and begin forging military alliances? What if either or both of these megastates find themselves racked by new internal conflict, while the other takes advantage? If the era ahead is indeed a US–China cold war, how will this play out in local struggles, perhaps even through proxy wars: civil conflicts in small states? As any number of weak states struggle with internal strife, or as a seemingly stable regime proves brittle and breaks, how will the effects flow out, and how will great powers keep out of each other's way if they intervene? Will new waves of repression and resistance inside greater China – Tibet, Xinjiang, Hong Kong – spill beyond China's borders, and how will China and the world react? Can China and Islam avoid collision in the long run? What if jihadist terrorists seize new territorial enclaves in Southeast Asia, such as the Philippines or Indonesia, close to the sea lanes, giving China a credible reason to join an international intervention?

How will climate change and resource insecurity compound rivalries among states? Could these shared challenges encourage China, India and America to put narrowly national interests aside? Alternatively, what if nations respond to environmental stress with unilateral 'geoengineering' measures to manipulate weather conditions in their favour? This could include some nations dispersing aerosols in the stratosphere above their territory to reduce local temperatures, regardless of possible effects on wider cross-border climate systems and the interests of other societies.[6] How long before nations compete openly for the barely touched seabed resources of the Indian and Pacific oceans? Demand is increasing for these resources, notably polymetallic nodules containing elements needed for smartphones and car batteries.[7] So is the feasibility of the technologies, such as undersea robotics, needed to find and extract them. China and India are already active in exploring the mineral-rich sea floor of the southwest

Indian Ocean. A joint study by Australian and French researchers in 2019 expressed concern that undersea prospecting could be a source of international tension, whether due to the value of the resources involved or because mining could been seen as cover for security activities, such as surveys for submarine operations, 'the positioning of undersea surveillance equipment or interference with undersea cables'.[8] And if data is the new oil, then submarine cables are new strategic chokepoints, especially for island nations connected by precious few.

Black swan risks will surely accumulate in the Southern Ocean and Antarctica, the latter currently protected from military activity and resource exploitation by a treaty regime due for renewal by 2048. Sovereignty over Antarctic territory is not resolved, merely suspended; the world has essentially agreed to disagree, for now. Most of the frozen continent was claimed in the 20th century by seven small or middle powers – Australia's territory is the largest, at 42 per cent – but 21st-century major powers such as China and India may have different ideas. Already, China and Russia have bases on the Australian Antarctic Territory and are exploring for minerals.[9] A worst-case scenario by mid-century would be a militarisation of Antarctica, with competing national bases using the continent not only for military communications and intelligence but potentially to deploy armed force for asserting new claims over resources. If the rules-based order continues to erode, and the Antarctica system relies on rules and restraint, then war on or over the ice may not always be so unthinkable. Whichever future the Antarctic holds, it is likely to be part of the Indo-Pacific power game, and access through the sea lanes of the Pacific and Indian oceans will be key to whether China and other Asian powers can pursue their Antarctic ambitions.

Globally, what disruptive technologies could shift the balance of national wealth or military power in ways yet barely conceivable? And if global warming opens viable Arctic sea lanes, how long will the Indo-Pacific remain the economic centre of gravity anyway?

Shakespeare knew something of the fray of nations: 'When sorrows come,' he wrote in Hamlet, 'they come not single spies but in battalions.'

Strategic shocks do not occur in isolation: in a hyperconnected world, they are likely to multiply and cascade with effects impossible to gauge in advance. Given the uncertainty, complexity and interdependence of this super-region's strategic puzzle – many layers, many players, the fast and unpredictable interplay of fear, confidence, nationalism, misinformation and power – all that can safely be foretold is that there is trouble ahead in the world's pivotal region. It's time for government and business alike to brace and hedge, to prepare for the risks of multiple plausible futures.

Falling together or apart: the insecurity continuum

Gloom makes headlines, and lists of woe are simple enough to summon. So it is worth stepping back and asking: is there really such a welter of insoluble problems here? After all, there remain deep divisions among experts and within governments about what China really wants, and whether the security future for the Indo-Pacific and world looks as troubling as this book suggests.

Officially, China wants what all nations deserve: a destiny of peace, prosperity, security, stability. But, through the Belt and Road and its grow-ing military footprint, China's problems are becoming the world's problems, and the world's problems are becoming China's. Moreover, even though China, like most nations most of the time, is not looking for conflict, it is proving willing to rely on coercion, whether in the form of armed force, geoeconomics or political interference. The vital question for others, then, becomes how to manage such coercion without it ending in conflict or capitulation.

To answer that question, we need a sense of how nations interact, and how these patterns can be encouraged towards desired outcomes. This is no straightforward matter – as argued in Chapter 5, there are pitfalls in reduc-ing international relations to something like the laws of physics. But at least it is worth trying to define the different types of relations that can occur among nations. These can be understood as a continuum of 'co' words, derived from *com*, Latin for 'together': from cooperation at one end, through degrees of coexistence, competition and confrontation, all the way to conflict. None of these alone can be described as the 'natural' condition of world affairs – typically several such dynamics occur at once – but there are circumstances in which, for instance, competition prevails over cooperation, and leads all the way to conflict.[10]

Cooperation is at the benign end: nations support each other's interests, even to the point that those interests are defined in common and the outcomes are positive-sum – everyone can win. The international system coordinates to address shared challenges: climate change, transnational crime, ecological stresses, resource pressures, energy needs, disease eradication, and raising the wellbeing and fulfilment of people everywhere across indicators of human development, such as health and education. Cooperation may occur among many nations through shared institutions – the United Nations, the European Union. Or it may work best between two nations or in small groups. Alliances and treaties may formalise and strengthen it. Not all cooperation need involve trust, but it does require at least those precursors of trust: predictability and reciprocity.

Coexistence is less ambitious but an essential starting point for cooperation. It connotes a degree of relatively benign indifference: nations may work together somewhat, but their first priority is to help themselves in ways that do not harm others. Most nations coexist most of the time. Coexistence is at the heart of the modern state system, captured in the Peace of Westphalia that ended Europe's ruinous Thirty Years' War in 1648. But it is also authentically Asian. The principles of peaceful coexistence have been preached by China, India and various non-aligned nations from Cold War days, based on the *Panchsheel* Treaty (Sanskrit for 'five virtues') signed in Bandung, Indonesia, in 1954: mutual respect for territory and sovereignty; non-aggression; non-interference in domestic affairs; equality and cooperation for mutual benefit; and, to sum it all up, peaceful coexistence itself. Sometimes breached in practice – especially as China becomes assertive – the principles nonetheless are an admirable starting point for a just and durable world order. It is time to revive them for the purpose of holding nations to their word.

Nations can compete even as they coexist. Indeed, even cooperation and competition can occur between the same countries at the same time on different issues or in different locations, with coexistence a connecting glue. Regular economic relations involve both – such is the logic of the World Trade Organization, where nations cooperate to set, follow and enforce the rules, then compete within those bounds. In such situations, the cooperation is not some kind of concession or weakness but a recognition of shared needs or common problems.[11]

Competition is an active quest for advantage, a contest among countries, and – along with coexistence – a traditional state of affairs in the international system. In trade and diplomacy, it can be respectful, or at least bound by rules and structures. Indeed, a standard assumption about international competition is that it is regulated and thus constrained. From trade to maritime disputes, there is in theory a body of agreed law and even umpires: appellate bodies and tribunals. A downside of competition is that nations may expend their energies against one another rather than for a common goal: consider, for example, the possible alternative uses for the resources thrown into national militaries and intelligence services with the overriding purpose of guarding against each other. That said, international competition can galvanise a country's capabilities to generate national achievements – such as America's Cold War advances in space exploration or the creation of the internet – that can later be harnessed for the common weal. A greater risk of competition among powerful states is that it pressures third countries to take sides. And the greatest is that competition can lead to conflict.

But first there is the crucial transition phase of confrontation: the heightening of tension, the forcing of crisis. This is when interests clash so intensely – and perhaps so suddenly – that a dangerous threshold is reached, and the door to conflict opens. Confrontation is a time of decisive choice. It would be naive to imagine it occurs solely through mishap or miscalculation. Confrontation can be a tool of statecraft, brinkmanship based on calculations that the other side is more averse to risk – or that pushing back is only going to get harder, so now is the time. Thus China has brought on maritime confrontations with Japan, Vietnam and the Philippines. India chose to confront China at Doklam. India–Pakistan confrontations are unnervingly frequent. In the domains of trade and technology, America has chosen to confront China repeatedly. And in its own smaller way, Australia confronted China in 2017 by taking a stand on foreign political interference.

Confrontation connects with coercion: the forceful constraining of choices, the use of threat to motivate a target to act in ways that suit the coercer's interests.[12] Coercion is the ability of one side to get another 'to do something it does not want to do'.[13] The strong can use confrontation as a coercive tactic, or confrontation can be a way to draw a line against prolonged bullying. Coercion may combine with that more subtle instrument collusion, in which the stronger power seeks to cajole or even corrupt the other's decision-makers to identify their interests with its own. Coercion works best when dominant voices within the weaker country declare the fight is not worth it – one interpretation of Duterte's failure to defy China's encroachments on the Philippines' maritime space.[14]

But when the fateful crossroads of confrontation are reached, the policy choices for each side boil down to three: conflict, capitulation or compromise.

Conflict can involve the use of armed force right up to the level of total war. Or it can refer mainly to nonviolent measures that nonetheless inflict grave harm, such as financial sanctions or cyber sabotage. Conflict differs from coercion (which may also use such geoeconomic instruments) in that it is two-sided: the target fights back. And although conflict may eventually resolve, the cost to all sides can be devastating, especially in an interdependent world armed with weapons of mass destruction and disruption. The point is to prevent it.

Capitulation involves one side recoiling at the prospect of conflict, choosing to lose without fighting. It may usher in new coexistence or even cooperation, but on starkly changed terms: one side has permanently accepted major damage to its interests and independence. Much has been said and written about the need to avoid conflict as China asserts itself.[15]

But nations large and small have a deep-seated need to protect their sovereignty – not only their territory but their ability to make independent decisions in line with their national interests, values and identity. Better to have discouraged confrontation in the first place. That is where deterrence comes in, which will be explained shortly.

Compromise sounds ideal, but can be especially difficult in the evolving Indo-Pacific. Here China has connected domestic social stability with the power of the Communist Party, that power with assertiveness abroad, and that assertiveness in turn with expansive geopolitical ambitions and intrusion into foreign societies. Second, and not just in China, nationalism and the amplification effect of constant media focus on every word and every move renders leaders ferociously careful not to lose face. The Trump administration seems to see its economic brinksmanship with China and nuclear brinksmanship with North Korea at least as much through the lenses of domestic electoral politics and presidential ego as through the lens of global stability. Third, the region's multipolar cast means compromise between any two nations – including China and America – may not be in the interests of third countries, and may even contravene them, sowing the seeds of future strife.

Ready or not

At the time of writing, on the eve of the 2020s, the danger signs are accumulating. The overall Indo-Pacific situation is somewhere at the competition point on the spectrum, with confrontation and conflict a rising danger and constant risk. It is neither peace nor war, but continuous and comprehensive competition, covering many aspects of national power.

To its credit, the United States has called out some of China's transgressions, especially in market manipulation, geoeconomic coercion and technology theft. But America's subsequent actions have been anything but reassuring to the world. If Donald Trump is, in his own words, 'the chosen one' to confront China, then heaven help us all.

To the detriment of America and most others, Washington is getting competition and confrontation back to front: America is stepping up to confront China without having done the vital preparatory work of competing with it first. That involves a long list of credibility gaps for the United States: getting its own house in order, demonstrating leadership, honouring its long-declared values, cultivating allies, respectfully wooing non-aligned nations, investing properly in infrastructure, rebuilding the national scientific research base, and prioritising the Indo-Pacific in defence deployments. Beijing may well have been caught off guard and off balance, with Washington declaring an end to constructive engagement before China was ready – but there's little sign that America or its allies are ready either.

Unreadiness does not stop war, however; it may even hasten it. In confrontation and conflict, the rules are largely cast aside. In that sense, we are already moving into territory more perilous than managed competition. Conflict rarely turns out the way either protagonist intended: any strategy is a plan an adversary seeks to thwart.[16]

Thus even as China seems to close its net on Taiwan – with missiles, submarines, amphibious forces, infiltrators and cyber threats – there would still be a daunting quotient of risk in outright invasion. Japan, India and Vietnam are weaker than China, but could still hold their own for long enough to at least call China's bluff or compel it to raise the stakes. And even a short-term 'success' in the use of force by China could unite much of the world against it. Attacking Taiwan, for instance, would effectively be an assault on part of the regional and global economy, entitling other nations to support Taiwan's defence by challenging a Chinese blockade, even while not recognising Taiwan as an independent nation. On the other hand, a military failure could critically harm the legitimacy of Communist Party rule. Use of force by the United States to defend its allies could escalate out of control, while American failure to fight – or an early loss of resolve – could wreck the credibility of its entire global alliance system. This truly would be world-changing, compelling anxious former allies to choose between provocatively arming up or compromising their sovereignty and accepting the dominance of China in Asia, Russia in Europe, and perhaps even Iran in the Middle East.

Setting course for coexistence

China makes no secret of being a revisionist power. It wants to change the international order to suit its expanding interests, and lays claim to territory over which others are willing to fight. It is driving one of the most formidable military transformations in history. At home, its political system is starting to resemble a new kind of 'networked totalitarianism', involving systematic and technology-enabled control, surveillance, fear, falsehood, and the fostering of outrage against enemies, real and perceived, in ways of which Mao, Stalin and Lenin could only have dreamed. The repression of the Uighur people has a chilling resonance with Nazi Germany's imprisonment of Jews and other minorities. The military has a grip on foreign policy, reminiscent at times of the hardline officer class in 1930s Tokyo, a thought doubly tragic given the suffering imperial Japan inflicted on the Chinese people. No matter how generous or jaded one's view of the world, there is no point pretending that this is a normal country in normal times.

Yet since its 20th-century wars against India, Vietnam and US-led UN forces in Korea, China has often shown strategic restraint, even as its capabilities and ambitions have grown. In the years ahead, it will likely keep seeking change through coercion. And it will need to manage carefully the heightened pride and nationalism of public opinion, namely the expectations that the PLA can protect China's interests and punish challengers anywhere, anytime – expectations China's Indo-Pacific push has inflated. Deep down, China's strategic thinkers are no doubt more conscious than those of empires past that their nation has everything to lose by recourse to war. Such war-aversion gives the world something to work with. China also has legitimate security needs: its history provides ample reason to feel constrained by American power, and it defies imagination that China would cede control of sea lanes to the US Navy forever. Fatefully, though, the Chinese leadership has conflated its own regime survival with infringement on other nations' security and interests. It is a recipe for perpetual mistrust.

Under these conditions, fully fledged cooperation is unrealistic for the foreseeable future. In the absence of fundamentally changed international behaviour by the China party-state, the idea that other nations should simply abandon their defensive mindsets or alleged 'Cold War thinking' and build new relations of strategic trust with Beijing is spurious and counter-productive.[17]

Instead, the overriding objective is both simple to define and difficult to attain.

In a word, it is coexistence.

This is about discouraging confrontation, maintaining a healthy level of competition, and moving the dial back closer to coexistence wherever possible. In practice, this may be more a kind of 'competitive coexistence', where a delicate balance is struck between deterring China from aggressive military action and reassuring it that its vital interests will not be attacked.[18] Competitive coexistence is a realistic state of affairs between not only China and America, but also China and Japan, and in the long run China and India.[19]

To sustain this, what is needed is a finely calibrated combination of three instruments: development, deterrence and diplomacy. These must be underpinned by two qualities: solidarity and resilience. In all, these are five new principles of coexistence for the Indo-Pacific age. On their own, none of these would succeed. Together, and in mutual reinforcement, they offer the best chance of preventing futures of conflict or capitulation.

Development: building the future

No amount of railing against China's geoeconomic powerplay, the Belt and Road, will succeed if it is simply about telling poor countries to say no to Beijing's loans and apparent largesse. Where poverty and underdevelopment remain pressing burdens for ordinary people, warnings about sovereignty, democracy, security and the balance of power will simply not fill the gap. For those nations that would manage or constrain Chinese power, therefore, development remains crucial. This does not mean an outright rejection of Chinese economic and aid programs. It will be important to distinguish those initiatives that have adjusted to involve the co-leadership of many nations – notably the Asian Infrastructure

Investment Bank (which America and Japan should join) – from those that remain China First in their objectives and impact.

The struggle will be fought with aid and loans, education and training, infrastructure and investment. Western nations that have long been accustomed to telling developing countries what's best for them – even when expressed in the most progressive and enlightened terms – need to think again. Conversely, a donor nation can undermine its own strategic aims if it loses patience and bluntly reminds aid recipients of its prerogatives – an important caution to America, Australia and others to stay humble as they seek to balance Chinese influence in the South Pacific.

But nor is there any point pretending that self-interest has nothing to do with the new race to help other nations. It makes perfect sense to focus on 'capacity building', such as Japanese and Australian efforts to train coast guard forces and provide boats, maritime monitoring and communications systems to partners from Vietnam to Indonesia, the Solomon Islands to Sri Lanka. This needs to be stepped up, so that more nations can protect their own sovereignty as China's capabilities and encroachments grow.

Deterrence: holding the line

Deterrence can be an ugly word, stirring the spectre of nuclear weapons and Cold War tension. But when it works, it is far preferable to conflict. Its basic message is that the costs of a certain course of action (typically military aggression) outweigh the benefits – so don't do it. Deterrence is about 'deliberate, purposive threats' that essentially succeed if they persuade the adversary not to act.[20] Deterrence is not simply about military power, threats and arms races. It goes hand in glove with diplomacy, requiring clear communication of capability, will and intent. The 'extended' deterrence of protecting allies – for decades an American military stock-in-trade – has often been more about reassuring them than dissuading those who would do them harm. Key questions are: what will effective deterrence look like in the future Indo-Pacific, and what can be done to promote it?

Undoubtedly the deterrence picture is changing. As the previous chapter outlines, China's military power has grown with breathtaking speed, and has provided a shield for assertive actions below provocation to full-blown conflict. At the end of the scale – a major air-sea battle, cyber conflict, nuclear threats – China almost certainly remains weaker than America, and in theory would lose. But harm would be mutual, perhaps immeasurable, and China may bank on America being unwilling to pay the price of 'victory'. China's dramatic capability advances, such as massed short- and medium-range missiles, fit well with a warfighting strategy of seeking a fait accompli. This would involve moving swiftly to knock frontline American forces out of the fight, then deterring America and its allies from assembling reinforcements and striking back.[21]

That is why it would be a fearsome folly for America to reduce its Indo-Pacific strategy to some kind of nuclear-armed pivot to Asia. Sad to say, nuclear weapons still matter; they cannot simply be wished away as catastrophic anachronisms of the 20th century. But nor can America or its allies afford to stake the credibility of their deterrence on a willingness to escalate conflict to the nuclear level. If nuclear weapons become the lone pillar for deterring China in the ocean of ambiguity between peace and Armageddon, then the contest is lost.

Instead, the United States and all those who favour its version of a balance of power need to regain an edge in conventional military force, in future technologies and in geoeconomic resilience – a capacity to resist pressure, and to exert it too. They need to restore deterrence in both its forms: the denial of gains to an adversary, and the ability to strike back.[22] This will involve sustained military modernisation, committed investment and a willingness to fail, with the new tools of warfare – such as cyber, artificial intelligence, space, new materials, robotics and advanced computing – in tandem with a new diplomacy to set rules about those very capabilities.

In any case, much of the important change in the region will be from third countries – powers in the middle – looking to their own devices. Deterrence of China is no longer unspoken in the military planning of other powers, such as Japan, Australia, Vietnam, Indonesia and Singapore. In India, it was always plainly put. What remains to be seen is whether they can build credible enough capabilities to discourage China in a crisis – or at least to demonstrate their willingness to keep it at bay and even hit back – all as a warning against conflict starting at all. The increased tempo of middle-player militaries training together is the most tangible manifestation of the diplomatic trend towards coalitions and collective self-help. This needs to extend now to a genuine willingness among small groups of nations to aggregate their forces, both to hold the line in the balance of power and to counter destabilising actions or outright aggression in a crisis.[23]

At the same time, can nations team up to balance against China with sufficient flexibility that alliance commitments don't unintentionally or irreversibly escalate tensions, a major cause of the First World War? How can frontline players such as Taiwan, Japan and Vietnam feel protected against aggression yet not so emboldened as to risk unnecessary provocation of China? How to reassure China's potential targets that they will not stand alone, while avoiding an action–reaction spiral of automatic mobilisation of alliances?

There is a fine line between solidarity and flexibility. This will require forthright and sophisticated diplomacy not only among treaty allies, notably the United States, Australia and Japan, but also with their emerging strategic partners such as India, Indonesia and Vietnam. Dialogue needs to be frequent and frank, including at the political level. This should be informed by practical working groups on issues like intelligence and logistics. Crisis scenarios need to be candidly considered and wargamed. The public would be surprised to know how little contingency planning is actually discussed between most nations. For many years, the polite assumption of diplomacy among Indo-Pacific countries seems to have been that talking about war would make it more likely; the opposite is now true. Partners need a clearer sense of each other's national priorities and decision processes, what they could reasonably expect of each other in a crisis, and what should be agreed thresholds for action.[24] Such assessment of future risk cannot revolve simply around scenarios of all-out war. Most frictions will fall short of major armed conflict, such as the serial micro-aggressions by paramilitary coast guard forces, state-backed fishing fleets and island-builders in the South China Sea. Nations, both alone and in partnership, need to plan their deterrence not only as a ladder of escalating steps but as a 'crosscutting web' of options for anticipating and discouraging a wide range of coercive activity in this 'grey zone'.[25]

Diplomacy: shared Indo-Pacific visions

On its own, diplomacy cannot avert conflict in the Indo-Pacific. But diplomatic avenues are a long way from exhausted.

The sheer scale of the Indo-Pacific – taking in fairly much half the world – does not lend itself to a single overarching organisation. Multilateral structures like the ASEAN Regional Forum have been found wanting, constrained by their lowest-common-denominator traditions of consensus, a 'pace comfortable to all', and the ASEAN custom of speak no evil.

Yet the interests of the region's many stakeholders cannot be left to the whim of great-power bilateralism, where the United States and China – or even, in the future, China and India – pursue their own harmony, however temporary, at the expense of others. A so-called Concert of Powers has sometimes been advocated.[26] This sounds harmonious and stable enough but, crudely, means a stitch-up among a handful of the most powerful to respect each other's spheres of influence and allow them to suppress smaller nations within that space. As such, it is unlikely to arise, or to function for long. The most renowned such concert arose in Europe from the ruins of the order-shattering Napoleonic wars, after successful balancing against a hegemon. It was based on regimes' shared (reactionary) values, and did not extend to overseas territories or maritime empires.[27] Now that China sees its Belt and Road sphere as impinging permanently on the interests of others, such as India and Japan, it is difficult to conceive how a 'concert' among them, or with America, would work.

Some hope lies in the new wave of minilateralism. These groups, such as trilaterals and the US–India–Japan–Australia quad, are islands of trust.

Their logic is largely about balancing China, a kind of latent deterrence. But they could potentially be stepping stones towards cooperative activity involving many countries. Of course, much depends on how carefully the associated diplomacy is handled: it is quite possible that less-aligned nations such as the Southeast Asians will remain wary of what they see as divisive blocs. Still, the option should be kept open for future minilateral cooperation that includes China: for instance, in disaster relief or evacuation missions. This would require basic agreement on rules and principles.

The more complete answer is a hybrid: a layered diplomacy with elements of bilateralism, multilateralism and practical minilateralism in between. This may be untidy and labour intensive – stretching the diplomatic resources of even large countries – but at least it is comprehensive and flexible.

In any case, endless meetings are not enough. So-called confidence-building measures for practical risk reduction need to be expanded, formalised and put to use. The whole point of such measures is not some utopia of complete trust among powerful nations, but to build stability and predictability under conditions of mistrust. Every foreign navy, air force and coast guard likely to encounter China's forces should pursue agreements, protocols and communication channels for managing incidents.[28] Sometimes such rules exist but remain poorly implemented. Hotlines may go unanswered. Codes to manage unplanned encounters at sea are useless when such clashes were planned. Political leaders need to take confidence-building measures seriously and not just treat them as convenient diplomatic agreements that are signed and not put into operation – these steps will more than prove their worth if they manage a single crisis. Dialogue is required on the exceptionally difficult work of extending CBMs and limitations to new capabilities: cyber, autonomous weapons, even the eventual use of artificial intelligence in war. What are the rules, what are the ethics? Is some kind of transparency and predictability possible? When it comes to regulating and limiting the new modes of combat, we are in an era akin to the nuclear 1950s – when atomic war was deemed winnable and arms control a distant dream.

The immediate danger remains at sea. Wherever China – or anyone – refuses to either agree on maritime risk-reduction measures or bother using them in a crisis, this needs to be exposed for what it is: recklessness and aggression. Such was the case in 2019 with incursions of a Chinese fishing fleet, coast guard escort and oil survey vessels into Vietnam's 200-nautical-mile exclusive economic zone.[29]

Despite China's island-building, the South China Sea remains a shared space, part of the global commons, the heart of the Indo-Pacific, a central commercial highway and every nation's business. Nations would be well within their rights to empower the ASEAN Regional Forum or the East Asia Summit to oversee the monitoring of its fisheries and endangered environment, or to maintain a public database of incidents and reported breaches of the peace. This would be an opportunity for Beijing to prove its win-win rhetoric. If China objected, that itself would prove a point.

Much will depend on how nations choose to use the current window of pan-regional awareness. The most elaborate diplomatic structures are useless if nations choose not to use them. This is a fertile time for diplomatic initiatives involving or led by middle players such as Australia, Indonesia, Singapore, India and Japan.

That is where the Indo-Pacific concept becomes a strength, with all its ambiguities and dualities. It is easy to pick up semantic differences in official statements to suggest that, rather than uniting against China, many nations want quite different things when they proclaim their visions for an Indo-Pacific order. Japan and America want an unabashedly 'free and open' region, casting China as the problem; the Southeast Asians favour harmony and inclusivity and seem especially uneager to kindle the wrath of the Chinese dragon; and Australia and India are somewhere in between, which positions them well to identify and expand common ground. Certainly, beneath all the talk, there is an unresolved tension. Is the Indo-Pacific framework a means to compel the many middle players to choose between the United States and China? Or is it a platform for all powers to engage both countries in efforts to manage their strategic competition, and prevent it from turning to confrontation or conflict?

In search of solidarity

Yet what is striking are the similarities across the various visions of the Indo-Pacific. It is a rallying call, a code for diluting and absorbing Chinese power. That is part of the point. Every nation that has joined the Indo-Pacific bandwagon – including America – has emphasised rules, norms, international law, the rights and sovereignty of small states and the rejection of coercion. Respect for the centrality of ASEAN and its regional institutions is another consistent refrain, including from non-ASEAN powers such as India, Japan, Australia and the United States. Connections across the two oceans are regularly acknowledged as a feature of the new era. Together, these principles chart a convergence of Indo-Pacific perspectives, providing a basis for solidarity.

This creation of a more unified regional approach to handling a strong China will demand give and take, particularly between an ASEAN that is too timid and an America that is too insensitive to other countries' views. If Southeast Asian nations are serious about respecting rules and rejecting coercion, they will need to use and strengthen their institutions, such as the East Asia Summit, to hold China to account for its acts of intimidation.[30] For its part, if the United States is genuine about promoting regional connectivity, development and prosperity, it will need to take much more notice of regional partners' interests in moderating its own long-term economic and technological competition with China.

In responding to China's power, Indo-Pacific solidarity provides an alternative to the extremes of containment or accommodation: a third way that could be termed 'incorporation' or 'conditional engagement'. This involves a calibrated combination of engagement and balancing. It would be about including China as a legitimate power across the region but in ways where there is mutual adjustment and mutual respect – China will have to adjust to the interests and sensitivities of others, such as India, just as others will need to adjust to China's. It means accepting a major role for China, but on the region's terms rather than on China's alone, while preparing for more active balancing if such engagement founders.

This approach is distinct from the simple geographic 'spheres of influence' idea propounded by some scholars, the notion that by sketching new lines on maps China can keep to one side, America (or Japan or India or whoever) to another, and peace will thus prevail. Variants of this include suggestions that China should be allowed to dominate East Asia, while India manages the Indian Ocean, America withdraws to the eastern Pacific and Taiwan finds itself abandoned to the PRC side of a revised 'defensive perimeter'.[31] Such demarcation does not work in a complex and dynamic Indo-Pacific region, where many players have interests and agency, and where Beijing has extended security, geoeconomic and political influence far from its shores (while moreover showing itself adept at shedding past agreements, such as over Hong Kong). Pursuing stability through conditional engagement would be based less on positioning and more on behaviour. This approach accepts that China will have a presence and interests in many places, and that others – including America, India and Japan – have the same right to a sustained and expansive role across the region. But where there is breach of the principle of non-coercion and the rights of smaller states, then multiple Indo-Pacific nations can be expected to pursue solidarity in resistance.

The counter-argument to solidarity is easy enough to conjure. Nations act in their own interests. A great power will coerce or co-opt them one at a time. No nation will risk its survival for the interests of another. Would America really be willing to chance major war over little Taiwan? For all their fraternal display, symbolised by the Modi–Abe train ride back in 2016, would Japan or India (or, for that matter, Australia) ever be so crazy-brave as to open a second front in someone else's conflict with China?

But solidarity among nations doesn't exist purely in the military realm. Alliances, coalitions and political courage are not only about force of arms. True, China's leverage is often about compelling smaller countries – or private entities – to submit in isolation. In this, Beijing has been intimidatingly creative. Where normal diplomacy does not go its way, it detains individual hostages – from Canada, Australia, even the local staff of the British consulate in Hong Kong. It mobilises nationalist anger to imperil the bottom line for foreign companies that don't toe its line against Taiwan or human rights or US alliances. It coerces nations singly in the grey zone that is neither peace nor war, with encroachment by state-backed civilian forces at sea, sometimes with gunboats too, or sanctions of economic disfavour, or simply by withholding diplomatic dialogue on important problems.

That is all the more reason for other powers to seek safety in numbers, to build a diplomatic phalanx of common cause. However discreetly, a priority should be dialogues to identify how nations can take a united stand against unacceptable behaviour in domains like geoeconomics and greyzone coercion. Too often there is a counsel of despair around cabinet tables and boardrooms: China can hurt us; it is big and we are small; we're on our own; there's nothing we can do except comply. The United Front Work Department could not script it better.

The way out is to set boundaries before confrontations begin, and to set them in solidarity: understandings or even formal agreements for collective and defensive action in such areas as geoeconomics, international law, cyber security, human rights, diplomacy and the countering of propaganda. Nations could agree on minimum common standards to engage with Belt and Road projects: India's 2017 statement about governance, transparency and the environment would be a good place to start. The Blue Dot Network, led by the United States, Japan and Australia, is a step in the right direction, but will only succeed with wider buy-in.[32] A common stance affirming the 'non-interference' principle of coexistence could prepare the ground for more concerted resistance against influence operations.

Nations could confer on applying uniform sanctions against entities implicated in China's coercion abroad, such as sand-dredging companies in the South China Sea, or agents of interference inside democracies. More contentious, given the non-interference principle, would be efforts to coordinate action against individuals or organisations involved in extreme cases of internal repression. Foreign ministries could coordinate on consular travel advice, moving together to warn their citizens of the dangers of arbitrary arrest and 'hostage diplomacy' in the new China. Perhaps most difficult of all, corporations could together declare common values on issues like human rights and freedom of expression, making it harder for

China to penalise them individually. Universities have been awoken by Hong Kong–related campus protests in such countries as Australia, Canada, New Zealand, Britain and America. This has compounded with direct experience of cyber attacks and ultimatums from government to encourage universities to set boundaries to their China connections.[33]

Collective or at least coordinated pushback against authoritarian power may sound idealistic and far-fetched, more hope than strategy. Some early efforts have been made, but they remain limited in scope and effectiveness. Europe is looking to establish its own sanction regime based on America's Global Magnitsky Act, a law targeting individuals operating at the nexus of espionage, organised crime and human rights abuses.[34] Pressure is mounting for the US administration to apply such sanctions to Chinese officials and businesses involved in repression in Xinjiang or Hong Kong, but how readily smaller powers will take similar measures remains to be seen. The 2016 international legal ruling favouring the Philippines against China in the South China Sea provided third nations a chance to collectively assert international rights of navigation, notably through a statement by the G7 countries, though this was somewhat undercut by Manila's failure to press its own claim. More promisingly, in December 2018, the governments of seven nations – the US-led Five Eyes intelligence alliance plus Japan and Germany – united in calling out China for massive cyber theft, collectively accusing the Chinese intelligence–backed hacking group ATP10 of ransacking the intellectual property of companies worldwide via managed service providers.[35]

At a human level, as solidarity grows with ordinary citizens bearing the brunt of CCP oppression – perhaps hastened by the highly visible trauma of Hong Kong – there is likely to be greater global mobilisation of public opinion to push governments and corporations to draw lines in their relations with China. Social mobilisation through social media in a connected world has achieved great things in civilising corporations on slave labour, racism and gender equality; it is not unimaginable that it could happen on other human rights issues too. It is an unpleasant reality that the private sector tends to prioritise human rights only when it chimes sufficiently with profit, reputation and business sustainability. But corporations are also beginning to learn that conceding to China's worldview only wins temporary reprieve, not permanent business advantage, and raises the expectation that further concessions will always be possible. Moreover, China may learn in time that serial bullying of foreign corporations is bad for its own business: damaging the international reputations of those companies most willing to tolerate its demands, and discouraging new foreign investors in China.[36]

Yet, it may reasonably be asked, would a middle-power government or lone corporation truly be so foolhardy as to make the first move in assembling a coalition against mighty China? The 'hostage diplomacy' against two Canadians is a case in point: some countries have openly sympathised with their plight and the coercion against Canada, but this has not led to any kind of effective international retaliation, or deterrence of further such acts. Meanwhile, Australia remains sensitive to Beijing's accusations that it is the 'ringleader' in international efforts to restrict Huawei. The Philippines under Duterte has almost disowned its own South China Sea legal victory. Over the Senkaku Islands, Doklam and the South China Sea, India, Japan and Vietnam have sometimes each stood their ground against China to the brink of war, but eventually rebalanced relations with conciliatory talk – until next time. Any nation, other than America, making itself the frontline target in setting limits to Chinese power can afford to do so only for a short time. For small countries and corporations alike, lone defiance seems more brave than sensible. Of course, international groupings or industry bodies would stand a better chance of effective defiance – but solidarity would need to be mustered first.

And solidarity is more likely and effective if big powers are involved, especially the United States. For the foreseeable future, the America factor remains vital. This need not always require US leadership but it does require US involvement. There are structural reasons for the United States to balance China in the Indo-Pacific – investment, trade, alliances, technology, security. These have been reflected in strong words and some measures from the Trump administration, as well as signals of Congressional bipartisanship. Yet important uncertainties linger. Will Trump's notorious unreliability – such as his abandonment of the Kurds – prove aberration or harbinger? Can America's continued Middle East entanglement complement rather than detract from Indo-Pacific commitment?

Prominent American security thinker Kori Schake has provided a blueprint for middle players to step up globally and hold the line in preserving a liberal rules-based order against China (and sometimes against America itself) as Washington recovers its sanity.[37] Middle powers are stronger than they think, she notes, and it's time to reverse the 'enfeeblement of middle powers in their own imagination'.

This revival of the middle could occur in different but mutually reinforcing ways at the global and regional levels. On global issues such as trade, environment, human rights and the protection of a rules-based order, Europe has a major role to play, and could yet position itself along with Japan, Canada and Australia at the core of middle-player coalitions, much as German foreign minister Heiko Maas has envisaged with what he terms an 'alliance for multilateralism'.[38] In the Indo-Pacific, a greater role looms for Japan, India, Indonesia, Vietnam, South Korea and Australia. It is worth reiterating that by the 2040s, the combination of Japan, India and Indonesia is projected to outweigh China in GDP, military spending and population. Add just one or two more nations and this would be a hefty coalition, especially given the natural advantages of geography, namely its combined oversight of much of the strategic waterways of the Indo-Pacific.

Of course, merely buying time for America's troubles to pass seems a somewhat desperate fallback, not a solution. How long do we have to wait? And what on earth would global order look like by the end of a second Trump administration? But perhaps these questions belie the current reality that the United States does remain active in the Indo-Pacific – unpredictable, yes, but not passive. Where it can be motivated to act, and to act responsibly, America retains enormous power as a potential prime mover and leader of balancing coalitions – or even just a major player among them. At the same time, beyond the 2020s, China may well become more constrained by its own internal challenges while struggling to control its proliferating interests abroad.

But if other Indo-Pacific nations end up attempting to set limits to Chinese power, with America or without, they need to be willing to pay a price, to endure short-term pain for long-term security. To do so, they need foresight, political will and, above all, resilience.

In the end, resilience

Resilience is a special kind of strength. When Vietnamese and Chinese coast guard ships were jostling to control oil and gas exploration close to Vietnam's coastline in the South China Sea, a Vietnamese diplomat fielded a barrage of questions in a meeting with foreign academics. If tomorrow his country got into a war with China, who would come to its aid? 'The answer is easy,' the diplomat replied, unfazed. 'The Vietnamese people.'

His nation, he explained, was thus working to increase its own power, and what it was seeking most from foreign friends was help in developing the capacity to protect itself. For those of us on the other side of the table, it was a credible reply. After all, Vietnam has seen (and done) it all – from coping with a thousand years of the vicissitudes of Chinese power to humbling a mighty America within living memory.[39]

Nations large and small need to make themselves less breakable. This is not about being particularly rich or powerful, or adopting a fortress mentality and obsessing about every risk. It is about being able to handle hardship and recover. Countries can no longer treat their different approaches to the world in isolation from each other – foreign affairs, economics, social policy, education, industry, technology, energy, national security. In a connected world, where a revisionist power is determined to knit together the strength of Party, state, military, diplomacy and commerce, others are at a disadvantage, liberal democracies especially so. (In that sense, there are limits to the example of communist Vietnam, although its resistance to foreign power seems more a manifestation of popular will and nationalism than of Party dictates.)

How can democratic nations improve their resilience? The answer is not to become more like Xi's party-state by insisting that regime survival equals national security and that national security overrides all other considerations. Rather, it is to strive to build a more inclusive narrative on what the nation is seeking to achieve and protect in a contested region. If defining and protecting the national interest remains the preserve of a small security caste of officials and experts, then it will be impossible to harness anything like the full extent of a nation's power to cope with coercion or the general turbulence of a contested Indo-Pacific.

Within governments, this means a genuine integration of policy across security, and economics, diplomacy and the information or narrative sphere. Policy-making needs to get beyond the false dichotomy of economics versus security, which handicaps a coherent response to the China challenge. The trap here lies in thinking that defensive decisions to limit Chinese power – for instance, curtailing PRC involvement in national infrastructure or dual-use technology research – will have unbearable economic consequences.

This zero-sum attitude, which pits prosperity against security, breaks down as soon as we look beyond the parochialism of the present. Prosperity and security may seem rivals in the short run, but they are interdependent over the long term. Over the time horizon of a generation – looking forward, say, twenty-five years – the consequences of granting an authoritarian giant dominance over technology and geography are not confined to security concerns (or threats to democratic values). They also threaten long-term economic disadvantage. On the other hand, policy-makers must not forget that blunt trade restrictions – notably, Trump-style tariffs – are not only grim for business, but in the long run are bad for security, reducing not only every country's ability to pay for its defences but also the goodwill of allies.

As well as thinking forward, into the future, governments need to think sideways when it comes to reimagining the national interest. Security is too important to be the purview of security agencies alone. Policy domains like environment, energy and education need to be understood not only for their intrinsic value but for their crucial contribution to national resilience. For example, there's no net national gain in talking a big talk diplomatically or modernising a military without also ensuring energy supply – including sustainable and renewable sources – or preparing a future workforce with skills from cyber to critical thinking. In universities, corporations and government agencies, it will be futile to block or regulate questionable links with Chinese research money if other funding sources more aligned with the national interest are not forthcoming.

Resilience requires not only a more connected approach across government, but an open and inclusive conversation within each nation about what is at stake in the new era of strategic competition. Within the cloisters of many intelligence services and other government departments there are now acute and well-informed concerns about the state of the world: both in big strategic pictures and detailed assessments. But this illumination is typically classified, for privileged eyes, and denied to citizens – even to most of their elected representatives. No wonder that when many people hear sound bites of the strategic powerplay – South China Sea, Belt and Road, foreign interference – they imagine the risks remote, exaggerated or not their problem. In a democracy like Australia, there is a desperate need for the strategic side of government to communicate better with civil society, business and across the political spectrum. It is short-sighted and counterproductive, for instance, that in Australia the government has not allowed the Opposition to receive China briefings from security agencies.[40] Such engagement has begun extending to business and universities – often frontline targets in cyber and influence operations. In federal systems, such as Australia and Canada, intelligence outreach needs to extend to state and provincial governments as well.

National conversations about security in an era of geopolitical struggle will demand high levels of political maturity. It is imperative not to reduce the discourse to partisan point-scoring or, worse still, to the kind of paranoia that makes citizens of Chinese origin feel that they are being made to look like part of the problem. In multicultural societies, this will be an acute challenge. Yet if in democracies the left and the moderate centre choose to be silent on issues of strategic competition with China and the CCP's export of repression and censorship, then the task of building an inclusive and resilient national response will only get harder.

Open waters

Call it what you will, the Asia-centric maritime zone we now call the Indo-Pacific is the place where the future of the world will be charted. This super-region is defined in part by China's expanding interests and power, the pushback of others, and the interplay of many rising players. But it is a map that won't be drawn by China alone. Indeed, China's greatest challenge in the Indo-Pacific may not be its imagined enemies but rather itself, as it expands into a space that tempts imperial overreach but ends up punishing it too. As with empires past, China's actions are helping to breed black swans and black elephants all over the Indo-Pacific. And the headlong speed of China's quasi-colonial expansion means that, for everyone, the chances and impacts of a collision are all the greater – especially when the new geopolitical motorway is being built faster than drivers can learn the rules of the road.

There's also the serious question of maintenance. Does China truly have a world-beating military edge? Given that more than half of the cost of a military is 'sustainment' – constantly maintaining and upgrading capabilities after they are built – can China retain a leading place even if it gets there? Already there are reports that the PLA's high-tech island fortresses in the South China Sea are struggling to cope with heat, humidity and storms.[41] The more a nation advances in its defence technology, the more it has to keep spending each year simply to stand still. America, for its part, has found that the bigger and costlier the force, the harder it is to prevent atrophy. Being a global power is constant and unforgiving.

One of the most pervasive achievements of Chinese soft and sharp power is the widespread belief that time is automatically on Beijing's side. Maybe it is. But there is good reason to consider the prospect that Chinese power, relative not to America but to the rest of the dynamic Indo-Pacific, has already peaked. China has had a transformative and disruptive effect in mapping the past decade but that provides no guarantee that it will lead or dominate in mapping the future.

Instead, if they are the grand strategists they are so often credited to be, the Communist Party's leaders should be giving much attention to these four factors. First, China's Indo-Pacific and Eurasian ambitions along the Belt and Road have a perilous momentum; pushback is happening and more is inevitable. Second, much of the rest of the Indo-Pacific is becoming wealthier and stronger too. China's power relative to its region may never be so great again. Third, America may be down but it is far from out, and it does not need to single-handedly dominate Asia, the Indo-Pacific or the world in order to work with others to balance Chinese power. Fourth, China's internal problems – debt, demographics, environmental stress, discontent – could well worsen, compounding the challenge of the three external factors of pushback, the rise of the rest, and American endurance.

These four factors combine to project a shadow of imperial overstretch. China will face extensive security tests across the vast Indo-Pacific, regardless of whether America sustains full-spectrum strategic rivalry. China will keep provoking anxieties from India and other consequential nations. Sooner or later, Beijing's decision-makers – in a moment either of confidence or nervousness – will likely authorise military action in one or more far-off places, with consequences hard to predict or control. And in a future confrontation with the United States or another major country, China's far-flung outposts and resource supply lines would instantly become liabilities and vulnerabilities. All this will need to be protected, plus borders with many mistrustful neighbours and a few unstable ones. Meanwhile, there will be the need to uphold 'internal' order in a greater China that includes more than a hundred million people with reason to resent the regime. Factor in slowing economic growth, an ageing population demanding that a greater share of wealth be allocated to welfare, and a hard but brittle political system, and the vision of long-term Chinese dominance becomes hazier still. The cost of empire could prompt domestic resentment; the need to retain regime legitimacy at home could encourage forceful action abroad; success in such action will stretch the empire further and worsen the contradictions in the long run, but failure will weaken the regime. It is an old story with a new twist. No nation has ever tried to go as far as fast as China. Yes, it commands stupendous resources. But it combines the complexities of manifold internal and external problems with the rigidities of an authoritarian party-state and a single point of failure at the top.

Of course, things may transpire differently. China may surprise the sceptics by sustaining for decades a techno-authoritarianism of surveillance and convenience, of conformity, intimidation and pride. And in any case, China need not fulfil all the global power ambitions of Xi's China Dream in order to bring wellbeing and stability to most of its people, or to be a continued engine of economic growth beyond its borders. It is an uncertain picture, but there are ways to look for clarity. Once the China-centric powerplay of strategic competition is seen through the wide Indo-Pacific lens and over a generation-long timeframe, the coordinates of a strategic settling point come into focus. If others' resistance to excessive and coercive actions by China can firm up into comprehensive competition, underpinned by resilience, solidarity and deterrence, then Indo-Pacific strategy becomes a kind of full-spectrum staring contest. This is not a happy situation for anyone, but it will give China as much pause as any nation.

Despite its one-party politics and proclaimed grand designs, China continues to have internal differences over what is really to be done. Indeed, it was not so long ago that some foreign analysts were arguing that China's external actions, far from being a strategy, were essentially the dissonant compromise of a cacophony of differing 'policy actors': not just the ruling party, but the military, business, provincial interests, academia and an opinionated online community, not entirely unlike the mix in a more pluralistic society.[42] One scholar went further and suggested that a 'vocal majority' of China's own policy experts wanted 'progressive reform' of Beijing's foreign policy and cooperation with America.[43]

Whatever the merit of such conclusions, the facts then changed. Xi's regime has spent the past seven years steamrolling much of the complexity and intellectual courage out of China's internal conversations on foreign policy. Still, the nation retains a great wealth of strategic talent. By pushing back against Chinese power, the aim for other countries should be to make China think twice. And if this resistance takes the form more of competition than of confrontation, then perhaps more prudent or even moderate voices will eventually be heard again. The debates of the pre-Xi era are suppressed but not dead; for instance, they are beginning to temper and recalibrate some of the recklessness of the early Belt and Road. China is likely to be a self-limiting empire. By protecting themselves, other states will help China find those limits sooner rather than later.[44]

Moreover, as China's challenges amass, so do the chances that there will be occasions when it needs other nations' help, and they its. In response to the 2008 Sichuan earthquake, China received assistance from nations it generally mistrusts. When it comes to disease outbreaks, China has provided help (against Ebola in Africa) and required it (with bird flu and recently swine fever). Chinese forces have become the largest national contribution to United Nations peacekeeping, most notably in South Sudan, but still operate in multinational deployments. In recent years, the Chinese navy's floating hospital, the *Peace Ark*, has provided much-needed medical assistance to coastal communities across several oceans – and scored soft-power gains for China. But large-scale humanitarian assistance functions best when many nations coordinate their public goods. After all, China's own such efforts were inspired by those of the United States (which has deployed hospital ships for decades) and its quad partners, Australia, India and Japan. It would make sense for future mass disaster relief on Indo-Pacific shores to involve coordinated action by, at a minimum, these five powers. Perhaps Beijing can somehow cope with the many things that will inevitably go wrong across the Belt and Road expanse. However, sometimes this will require voluntary cooperation with nations whose interests may otherwise not align with China's.

One last time, Australia's experience is illustrative. In late 2013, Beijing essentially froze diplomatic relations with Canberra after Australia had shown overt solidarity with Japanese and American criticism of China's efforts to control disputed airspace above the East China Sea. On 8 March 2014, Malaysia Airlines Flight 370, with 153 Chinese nationals among its passengers, went missing and was later believed to have crashed into the Indian Ocean. It was a traumatic disaster within China, and a consular

*Dialogue despite mistrust: Australian foreign minister Julie Bishop
and her Chinese counterpart, Wang Yi, in February 2017*

nightmare for a regime increasingly expected to protect its people and their
interests anywhere in the world. Many nations, including China, accepted
Australian coordination of the international search: Australia had the
capacity, the partnerships and the proximity, and the plane had disappeared
somewhere within Australia's huge zone of search and rescue responsibility.
Suddenly, China needed to rapidly rediscover friendship with the southern
land: Chinese foreign minister Wang Yi found himself reaching out to the
same Australian counterpart, Julie Bishop, whom he had earlier shunned.
China's aircraft and ships were invited to join the operation – a coalition
including Japan, South Korea, France, Britain, America and Malaysia –
based out of the very part of Australia, its southwest corner, that is a prime
habitat of the black swan.

The Indigenous people of that place, the Noongar, have a mythology of
ancestral Dreaming stories that imbue this bird, called maali, with subtler
characteristics than some one-dimensional symbol of surprise. The swans
were originally white, but their conceit provoked the fearsome wedge-tailed
eagles to attack and pluck out their feathers. The tale involves cooperation

as well as conflict: the crows intervened, providing black feathers to protect and reclothe the wounded swans. Today their white tail feathers remain as reminders that the black swans are not what they appear, while their beaks remain red from the fight.[45]

The history of geopolitics provides its own lessons. Pride, blowback and rebalancing seem to accompany every empire that tries to rule the Indo-Pacific. This super-region is too vast and complex for any country to succeed in protecting its interests alone. There will be a premium on partnerships. Each nation, each society, will need to help and be helped in navigating new turbulence as power balances adjust. Their watchwords should be multipolarity, solidarity and a confident kind of strategic patience. A path can be charted between conflict and capitulation. The future is not solely in the hands of an authoritarian China or an unpredictable, self-centred America. In the end, the Indo-Pacific is both a region and an idea: a metaphor for collective action, self-help combined with mutual help. If things go badly awry, it could be the place of the first general and catastrophic war since 1945. But if its future can be secured, it can flourish as a shared space at the heart of a reconnected world, in ways its early voyagers could have scarcely imagined.

ACKNOWLEDGEMENTS

This book began in 2012 as a short blog post, which grew to a public lecture and then an array of articles, reports, speeches and university courses. My ambition to bring it all together between two covers kept being deferred, which gave me so much more to write about when the time came. In the interval, the Indo-Pacific has evolved from an intriguing idea into something approaching orthodoxy in the foreign policy settings of many countries. Of course, the tides of world affairs never stop shifting, and when the facts change again, I hope I will be ready to change my mind.

My career has roamed widely, but its path has always been about engaging with history's first draft. Diplomatic assignments brought me to India and Japan and back to the land of my birth, Papua New Guinea. As an intelligence analyst, I watched China and Southeast Asia through the prism of regional security. Since 2007, life in the diplomatic 'second track' of think tanks and universities has unlocked insights from countless experts and officials in dialogues, roundtables, conferences and myriad informal conversations. This is the grey zone – unpublished and often off the record – that provides invaluable early interpretation of world events. My more specialised security research projects – on maritime confidence-building measures, nuclear deterrence, India, China and Australia – have all fed into the Indo-Pacific stream.

Indo-Pacific Empire thus draws together many strands of my experience. But it is far from a solo effort. Its imperfections are of my making, while its better qualities synthesise the contributions of many.

Some brilliant younger analysts have informed and influenced. Notable among them are Fiona Cunningham, Ashley Townshend, Katherine Mansted, James Brown, Danielle Rajendram, Brendan Thomas-Noone, Marty Harris, Darshana Baruah, Dhruva Jaishankar, Geng Chen and Shannon Tow.

Students at the National Security College, Australian National University (ANU), have been kind enough to road-test Indo-Pacific ideas in their coursework. I commend their critical thinking.

Many wise policy-makers and experts have refined my worldview, through inspiration and provocation. They include C. Raja Mohan, Peter Varghese, Doug Kean, Allan Gyngell, Richard Maude, Bruce Miller, James Goldrick, Brendan Sargeant, Kanehara Nobukatsu, Ian Hall, Ric Smith, Ashok Malik, Samir Saran, Tanvi Madan, Nitin Pai, Sujan Chinoy, Anthony Bergin, Allan Behm, Darren Lim, Oriana Skylar Mastro, Anthea Roberts, Bill Tow, Mohan Malik, Andrew Shearer, Hugh White, Euan Graham, David Brewster, Richard Rigby, Richard McGregor, Malcolm Cook, Anthony Bubalo, Gordon Flake, You Ji, Dino Patti Djalal, Ashley Tellis, Mike Green, Zack Cooper, Bonnie Glaser, Ely Ratner, Shen Dingli, Yamato Taro, Tom Wright, Brendan Taylor, Bruno Tertrais and Valérie Niquet.

Extra thanks are due to Katherine Mansted, Darren Lim, James Goldrick, Eva Medcalf, Bruce Miller, Allan Gyngell and Ian Hall for their constructive critiques of the manuscript.

For big thinking, I pay tribute to the late Coral Bell, whose last major work, 'The end of the Vasco da Gama era', was the first paper I edited at the Lowy Institute.

I am proud to lead the ANU National Security College and I commend my colleagues there. They do exceptional work – trusted, independent and without fanfare – in developing new generations of security expertise for Australia's long-term national interest. Particular mention goes to my executive assistant, Laura Florance, and our chief operating officer, Sharon Dean, for their added commitment when I was diverted to book-writing.

Two institutions have been formative in my intellectual journey. The Office of National Assessments, now the Office of National Intelligence, is a stronghold of first-rate analysis, writing and collegiality. I also cannot overlook the Lowy Institute, now led by Michael Fullilove and founded with such vision by Frank Lowy. It gave me space to think anew about policy, push Indo-Pacific boundaries, and join the public debate. For their part in the pivotal decisions that led me to those places, I will always thank Doug Kean and Allan Gyngell.

My thanks also to Kay Dancey and ANU CartoGIS Services, my university's own geospatial agency, for such professionalism in preparing some of this book's key maps.

Too much security research and commentary is removed from direct experience. The Royal Australian Navy is on a mission to correct that. My thanks to the Chief of Navy, Vice Admiral Michael Noonan, Captain Sean Andrews of the Sea Power Centre, and the crew and then commanding officer, Captain Ashley Papp, of HMAS *Canberra*, for the opportunity to 'sea ride', as they say, in May 2019.

I've learned that authors mean it when they thank their publishers. Black Inc. and La Trobe University Press have done a superlative job. Chris Feik stopped my tiresome talk about writing a book through the canny means of commissioning one. But special thanks to the project's talented and tolerant editor, Jo Rosenberg, who did so much to compel clarity and make the book real. And acknowledgement too of Manchester University Press, and notably Jonathan de Peyer, for taking the leap with this international edition.

I am grateful to many people for many things, but above all to my cherished family. My dear parents, Faith and Max, for their long confidence in all my endeavours. My marvellous children, Edgar and Frida, for making everything worthwhile. And to my wife, Eva, whose love, wit, patience and uncommon sense steer us through every strait, always to splendid horizons.

IMAGE CREDITS

Inside front cover: Map by Abraham Ortelius of Antwerp, *Indiae Orientalis Insularumque Adiacientium Typus*, from the atlas *Theatrum Orbis Terrarum*, 1570

p. 2: Abe Shinzō and Narendra Modi
Copyright: unknown; source: Raveesh Kumar's Twitter, @MEAIndia

p. 32: Thomas Mitchell's map
Thomas Mitchell, *Journal of an Expedition into the Interior of Tropical Australia in Search of a Route from Sydney to the Gulf of Carpentaria*, Longman, Brown, Green and Longmans, London, 1848

p. 61: Gandhi addressing the Asian Relations Conference
Copyright: unknown; source: WikiCommons

p. 87: Chinese crewmen being held captive by Somali pirates
Copyright: Mass Communication Specialist 2nd Class Jason R. Zalasky; source: Wikicommons

p. 107: Indo-Pacific shipping lanes map
Adapted from a map published by the Australian government in official documents in 2012 and 2013, notably Commonwealth of Australia, '2013 Defence White Paper', Canberra. Map prepared by CartoGIS Services, College of Asia and the Pacific, The Australian National University

p. 127: Xi Jinping in military uniform
Copyright: unknown; source: AP

p. 163: Joko Widodo's inauguration speech
Copyright: Adi Weda/EPA/AAP

p. 177: The Australian navy flagship entering Tanjung Priok
Copyright: Rory Medcalf

p. 197: The Belt and Road
This map, showing some of the key corridors and features of the Chinese Belt and Road Initiative, is adapted from a 2018 map published by the Mercator Institute for China Studies (MERICS). Map prepared by CartoGIS Services, College of Asia and the Pacific, The Australian National University

p. 200: The opening ceremony at China's Djibouti military base
Copyright: Voice of America

p. 213: China's first aircraft carrier
Copyright: AFP Contributor/Contributor/Getty

p. 267: Julie Bishop and Wang Yi
Copyright: Mick Tsikas/AAP

Inside back cover: Map by Hao Xiaoguang, Institute of Geodesy and Geophysics, Chinese Academy of Sciences, 'A new version of world map published', 2013

NOTES

Chapter 1: Of Names, Maps and Power

1   Ministry of External Affairs of the Republic of India, 'India–Japan joint statement during the visit of Prime Minister to Japan', 11 November 2016.

2   This analysis builds on several previous publications by the author, including 'Pivoting the map: Australia's Indo-Pacific system', Centre of Gravity Series, No. 1, Strategic and Defence Studies Centre, Australian National University, November 2012; 'The Indo-Pacific: What's in a name?' *American Interest*, October 2013; 'Reimagining Asia: From Asia-Pacific to Indo-Pacific', *Asian Forum*, 26 June 2015; '*La Chine et l'Indo-Pacifique: Multipolarité, solidarité et patience stratégique*' [China and the Indo-Pacific: Multipolarity, solidarity and strategic patience], *Revue Défense Nationale*, No. 811, 2018; and 'Indo-Pacific visions: Giving solidarity a chance', *Asia Policy*, Vol. 14, No. 3, July 2019.

3   Geoff Raby, 'China relations can only be unfrozen with Julie Bishop's sacking', *Australian Financial Review*, 14 May 2018. Raby runs a Beijing-based business advisory firm and is a former Australian ambassador to China.

4   Bill Birtles, 'China mocks Australia over "Indo-Pacific" concept it says will "dissipate"', ABC News, 8 March 2018. Some analysts suggest China's response to the Indo-Pacific is merely 'nonchalance', although if this were the case then perhaps China's official position would be either to ignore the construct or to accept it as harmless. Feng Zhang, 'China's curious nonchalance towards the Indo-Pacific', *Survival*, Vol. 61, No. 3, 2019.

5   Robert Kaplan, 'Center stage for the 21st century: Power plays in the Indian Ocean', *Foreign Affairs*, March/April 2009.

6   Barry Buzan, 'Security architecture in Asia: The interplay of regional and global levels', *The Pacific Review*, Vol. 16, No. 2, 2003, pp. 145–148.

7   A similar point is made by Amitav Acharya, *The End of American World Order*, Polity Press, London, 2014, p. 82.

8   Mu Chunshan, 'What is CICA (and why does China care about it)?', *The Diplomat*, 17 May 2014.

9   Bilahari Kausikan, 'An expose of how states manipulate other countries' citizens', *The Straits Times*, 1 July 2018.

10   For instance, Australian government Treasury estimates about the relative size of the two economies provide a starting point for prominent Australian scholar Hugh White in his case for his country to fashion a defence policy that assumes the absence or irrelevance of a US alliance. Hugh White, *How to Defend Australia*, La Trobe University Press, Melbourne, 2019, p. 9. Some other experts reach very different conclusions. For instance, American scholar Michael Beckley has developed a 'balance sheet' approach to measuring power, subtracting liabilities like welfare and domestic security from GDP, and accordingly concludes that the United States will continue to outrank China in power by an order of magnitude. Michael Beckley, *Unrivaled: Why America Will Remain the World's Sole Superpower*, Cornell University Press, Ithaca, 2018, pp. 1–3.

11   Data combined from multiple sources, including: United Nations, Department of Economic and Social Affairs, Population Division, 'World population prospects 2019',

Medium fertility variant; PricewaterhouseCoopers, 'The long view: How will the global economic order change by 2050?', February 2017, pp. 23, 68; Stockholm International Peace Research Institute, 'Military expenditure by country, in constant 2017 US$ 1988–2018'.

12 There is much debate over the reliability of official Chinese data. On possible fabrication of economic statistics, see Yi Fuxian, 'China's population numbers are almost certainly inflated to hide the harmful legacy of its family planning policy', *South China Morning Post*, 20 July 2019.

13 This section builds on an analysis originally provided in Rory Medcalf and C. Raja Mohan, 'Responding to Indo-Pacific rivalry: Australia, India and middle power coalitions', Lowy Institute Analysis, 2014.

14 Author's private conversation with a senior government official well placed to analyse the November 2016 Modi–Abe meeting.

15 Abe Shinzō, 'Address by Prime Minister Shinzō Abe at the opening session of the Sixth Tokyo International Conference on African Development (TICAD VI)', Nairobi, 27 August 2016.

16 Brahma Chellaney, 'Building a "Free and Open" Indo-Pacific', *The Japan Times*, 21 November 2018.

17 There is reportedly even a designated 'Japan ombudsman' empowered to champion the relationship on all issues within India's Ministry of External Affairs; see Thomas F. Lynch III, 'An Indo-Pacific romance', *The National Interest*, March/April 2019, p. 53.

18 No single scholar or official can claim fully to have coined the term 'Indo-Pacific' in its 21st-century strategic sense. The first modern academic article to mention the Indo-Pacific as a geopolitical term was by Canadian naval scholar James Boutilier in 2004, followed by New Zealand maritime expert Peter Cozens and Australian journalist Michael Richardson in 2005, and Indian naval officer Gurpreet Khurana in 2007. Prominent Indian and American strategic thinkers, such as C. Raja Mohan and Michael Auslin, also began publishing the term around 2008. The author was aware of some Australian and Canadian government analysts using Indo-Pacific terminology in internal documents from 2005 onwards, and began further developing and promoting it from 2007, beginning with an open letter to Australia's then foreign minister. See James A. Boutilier, 'Reflections on the new Indo-Pacific maritime and naval environment', *Journal of the Australian Naval Institute*, Issue 114, 2004; Peter Cozens, 'Some reflections on maritime developments in the Indo-Pacific during the past sixty years', *Maritime Affairs*, Vol. 1, No. 1 2005; Michael Richardson, 'Australia-Southeast Asia relations and the East Asian Summit', *Australian Journal of International Affairs*, Vol. 59, No. 3, 2005; Gurpreet S. Khurana, 'Security of sea lines: Prospects for India-Japan cooperation', *Strategic Analysis*, Vol. 31, No. 1, 2007; Michael Auslin, 'Security in the Indo-Pacific commons: Toward a regional strategy', American Enterprise Institute, 2010; C. Raja Mohan, *Samudra Manthan: Sino-Indian Rivalry in the Indo-Pacific*, Carnegie Endowment for International Peace, Washington, 2012; Rory Medcalf, 'Incoming government brief: Australia's relations with India', *The Interpreter* (Lowy Institute blog), 21 December 2007.

19 Commonwealth of Australia, 'Defence White Paper 2013', Canberra, pp. 7, 13.

20 'National Security Strategy of the United States of America', December 2017, pp. 45–47.

21 Department of Defense, 'Indo-Pacific Strategy Report: Preparedness, partnerships, and promoting a networked region', 1 June 2019.

22 Editorial Board, East Asia Forum, 'India's cautious courtship with the US-led order in Asia', East Asia Forum (blog), 24 September 2018.

23 Narendra Modi, keynote address at the Shangri-La Dialogue, Singapore, 1 June 2018.

24 Association of Southeast Asian Nations, 'ASEAN outlook on the Indo-Pacific', 23 June 2019; Melissa Conley Tyler, 'The Indo-Pacific is the new Asia', *The Interpreter* (Lowy Institute blog), 28 June 2019.

25 J.R. Logan, *Ethnology of the Indo-Pacific Islands*, Jacob Baptist, Singapore, 1852.

26 Anthea Roberts, Henrique Choer Moraes and Victor Ferguson, 'The geoeconomic world order', *Lawfare* (blog), 19 November 2018.

27 Robert D. Blackwill and Jennifer M. Harris, *War by Other Means: Geoeconomics and Statecraft*, Harvard University Press, Cambridge, Massachusetts, 2016, p. 20.

28 As argued also in Bruno Maçães, *Belt and Road: A Chinese World Order*, Hurst and Company, London, 2018.

29 Cuiping Zhu, *India's Ocean: Can China and India Coexist?*, Springer/Social Sciences Academic Press, Singapore, 2018, pp. 142–143.

30 Darren J. Lim and Rohan Mukherjee, 'What money can't buy: The security externalities of Chinese economic statecraft in post-war Sri Lanka', *Asian Security*, Vol. 15, No. 2, 2019.

31 State Council, People's Republic of China, *China's Military Strategy*, 2015.

32 For instance, 'Power projection in the Indo-Pacific region: Aircraft carriers and amphibious ships', in *Asia-Pacific Regional Security Assessment 2019*, International Institute for Strategic Studies.

33 General Angus Campbell, Chief of the Australian Defence Force, 'You may not be interested in war, but war is interested in you', Speech to the Australian Strategic Policy Institute's 'War in 2025' conference, Canberra, 13 June 2019.

34 Rory Medcalf, 'China's influence in Australia is not ordinary soft power', *Australian Financial Review*, 7 June 2017. The concept of sharp power was further developed by the US National Endowment for Democracy in its report 'Sharp power: Rising authoritarian influence' in December 2017.

35 Peter Harris, 'Conflict with China is not about a clash of civilisations', *The National Interest* online, 3 June 2019.

36 Bilahari Kausikan, 'No sweet spot for Singapore in US–China tension', *The Straits Times*, 30 May 2019.

37 Brendan Taylor, *The Four Flashpoints: How Asia Goes to War*, La Trobe University Press, Melbourne, 2018.

38 Hal Brands, 'The too-good-to-be-true way to fight the Chinese military', *Bloomberg*, 10 July 2019.

39 Commonwealth of Australia, 'Opportunity, security, strength: The 2017 foreign policy white paper', Canberra, 2017.

40 The 'sphere of influence' argument has been advanced as a basis for a view that countries like Australia will need to prepare to face China alone; see Hugh White, *How to Defend Australia*, pp. 38–42.

41 For example, Michael D. Swaine, 'A counterproductive Cold War with China: Washington's "Free and Open Indo-Pacific" strategy will make Asia less open and less free', *Foreign Affairs*, 2 March 2018.

42 Philip Bowring, *Empire of the Winds: The Global Role of Asia's Great Archipelago*, I.B. Tauris, London, 2019, p. 61.

43 Shyam Saran, *How India Sees the World: Kautilya to the 21st Century*, Juggernaut, New Delhi, 2017.

44 Rose George, *Ninety Percent of Everything: Inside Shipping, the Invisible Industry that*

Puts Clothes on Your Back, Gas in Your Car and Food on Your Plate, Metropolitan Books, New York, 2013.

45 Will Doig, *High-Speed Empire: Chinese Expansion and the Future of Southeast Asia*, Columbia Global Reports, New York, 2018.

Chapter 2: A Submerged History of Asia

1 Borrowing from Thomas Mitchell, the author reintroduced a pivoted map of Asia in a public lecture at the Australian National University in 2012: Rory Medcalf, 'Pivoting the map: Australia's Indo-Pacific system', Centre of Gravity Paper No. 1, Strategic and Defence Studies Centre, Australian National University, November 2012. See also Thomas Mitchell, *Journal of an Expedition into the Interior of Tropical Australia in Search of a Route from Sydney to the Gulf of Carpentaria*, Longman, Brown, Green and Longmans, London, 1848.

2 Institute of Geodesy and Geophysics, Chinese Academy of Sciences, 'A new version of world map published', 2013, website accessed 16 January 2019. http://english.whigg.cas.cn/ns/es/201312/t20131211_114311.html. See inside back cover.

3 Pepe Escobar, 'Chinese scholar offers insight into Beijing's strategic mindset', *Asia Times*, 5 January 2019.

4 Andrew Phillips and J.C. Sharman, *International Order in Diversity: War, Trade and Rule in the Indian Ocean*, Cambridge University Press, Cambridge, 2015, p. 9.

5 Tansen Sen, 'The "Indo-Pacific" is really nothing new, just ask the fish', *South China Morning Post*, 30 December 2017.

6 Kalidas Nag, *India and the Pacific World*, Book Company Ltd., Calcutta, 1941, p. 18. In 1924, Nag had travelled by sea with Indian poet and pan-Asian visionary Rabindranath Tagore to rediscover India's cultural and historical connections to East Asia; see T.C.A. Raghavan, 'The changing seas: Antecedents of the Indo-Pacific', *The Telegraph* (Kolkata), 17 July 2019.

7 D. Fuller, N. Boivin, T. Hoogervorst and R. Allaby, 'Across the Indian Ocean: The prehistoric movement of plants and animals', *Antiquity*, Vol. 85, No. 328, 2011, pp. 544–558.

8 Bill Hayton, *The South China Sea: The Struggle for Power in Asia*, Yale University Press, New Haven and London, 2014, p. 6.

9 Angela Clark et al., 'Biological anthropology in the Indo-Pacific region: New approaches to age-old questions', *Journal of Indo-Pacific Archaeology*, Vol. 41, 2017, pp. 78–94.

10 Bill Hayton, *The South China Sea*, pp. 6–8.

11 Quoted in Pepe Escobar, 'Chinese scholar offers insight into Beijing's strategic mindset'.

12 Ellen L. Frost, *Asia's New Regionalism*, National University of Singapore Press, Singapore, 2008, p. 47.

13 Kautilya, *The Arthashastra*, Book 6; Shyam Saran, *How India Sees the World*, pp. 11–14.

14 Herodotus, *The Histories*, Aubrey de Sélincourt (trans.), Penguin Classics, London, 1954, pp. 187, 213, 440–441.

15 Tansen Sen, *India, China, and the World: A Connected History*, Roman and Littlefield, Lanham, 2017, p. 6.

16 K.M. Panikkar, *Asia and Western Dominance: A Survey of the Vasco da Gama Epoch of Asian History 1498–1945*, George Allen & Unwin, London, 1953 (1959 edition), p. 29.

17 The News Minute/Indo-Asian News Service, 'Navigation began in India: Indians used monsoon winds for sailing long before Greeks', 4 December 2017.

18 Chinese intellectual Liang Qichao speaking in 1924, quoted in Tansen Sen, *India, China, and the World*, p. 1.

19 Ibid., pp. 125–127.

20 Howard W. French, *Everything Under the Heavens: How the Past Helps Shape China's Push for Global Power*, Vintage Books, New York, 2017 (2018 edition), pp. 114–117.

21 Philip Bowring, *Empire of the Winds*, pp. 57–64.

22 This section draws on Howard W. French, *Everything Under the Heavens*, pp. 117–119.

23 Timothy Brook, *Great State: China and the World*, Profile, London, 2019, pp. 36–42, 45–52.

24 Ibid., pp. 44–45, 83–84.

25 'Full text of President Xi's speech at opening of Belt and Road Forum', *Xinhua*, 14 May 2017.

26 'Full text: Hu's speech', *The Sydney Morning Herald*, 24 October 2003.

27 Bill Hayton, *The South China Sea*, pp. 24–26; Howard W. French, *Everything Under the Heavens*, pp. 101–104; Tansen Sen, *India, China, and the World*, pp. 195–222: Geoff Wade, 'The Zheng He voyages: A reassessment', *Journal of the Malaysian Branch of the Royal Asiatic Society*, Vol. 78, No. 1, 2005, pp. 37–58; Timothy Brook, *Great State*, pp. 79–83.

28 Xi Jinping, Speech to the Indonesian Parliament, Jakarta, 2 October 2013.

29 Howard W. French, *Everything Under the Heavens*, p. 101.

30 Ibid., pp. 98–109; Bill Hayton, *The South China Sea*, pp. 24–26; Timothy Brook, *Great State*, p. 105.

31 K.M. Panikkar's *Asia and Western Dominance* is a compelling account, the first comprehensive history of colonialism by an Asian scholar.

32 'Speech by Chairman of the delegation of the People's Republic of China, Deng Xiaoping, at the Special Session of the UN General Assembly', New York, 10 April 1974.

33 See, for instance: James A. Millward, 'Is China a colonial power?', *The New York Times*, 4 May 2018; Richard McGregor, 'Mahathir, China and neo-colonialism', *Nikkei Asian Review*, 30 August 2018; Mihir Sharma, 'China should beware what it wishes for', *Bloomberg*, 19 May 2017.

34 Isabel Hilton, 'The myth of China's "great state"', *New Statesman*, 18 September 2019; Timothy Brook, *Great State*.

35 Admiral James Stavridis, *Sea Power: The History and Geopolitics of the World's Oceans*, Penguin Books, New York, 2017, p. 103.

36 K.M. Panikkar, *Asia and Western Dominance*, p. 49.

37 Robert D. Kaplan, *Monsoon: The Indian Ocean and the Future of American Power*, Random House, New York, 2010, p. 55.

38 K.M. Panikkar, *Asia and Western Dominance*, pp. 40–41.

39 J.C. Sharman, *Empires of the Weak: The Real Story of European Expansion and the Creation of the New World Order*, Princeton University Press, Princeton and Oxford, 2019.

40 Ellen L. Frost, *Asia's New Regionalism*, p. 54.

41 Michael Wesley, *Restless Continent: Wealth, Rivalry and Asia's New Geopolitics*, Black Inc., Melbourne, 2015, pp. 43–44.

42 Jawaharlal Nehru, Speech to the first Asian Relations Conference, New Delhi, 24 March 1947.

43 K.M. Panikkar, *Asia and Western Dominance*, p. 52; Bill Hayton, *The South China Sea*, p. 35.

44 Ellen L. Frost, *Asia's New Regionalism*, p. 55.

45 Tansen Sen, *India, China, and the World*, p. 4.

46 Amitav Acharya, 'Asia is not one', *The Journal of Asian Studies*, Vol. 69, No. 4, 2010, p. 1003; John M. Steadman, *The Myth of Asia*, London, Macmillan, 1969, pp. 32–33.

47 Matteo Ricci (trans. Louis J. Gallagher), *China in the Sixteenth Century: The Journals of Matthew Ricci 1583–1610*, Random House, New York, p. 364.

48 Timothy Brook, *Great State*, pp. 2–5.

49 J.R. Logan, *Ethnology of the Indo-Pacific Islands*, Jacob Baptist, Singapore, 1852; J.R. Logan, 'The Ethnology of the Indian Archipelago: Embracing enquiries into the continental relations of the Indo-Pacific Islanders', *Journal of the Indian Archipelago and Eastern Asia*, Vol. 4, 1850, pp. 252–347.

50 C. Raja Mohan, *Samudra Manthan: Sino-Indian Rivalry in the Indo-Pacific*, Carnegie Endowment for International Peace, Washington, 2012; 'Return of the Raj', *The American Interest*, Vol. 5, No. 5, May 2010.

51 Robert Kaplan, *Monsoon*, pp. 181–185.

52 This section draws on Michael J. Green, *By More than Providence: Grand Strategy and American Power in the Asia Pacific since 1783*, Columbia University Press, New York, 2017, pp. 21–31.

53 Ibid., pp. 64–77.

54 For a thorough account of the neglected subject of the Battle of Tsushima and the Russian fleet's voyage to disaster, see Constantine Pleshakov, *The Tsar's Last Armada: The Epic Voyage to the Battle of Tsushima*, Basic Books, New York, 2002.

55 Alistair Horne, *Hubris: The Tragedy of War in the Twentieth Century*, Weidenfeld & Nicolson, London, 2015, pp. 66–87.

56 Hans Weigert, 'Haushofer and the Pacific: The future in retrospect', *Foreign Affairs*, July 1942.

57 K.M. Panikkar, *India and the Indian Ocean: An Essay on the Influence of Sea Power on Indian History*, George Allen & Unwin, London, 1945.

58 Dennis Rumley, Timothy Doyle and Sanjay Chaturvedi, '"Securing" the Indian Ocean? Competing regional security constructions', *Journal of the Indian Ocean Region*, Vol. 8, No. 1, 2012, pp. 1–20.

59 Karl Haushofer, *Geopolitics of the Pacific Ocean*, edited and updated by Lewis A. Tambs, translated by Ernst J. Brehm, 2002, Edwin Mellen Press, New York, 1924; K.M. Panikkar, *India and the Indian Ocean*, p. 18.

60 Pankaj Mishra, *From the Ruins of Empire: The Revolt Against the West and the Remaking of Asia*, Penguin, London, 2012, pp. 230–231.

61 K.M. Panikkar, *Asia and Western Dominance*, pp. 197–199.

62 Ashok Malik, 'Under China's shadow, India looks to Australia', *Yale Global Online*, 8 February 2013.

63 K.M. Panikkar, *India and the Indian Ocean*, p. 85.

64 Admiral James Stavridis, *Sea Power*, p. 111.

65 For instance, '1942 Map of the Assembled Greater East Asia Co-Prosperity Sphere'. This propaganda map, released on 20 June 1942 by the government of Imperial Japan, was used at community meetings to convince the population that conquest was necessary to secure raw materials.

66 C. Raja Mohan, 'Return of the Raj'.

Chapter 3: Odyssey of Nations: The Quest for a Regional Home

1 Phillips Talbot, '1947 India conference that marked end of colonialism', *The New Republic*, 29 April 1947.

2 Ibid.

3 Ibid.

4 Vineet Thakur, 'An Asian drama: The Asia Relations Conference, 1947', *The International History Review*, Vol. 41, No. 6, pp. 673–695.

5 Jawaharlal Nehru, Speech to the First Asian Relations Conference, New Delhi, 24 March 1947.

6   Historian Frank Dikötter estimates that the PRC regime was responsible for the killings of at least 5 million civilians in the purges, terror and enforced land redistributions from 1949 to 1959: Frank Dikötter, *The Tragedy of Liberation: A History of the Chinese Revolution 1945–1957*, Bloomsbury, London, 2013, pp. xi–xv.

7   Victor D. Cha, *Powerplay: The Origins of the American Alliance System in Asia*, Princeton University Press, Princeton, 2016, p. 4.

8   Amitav Acharya, 'Asia is not one', p. 1009.

9   For an insider account of both initiatives, by Australia's then external affairs minister, see Percy Spender, *Exercises in Diplomacy*, Sydney University Press, Sydney, 1969.

10 Allan Gyngell, *Fear of Abandonment: Australia in the World since 1942*, La Trobe University Press, Melbourne, 2017, pp. 84–85.

11 Julie Suares, *J.B. Chifley: An Ardent Internationalist*, Melbourne University Publishing, 2019, pp. 5–7.

12 Tansen Sen, *India, China, and the World*, pp. 396–398.

13 'India: Never again the same', *Time*, 30 November 1962.

14 Neville Maxwell, *India's China War*, Jonathan Cape, London, 1970, pp. 11–14, 286–288.

15 Jeff Smith, *Cold Peace: China–India Rivalry in the 21st Century*, Lexington Books, Lanham, 2013.

16 C. Raja Mohan, *Samudra Manthan*, p. 39.

17 Michael Wesley, *Restless Continent*, pp. 47–48.

18 K.M. Panikkar, *India and the Indian Ocean*, pp. 14–15, 85.

19 Defence Studies Project, *Proceedings of the Seminar on Nuclear Dispersal in Asia and the Indo-Pacific Region*, The Australian Institute of International Affairs and the Australian National University, Canberra, 1965; Defence Studies Project, *Proceedings of the Seminar on Commonwealth Responsibilities for Security in the Indo-Pacific Region*, The Australian Institute of International Affairs and the Australian National University, Canberra, 1966.

20 UK Cabinet Office, 'Indo-Pacific strategy', 6 October 1965, National Archives Ref. CAB148 52 C614951.

21 See also Alessio Patalano, 'Days of future past: British strategy and the shaping of Indo-Pacific security', Policy Exchange report, 2019.

22 UK Cabinet Office, 'Indo-Pacific Strategy', p. 2.

23 Ibid.

24 Richard M. Nixon, 'Asia after Viet Nam', *Foreign Affairs*, October 1967.

25 J.D.B. Miller (ed.), *India, Japan, Australia: Partners in Asia? Papers from a Conference at the Australian National University, September 1967*, ANU Press, Canberra, 1968, p. vii.

26 Allan Gyngell, *Fear of Abandonment*, p. 113.

27 Ibid.

28 Interviews and selections by Graham Allison and Robert D. Blackwill, with Ali Wyne, *Lee Kuan Yew: The Grand Master's Insights on China, the United States and the World*, Belfer Center Studies in International Security, The MIT Press, Cambridge, Massachusetts, 2012, p. 63.

29 Sunanda Datta-Ray, *Looking East to Look West: Lee Kuan Yew's Mission India*, Institute of Southeast Asian Studies and Penguin, Singapore, 2009.

30 Google Books, Ngram Viewer, using search terms 'Asia-Pacific', 'Indo-Pacific', 1800–2008.

31 Sue Thompson, 'The Western powers and the development of regional cooperation in Southeast Asia: The international dimension, 1945–67', *Global Change, Peace and Security*, Vol. 23, No. 1.

32 Amitav Acharya, 'Asia is not one', pp. 1009–1010.

33 Ibid., p. 1009.
34 Paul Keating, *Engagement: Australia Faces the Asia-Pacific*, Macmillan, Sydney, 2000.
35 Yen Makabenta, 'At 26, APEC is still looking for a noun', *Manila Times*, 6 November 2015. Of course, a pedant would note that 'cooperation' is a noun, but Evans was presumably pointing out the lack of a named structure such as 'organisation' at the end of the title, with the consequence that APEC was not well empowered to bind its participants to act.
36 Gaye Christoffersen, 'China and the Asia-Pacific: Need for a grand strategy', *Asian Survey*, Vol. 36, No. 11, 1996, pp. 1067–1076.
37 'Condi entertains at Asean Forum', BBC News, 28 July 2006.
38 'Towards an East Asian Community' (report of the East Asia Vision Group), 2001, p. 15.
39 For an authoritative account of the George W. Bush administration's Asia policy, see Michael J. Green, *By More than Providence*, pp. 482–517.
40 Australian academic Michael Wesley has aptly described Malaysia, Thailand and Singapore as encompassing an 'Indo-Pacific peninsula'; see Michael Wesley, *Restless Continent*, p. 146.
41 Years afterward, former Indonesian foreign minister Marty Natalegawa said that the shaping of the EAS was a conscious act of Indo-Pacific diplomacy by Southeast Asian states; see Marty Natalegawa, 'An Indonesian perspective on the Indo-Pacific', Speech to the Centre for Strategic and International Studies Indonesia Conference, Washington, DC, 16 May 2013. Indeed, as early as September 2005, even before the leaders had actually met, Australian journalist Michael Richardson was the first observer to note that the emerging forum marked a shift to an Indo-Pacific construct; see Michael Richardson, 'Australia–Southeast Asia relations and the East Asia Summit', *Australian Journal of International Affairs*, Vol. 59, No. 3, 2005.

Chapter 4: Rise of the Indo-Pacific

1 'Chinese navy sets sail for anti-piracy mission off Somalia', *Xinhua*, 26 December 2008.
2 Rory Medcalf, 'China's gunboat diplomacy', *The New York Times (International Herald Tribune)*, 28 December 2008.
3 'Chinese ship uses Molotov cocktails to fight off Somali pirates', *The Telegraph*, 19 December 2008.
4 James Mulvenon, 'Chairman Hu and the PLA's "New Historic Missions"', *China Leadership Monitor*, Vol. 27, Hoover Institution, 2009.
5 United Nations Security Council Resolution 1851, 'The situation in Somalia', 2008.
6 United States Government, 'A cooperative strategy for 21st century seapower', October 2007.
7 Robert Zoellick, 'Whither China: From membership to responsibility?' Remarks to National Committee on US–China relations, 21 September 2005.
8 For instance, Brendan Taylor, *The Four Flashpoints: How Asia Goes to War*; Bill Hayton, *The South China Sea*; Richard McGregor, *Asia's Reckoning: The Struggle for Global Dominance*, Penguin, London, 2017.
9 A considered account of the *Impeccable* incident is provided in Michael J. Green, Kathleen H. Hicks and John Schaus, 'Countering coercion in maritime Asia: The theory and practice of gray-zone deterrence', Center for Strategic and International Studies, 2017.
10 'How much trade transits the South China Sea?' China Power website, Center for Strategic and International Studies, https://chinapower.csis.org/much-trade-transits-south-china-sea.
11 Bill Hayton, *The South China Sea*, pp. 59–60.
12 Navin Rajagobal, 'The 2009 claims that changed the dynamics in the South China Sea', *The Straits Times*, 12 July 2016.

13 Linda Jakobson, 'China's unpredictable maritime security actors', Lowy Institute Report, 2014.

14 Richard Halloran, 'What is Hatoyama's foreign policy?', *Real Clear Politics*, 6 September 2009.

15 Abe Shinzō, 'Asia's democratic security diamond', *Project Syndicate*, 27 December 2012.

16 'In 2010 the US surfaced three missile submarines as a warning to China', *The National Interest* online, 14 August 2017.

17 'US here to stay, says Clinton, Ha Noi', ASEAN website, 23 July 2010.

18 Joshua Kurlatzick, 'The belligerents', *New Republic*, 27 January 2011.

19 Kurt M. Campbell, *The Pivot: The Future of American Statecraft in Asia*, Twelve, New York, 2016.

20 The White House, 'Remarks by President Obama to the Australian Parliament', 17 November 2011.

21 Michael J. Green, *By More than Providence*, pp. 482–517; Nina Silove, 'The pivot before the pivot: US strategy to preserve the balance of power in Asia', *International Security*, Vol. 40, No. 4, 2016, pp. 45–88.

22 For example, Malcolm Fraser, 'Our star spangled manner', *The Sydney Morning Herald*, 7 June 2012.

23 Hillary Clinton, 'America's Pacific century', *Foreign Policy*, 11 October 2011.

24 'Nuclear anxiety: Indian's letter to Clinton on the nuclear testing', *The New York Times*, 13 May 2013.

25 The author observed this rapid geopolitical shift up close as an Australian diplomat in New Delhi from 2000 to 2003.

26 Shyam Saran, *How India Sees the World*, pp. 194–195.

27 As US Ambassador Robert Blackwill foreshadowed: 'Achieving this objective requires the United States to particularly strengthen political, economic, and military-to-military relations with those Asian states that share our democratic values and national interests. That spells India. A strong US–India partnership contributing to the construction of a peaceful and prosperous Asia binds the resources of the world's most powerful and most populous democracies in support of freedom, political moderation, and economic and technological development.' See Robert Blackwill, 'The quality and durability of the US–India relationship', Speech in Kolkata, 27 November 2002. See also Ashley Tellis, 'India as a new global power: An action agenda for the United States', Carnegie Endowment for International Peace, 2005.

28 'US to help make India "a major world power"', *China Daily*, 26 March 2005.

29 Author's discussion with senior Chinese diplomat, New Delhi, 2003.

30 Amit Baruah, 'Only "escort duties" in Malacca Straits', *The Hindu*, 23 April 2002.

31 Tanvi Madan, 'The rise, fall and rebirth of the "quad"', *War on the Rocks*, 16 November 2017.

32 For Rudd's view, see Kevin Rudd, 'The convenient rewriting of the history of the "Quad"', *Nikkei Asian Review*, 26 March 2019.

33 Rory Medcalf, 'Chinese ghost story', *The Diplomat*, 14 February 2008.

34 Coral Bell, *The End of the Vasco da Gama Era: The Next Landscape of World Politics*, Lowy Institute Paper 21, Sydney, 2007, p. 22. Dr Bell has been described affectionately as Australia's 'George Kennan in thick glasses, blue floral dress, white sneakers and a string of pearls'; see Minh Bui Jones, *The Interpreter* (Lowy Institute blog), 5 October 2012.

35 James Brown, 'Pirates and privateers: Managing the Indian Ocean's private security boom', Lowy Institute Analysis, Sydney, 12 September 2012.

36 June Park and Ali Ahmad, 'Risky business: South Korea's secret military deal with UAE', *The Diplomat*, 1 March 2018.

37 Statistics provided by China scholar Andrew Erickson, 'The China anti-piracy bookshelf: Statistics and implications from ten years' deployment … and counting', 2 January 2019, http://www.andrewerickson.com/2019/01/the-china-anti-piracy-bookshelf-statistics-implications-from-ten-years-deployment-counting.

38 Rajat Pandit, 'India suspicious as Chinese submarine docks in Sri Lanka', *The Times of India*, 8 November 2014.

39 Rory Medcalf and Raja Mohan, 'Sea change of China power', *The Australian*, 11 February 2014.

40 'China builds up strategic sea lanes', *The Washington Times*, 17 January 2005.

41 Shen Dingli, 'Don't shun the idea of setting up overseas military bases', *China.org.cn*, 28 January 2010.

42 Howard French, *China's Second Continent: How a Million Migrants Are Building a New Empire in Africa*, Knopf, New York, 2014.

43 Xi Jinping, Speech to Indonesian Parliament, Jakarta, 2 October 2013.

44 'Promote friendship between our people and work together to build a bright future', Xi Jinping, Speech at Nazarbayev University, Astana, Kazakhstan, 7 September 2013.

45 Bruno Maçães, *Belt and Road*, p. 24.

46 Rachel Will, 'China's stadium diplomacy', *World Policy*, 6 June 2012; Thomas Fuller, 'Myanmar backs down, suspending dam project', *The New York Times*, 30 September 2011; Lermie Shayne Garcia, 'Chinese aid in Southeast Asia before the Belt and Road Initiative: Solidarity or business as usual?', *Asian Studies: Journal of Critical Perspectives on Asia*, Vol. 53, No. 1, 2017.

47 National Development and Reform Commission, Ministry of Foreign Affairs and Ministry of Commerce, People's Republic of China, with State Council authorisation, 'Vision and actions on jointly building Silk Road Economic Belt and 21st Century Maritime Silk Road', 28 March 2015.

48 Bruno Maçães, *Belt and Road*, p. 24.

49 David Zweig, 'Spooked by China's hawks? So are the Chinese', *The Wall Street Journal (Asia)*, 11 November 2010. The author encountered similar views among Chinese scholars during research meetings in China in late 2010.

50 For example, Qi Jianguo, 'An unprecedented great changing situation: Understanding and thoughts on the global strategic situation and our country's national security environment', in James A. Bellacqua and Daniel M. Hartnett, 'Article by LTG Qi Jianguo on international security affairs', *CNA China Studies*, April 2013; and Kui Jing, 'Welcoming the US into the Indo-Asia-Pacific', *Sohu*, 19 March 2013.

51 Minghao Zhao, 'The emerging strategic triangle in Indo-Pacific Asia', *The Diplomat*, 4 June 2013.

52 See, for example, Lü Yaodong, 'Japan's "Indo-Pacific" concept another platform for containing China', *Global Times*, 13 October 2014; another Chinese scholar claimed India was the 'key' for a US 'Indo-Pacific strategy' aimed at containing China and 'balancing Beijing's Silk Road push into the Indian Ocean'. See 'Obama's India visit aimed at containing China: Report', *The Times of India*, 25 January 2015.

53 Minghao Zhao, 'The emerging strategic triangle in Indo-Pacific Asia'.

54 Commonwealth of Australia, 'Australia in the Asian Century: white paper', Canberra, October 2012.

55 The map, commissioned by senior defence official Brendan Sargeant, was initially controversial within parts of the Australian defence establishment, and reportedly met bewilderment among American officials still focused on the Middle East. An alternative and rather conspiratorial view has it that Australian defence officials promoted the

Indo-Pacific to gain ascendancy over economic agencies that had pushed the Asian Century idea – but this overlooks that the Indo-Pacific had already been aired in the Asian Century white paper and was being taken seriously in foreign policy circles too. See Graeme Dobell, 'Sunny Asian century versus dark Indo-Pacific', *The Strategist*, 8 July 2019.

56 Dennis Rumley, Timothy Doyle and Sanjay Chaturverdi, '"Securing" the Indian Ocean?: Competing regional security constructions', Indo-Pacific Governance Research Centre Policy Brief, University of Adelaide, 2012.

57 Nick Bisley and Andrew Phillips, 'Rebalance to where? US strategic geography in Asia', *Survival*, Vol. 55, No. 5, 2013, p. 96.

58 Commonwealth of Australia, 'Opportunity, security, strength: Foreign policy white paper', Canberra, 2017.

59 For example, Michael Auslin, 'Tipping point in the Indo-Pacific', *The American Interest*, March 2011. Author Robert Kaplan had an impact on US policy thinking through a timely journal article: Robert Kaplan, 'Center stage for the 21st century: Power plays in the Indian Ocean', *Foreign Affairs*, March 2009.

60 'President Obama, PM Modi's joint statement: full text', 25 January 2015.

61 Marty Natalegawa, 'An Indonesian perspective on the Indo-Pacific', keynote address at the Conference on Indonesia, Washington DC, 16 May 2013.

62 Narendra Modi, Speech to the Australian Parliament, Canberra, 18 November 2014.

63 C. Raja Mohan, *Samudra Manthan*.

64 Shyam Saran, 'Mapping the Indo-Pacific', *Indian Express*, 29 October 2011.

65 Gurpreet S. Khurana, 'Security of sea lanes: Prospects for India-Japan cooperation', *Strategic Analysis*, Vol. 31, No. 1, 2007.

66 Abe Shinzō, 'Confluence of the two seas', Speech to the Parliament of the Republic of India, New Delhi, 22 August 2007.

67 'Movers of Abe's diplomacy', *The Japan Times*, 11 February 2013.

68 Shiraishi Takashi, 'Japan's Indo-Pacific policy', Center for Strategic and International Studies, 1 March 2016.

69 Michael J. Green, Kathleen H. Hicks and John Schaus, 'Countering coercion in maritime Asia: The theory and practice of gray-zone deterrence'.

70 Barack Obama, 'Commencement speech: West Point', New York, 28 May 2014.

71 Ashley Townshend and Rory Medcalf, 'Shifting waters: China's new passive assertiveness in Asian maritime security', Lowy Institute Analysis, 2016.

72 Address by Abe Shinzō at the Opening Session of the Sixth Tokyo International Conference on African Development, Nairobi, 27 August 2016.

73 Kori Schake, *America vs the West*, Lowy Institute Paper, 2018.

74 Commonwealth of Australia, *Opportunity, Security, Strength: Foreign Affairs White Paper*, 2017, p. 4.

75 Louis Nelson, 'In Asia, Trump keeps talking about Indo-Pacific', *Politico*, 7 November 2017.

76 The White House, 'Remarks by President Trump, APEC CEO summit, Da Nang Vietnam', 10 November 2017.

77 National Security Strategy of the United States of America, December 2017, p. 45.

78 Lindsey Ford, 'Promise vs. experience: How to fix the "free and open Indo-Pacific"', *War on the Rocks*, 10 April 2018.

79 Jansen Tham, 'What's in Indonesia's Indo-Pacific concept?', *The Diplomat*, May 2018.

80 Bill Birtles, 'China mocks Australia over "Indo-Pacific" concept it says will "dissipate"'.

81 Raja Mohan, Rory Medcalf and Bruno Tertrais, 'New Indo-Pacific axis', *Indian Express*, 8 May 2018.

82 Richard Heydarian, 'The Indo-Pacific era debuts at Shangri-La Dialogue', *Asian Maritime Transparency Initiative*, 8 June 2018.

83 Sam Sachdeva, 'Peters pushes trade, pokes China in latest US trip', *Newsroom*, 18 July 2019.

84 A survey of Southeast Asian policy elites suggested than 61 per cent considered the Indo-Pacific concept to need more explanation. About 17 per cent also said the concept could undermine ASEAN, with around the same number seeing it as a viable basis for a new regional order. About one in four considered that it was intended to 'contain' China. Only 11.8 per cent considered it would 'fade away'. See *The State of Southeast Asia: Survey Report*, Institute of Southeast Asian Studies, Singapore, 2019, p. 25.

85 John Garnaut, 'Australia's China reset: The rest of the world is watching how we counter Beijing's campaign of influence', *The Monthly*, August 2018.

86 The White House, 'Remarks by Vice President Pence on the administration's policy towards China', 4 October 2018.

87 US Department of Defense, 'Indo-Pacific Strategy report: Preparedness, partnerships, and promoting a networked region', 1 June 2019.

88 US Congress, *John S. McCain National Defense Authorization Act for Fiscal Year 2019*.

89 David Wroe, 'China eyes Vanuatu military base in plan with global ramifications', *The Sydney Morning Herald*, 9 April 2018; 'Outflanking China, U.S. allies – including Japan – pledge to provide electricity to Papua New Guinea', *The Japan Times*, 18 November 2018.

Chapter 5: Games and Giants

1 See, for instance, David Scott, 'The great power "Great Game" between China and India: The logic of geography', *Geopolitics*, Vol. 13, No. 1, 2008; Robert Kaplan, 'Center stage for the 21st century: Power plays in the Indian Ocean', *Foreign Affairs*, March/April 2009; Bertil Lintner, *Great Game East: India, China and the Struggle for Asia's Most Volatile Frontier*, HarperCollins India, Delhi, 2012, p. xxv; Rani D. Mullen and Cody Poplin, 'The new Great Game: A battle for access and influence in the Indo-Pacific', *Foreign Affairs* online, 29 September 2015; Garima Mohan, 'Great Game in the Indian Ocean', Global Public Policy Institute, 11 June 2018.

2 Peter Hopkirk, *Quest for Kim: In Search of Kipling's Great Game*, Oxford University Press, Oxford, 1996, pp. 2, 6.

3 The Go analogy is noted, for instance, by You Ji, 'The Indian Ocean: A grand Sino-Indian game of "Go"', in David Brewster (ed.), *India and China at Sea: Competition for Naval Dominance in the Indian Ocean*, Oxford University Press, Delhi, 2018.

4 American policy scholar Mike Green makes a similar point in relation to US strategy in the region, describing it as 'at least as complex as three-dimensional chess': Washington must simultaneously support rules, engage with China and sustain military strength. See Michael J. Green, *By More than Providence*, p. 543.

5 The 'quintessential smart power' appellation for Japan was bestowed by the Lowy Institute Asia Power Index 2019, p. 8.

6 John J. Mearshemier, *The Tragedy of Great Power Politics*, W.W. Norton and Company, New York, 2014, pp. 1–5.

7 Alexander Wendt, 'Anarchy is what states make of it: The social construction of power politics', *International Organization*, Vol. 46, No. 2, 1992.

8 One of the most comprehensive efforts to assess the many factors that make up national power was one of the first: Hans Morgenthau, *Politics among Nations: The Struggle for Power and Peace*, Knopf, New York, 1948. More recently, a useful online device for

estimating power relativities in the Indo-Pacific, and how these shift according to the weightings placed on different factors, is the Lowy Institute's Asia Power Index: https://power.lowyinstitute.org.

9   Kenneth Waltz, quoted in George Perkovich, 'Is India a major power?', *The Washington Quarterly*, Vol. 27, No. 1, 2003, p. 129.

10 Michael Beckley, *Unrivaled: Why America Will Remain the World's Sole Superpower*, Cornell University Press, Ithaca, 2018, pp. 10–13.

11 The billiard ball analogy has been famously invoked in all seriousness by the doyen of realist scholars of international relations; see John J. Mearshemier, *The Tragedy of Great Power Politics*, p. 18.

12 Hal Brands and Charles Edel, *The Lessons of Tragedy: Statecraft and World Order*, Yale University Press, New Haven, 2019, p. 6.

13 David Fickling, 'China could outrun the US next year. Or never', *Bloomberg Opinion*, 9 March 2019.

14 Michael Beckley, *Unrivaled*, p. 61.

15 Wei Chen et al., 'A forensic examination of China's national accounts', Brookings Papers on Economic Activity, 2019.

16 Sebastian Heilmann (ed.), *China's Political System*, Rowman & Littlefield, Lanham, 2017, p. 23.

17 Frank Dikötter, *The Age of Openness: China Before Mao*, University of Chicago Press, Berkeley, 2008.

18 Vicky Xiuzhong Xu, 'China's youth are trapped in the cult of nationalism', *Foreign Policy*, 1 October 2019.

19 Xi Jinping, 'Secure a decisive victory in building a moderately prosperous society in all respects and strive for the great success of socialism with Chinese characteristics for a new era', Report delivered at the 19th National Congress of the Communist Party of China, 18 October 2017.

20 Ibid.

21 Bates Gill and Linda Jakobson, *China Matters: Getting It Right for Australia*, La Trobe University Press, Melbourne, 2017, p. 46 (ebook).

22 Richard McGregor, *Asia's Reckoning: China, Japan and the Fate of US Power in the Pacific Century*, Penguin, New York, 2017, pp. 129–132.

23 Carl Minzner, *End of an Era: How China's Authoritarian Revival Is Undermining Its Rise*, Oxford University Press, New York, 2018, pp. 21, 168–169.

24 Thomas J. Christensen, *The China Challenge: Shaping the Choices of a Rising Power*, Norton, New York, 2015, p. 13.

25 Elizabeth E. Economy, *The Third Revolution: Xi Jinping and the New Chinese State*, Oxford University Press, New York, 2018, p. 188; Richard N. Haas, *Foreign Policy Begins at Home: The Case for Putting America's House in Order*, Basic Books, New York, 2013, p. 32.

26 Chris Buckley and Keith Bradsher, 'Xi Jinping's marathon speech: Five takeaways', *The New York Times*, 18 October 2017.

27 Elizabeth E. Economy, *The Third Revolution*.

28 Kai Strittmatter, *We Have Been Harmonised: Life in China's Surveillance State*, Old Street Publishing, London, 2019, p. 6.

29 Wang Jisi, quoted in Richard McGregor, *Xi Jinping: The Backlash*, Penguin/Lowy Institute Paper, Sydney, 2019, p. 112.

30 '"Arrogant demands" by US "invade" China's economic sovereignty, state news agency says', *South China Morning Post*, 26 May 2019.

31   Richard McGregor, *Xi Jinping*, p. 114.

32   From Xi's 2017 report: 'With a view to realizing the Chinese Dream and the dream of building a powerful military … We have strengthened military training and war preparedness, and undertaken major missions related to the protection of maritime rights, countering terrorism, maintaining stability, disaster rescue and relief, international peacekeeping, escort services in the Gulf of Aden, and humanitarian assistance.'

33   You Ji, 'The Indian Ocean: A grand Sino-Indian game of "Go"', p. 90; Michael Peck, 'China is tripling the size of its Marine Corps', *The National Interest*, 29 August 2018.

34   Hugh White, *How to Defend Australia*, pp. 39. 42.

35   State Council of the People's Republic of China, 'China's national defense in the new era' (Chinese defence white paper), July 2019.

36   Howard French, *Everything Under the Heavens*, p. 274.

37   Ibid., pp. 278–283. It is worth noting that China's 'Gini coefficient', a measure of income inequality, is worse than that of India.

38   David Shambaugh, *China's Future?*, Polity, Cambridge, 2016, pp. 50–51, 125–129; Carl Minzner, *End of an Era*, pp. 164–172.

39   Bill Birtles, 'China's security obsession is now a point of national pride', ABC News, 10 October 2017; Lily Kuo, 'China is spending more on policing its own people than on its defense budget', *Quartz*, 6 March 2013.

40   For instance, the Pew Research Center's Global Attitudes and Trends polling, conducted in China from 2011 to 2014, indicated that between 82 and 92 per cent of respondents had confidence in the Chinese leader. This, however, was in the early phase of Xi's rule, before repression heightened and economic growth slowed, and may reflect among other things the limitations of obtaining reliable polling responses in an authoritarian surveillance state. https://www.pewresearch.org/global/database/indicator/69/country/CN.

41   '20 years on, Falun Gong survives underground in China', *The Japan Times*, 23 April 2019.

42   Tom Blackwell, '"Don't step out of line": Confidential report reveals how Chinese officials harass activists in Canada', *National Post*, 5 January 2018.

43   Peter Pomeranstev, *This Is Not Propaganda: Adventures in the War Against Reality*, Faber & Faber, London, 2019, pp. 246–247.

44   These highly popular films in 2017 and 2018 depicted heroic Chinese special forces soldiers venturing to Africa and the Arabian Peninsula to rescue hostages from such villains as American mercenaries and Islamic terrorists. *Wolf Warrior 2* was promoted with the line, 'Anyone who attacks China will be killed, no matter how far away he is.' See Kai Strittmatter, *We Have Been Harmonised*, pp. 56–57.

45   'Headlines from China: Will China ban *Wolf Warrior 3*?' *ChinaFilmInsider*, 3 December 2018.

46   US Department of Defense, 'Indo-Pacific Strategy Report', Washington DC, June 2019.

47   Wu Xinbo, 'The end of the silver lining: A Chinese view of the US–Japan alliance', *The Washington Quarterly*, Vol. 29, No.1, 2005.

48   Robert Jervis, 'Cooperation under the security dilemma', *World Politics*, Vol. 30, No. 2, 1978.

49   George Perkovich, 'Is India a major power?', p. 130.

50   There is no single Indian national security strategy document that formally sets out this spectrum of challenges. One comprehensive if unofficial survey of India's security challenges is set out in a multi-authored report: Sunil Khilnani et al., 'Nonalignment 2.0: a foreign and strategic policy for India in the 21st century', Center for Policy Research, New Delhi, 2012. Another useful recent tour of the nation's security horizon is set out in Gurmeet Kanwal, *The New Arthashastra: A Security Strategy for India*, HarperCollins India, Noida, 2016.

51 Shivshankar Menon, *Choices: Inside the Making of India's Foreign Policy*, Brookings Institution Press, Washington DC, 2016, pp. 37–38.

52 Annie Gowen, 'In Modi's India, journalists face bullying, criminal cases and worse', *Washington Post*, 16 February 2018.

53 'India is world's second-largest arms importer', *The Hindu*, 11 March 2019.

54 Niall McCarthy, 'Report: India lifted 271 million people out of poverty in a decade', *Forbes*, 12 July 2019.

55 World Bank, 'Poverty and equity brief: South Asia: India', 2019.

56 'India's oil import dependence jumps to 86 per cent', *Economic Times*, 5 May 2019.

57 Rory Medcalf, 'India Poll 2013', Lowy Institute and Australia–India Institute, May 2013, https://www.lowyinstitute.org/publications/india-poll-2013.

58 Shyam Saran, *How India Sees the World*, p. 106.

59 C. Raja Mohan, 'Explained: How Balakot changed the familiar script of India–Pakistan military crises', 4 March 2019.

60 Ravi Agrawal and Kathryn Salam, 'Is India becoming more like China?' *Foreign Policy*, 22 October 2019.

61 'Air strikes on Pakistan may win Narendra Modi India's election', *The Economist*, 14 March 2019.

62 Sumit Ganguly, 'Why the India-Pakistan crisis isn't likely to turn nuclear', *Foreign Affairs*, 5 March 2019.

63 Tanvi Madan, 'Doklam standoff: The takeaways for India', *LiveMint*, 4 September 2017.

64 Ian Hall, *Modi and the Reinvention of Indian Foreign Policy*, Bristol University Press, Bristol, 2019, p. 142.

65 Subrahmanyam Jaishankar, remarks at launch of 'Indian Foreign Policy: the Modi Era', Observer Researcher Foundation, New Delhi, 24 April 2019.

66 Amartya Sen, 'Contrary India', *The Economist*, 18 November 2005.

67 Subrahmanyam Jaishankar, remarks at launch.

68 Sadanand Dhume, 'The dueling narratives of India's Kashmir crackdown', *The Atlantic*, 5 September 2019.

69 Kishan Rana, 'The Indian foreign service: The glass gets fuller', *The Foreign Service Journal*, June 2014.

70 Ashok Malik and Rory Medcalf, 'India's new world: Civil society in the making of foreign policy', Lowy Institute Analysis, May 2011.

71 Ministry of External Affairs, Government of India, 'Official spokesperson's response to a query on participation of India in OBOR/BRI forum', 13 May 2017; 'With China still opposed, India's NSG membership application remains in cold storage', *The Wire*, 22 June 2019.

72 Kenneth Waltz, quoted in George Perkovich, 'Is India a major power?', p. 129.

73 In 2009, Admiral Sureesh Mehta was Chairman of the Chiefs of the Staff Committee – India's senior-most military role. He caused controversy by stating publicly that it would be foolhardy for India to compare itself directly with a stronger, wealthier China, and made a strategic recommendation that has proven prescient: 'The traditional or "attritionist" approach of matching "Division for Division" must give way to harnessing modern technology for developing high situational awareness and creating a reliable stand-off deterrent.' See Sureesh Mehta, 'India's national security challenges: An armed forces overview', Paper presented at the Indian Habitat Centre, New Delhi, 10 August 2009.

74 Michael J. Green, *By More than Providence*, p. 5.

75 Victor Cha, *Powerplay: The Origins of the American Alliances System in Asia*, Princeton University Press, Princeton, 2016, p. 18.

76 Thomas J. Wright, *All Measures Short of War: The Contest for the 21st Century and the Future of American Power*, Yale University Press, Connecticut, 2017, pp. 154–155.

77 Barry Posen, *Restraint: A New Foundation for US Grand Strategy*, Cornell University Press, Ithaca, 2014, p. xiii. See also James Steinberg and Michael E. O'Hanlon, *Strategic Reassurance and Resolve: US–China Relations in the 21st Century*, Princeton University Press, Princeton, 2014, pp. 48–55; John J. Mearsheimer and Stephen M. Walt, 'The case for offshore balancing: A superior US grand strategy', *Foreign Affairs*, July/August 2016.

78 Ibid., p. 98.

79 The White House, 'National Security Strategy of the United States', December 2017, p. 45.

80 Poll conducted by Pew Research Center, 2019: https://www.people-press.org/2019/07/30/climate-change-and-russia-are-partisan-flashpoints-in-publics-views-of-global-threats.

81 Audrey McAvoy, 'Diversion of funds for wall puts Guam projects on hold', *The Boston Globe*, 28 September 2019.

82 For implicit acknowledgement of this point, see Aaron L. Friedberg, *A Contest for Supremacy: China, America and the Struggle for Mastery in Asia*, Norton, New York, 2011, pp. 274–275.

83 Patrick M. Shanahan, 'Acting Secretary Shanahan's remarks at the IISS Shangri-la Dialogue 2019', 1 June 2019.

84 James Stavridis, 'China and Russia want to control the world island', *Bloomberg Opinion*, 11 June 2019.

85 Barry Posen, *Restraint*, p. 95.

86 'Kremlin hails special relationship with China amid missile system cooperation', *Moscow Times*, 4 October 2019.

87 'In Washington, talk of a China threat cuts across the political divide', *The Economist*, 18 May 2019.

Chapter 6: Many Players

1 See, for instance, Karl W. Deutsch and J. David Singer, 'Multipolar systems and international stability', *World Politics*, Vol. 16, No. 3, April 1964.

2 An influential Japanese policy adviser even grandly declares that Japan's creation of a Freeand Open Indo-Pacific is 'the greatest challenge of this century', and is the next stage in the spread of liberal ideals of human rights, racial equality, Asian post-colonial self-determination and the consent of the governed. Kanehara Nobukatsu, 'A Free and Open Indo-Pacific Region: Japan's grand strategy', Speech at the United States Military Academy at West Point, 5 February 2018 (unpublished, author given permission to cite).

3 Ebuchi Tomohiro and Hadano Tsukasa, 'Japan to end China aid, and proposes joint assistance for others', *Nikkei Asian Review*, 23 October 2018.

4 Government of Japan, 'National defense program guidelines for FY2019 and beyond', 18 December 2018 (provisional translation), pp. 6–7.

5 Based on data from US Energy Information Administration, Japan Overview report, 2 February 2017.

6 Japan's need to prevent Chinese control of the waterways that are its energy lifelines is acknowledged even by some who advocate allowing China more strategic space, a 'sphere of influence'. In the words of Australian scholar Hugh White, to concede to China 'a sphere of influence that extended to the waters around China … would be to concede

more than is compatible with the vital interests of other great powers, especially Japan';
see Hugh White, *The China Choice: Why America Should Share Power*, Black Inc.,
Melbourne, 2012, p. 151.

7   Michelle Jamrisko, 'China no match for Japan in Southeast Asia infrastructure race',
Forbes, 23 June 2019.

8   Michishita Narushige, 'Cooperate and compete: Abe's new approach to China', *The Straits Times*, 13 November 2018.

9   Kanehara Nobukatsu, 'The most important relationship of the 21st century – triangular
cooperation among US, India and Japan', Speech to the Hudson Institute, Washington
DC, 19 February 2019 (unpublished, author given permission to cite).

10 'Japan needs more "quasi-allies"', *Nikkei Asian Review* (editorial), 16 October 2018.

11 Anthony Richardson, 'Australia imports almost all of its oil and there are pitfalls all over
the globe', *The Conversation*, 24 May 2018; Alan Dupont, 'Fuelled for action', *The Weekend Australian*, 5–6 October 2019.

12 Allan Gyngell, 'Scott Morrison strikes an anxious and inward-looking tone', *The Interpreter* (Lowy Institute blog), 4 October 2019.

13 Commonwealth of Australia, 'Opportunity, security, strength: Foreign policy white
paper', Canberra, 2017.

14 Marise Payne, 'Ensuring security, enabling prosperity', Speech to the United States
Studies Centre, University of Sydney, 29 October 2019.

15 Allan Gyngell, *Fear of Abandonment*.

16 Rory Medcalf and C. Raja Mohan, 'Responding to Indo-Pacific rivalry'.

17 Penny Wong, 'Protecting and promoting regional interests in a time of US–China
strategic competition', Speech to the Centre for Strategic and International Studies in
Jakarta, Indonesia, 24 September 2019.

18 Scott Morrison, 'In our interest', Speech to the Lowy Institute, Sydney, 3 October 2019.

19 Sam Roggeveen, 'National security: Australians and their elites', *The Interpreter* (Lowy
Institute blog), 28 June 2019.

20 'China Fact Sheet', Australian Department of Foreign Affairs and Trade, Canberra, 2019.

21 For instance, Australian exports equal just 21.7 per cent of gross domestic product,
making the country's overall economy more able to withstand demand disruption than,
say, South Korea's (44 per cent), Malaysia's (69.7 per cent), Germany's (47 per cent) or, at
the extreme end, Singapore's (176.4 per cent). See World Bank Data, 'Exports of goods
and services as a % of GDP', 2018, https://data.worldbank.org/indicator/ne.exp.gnfs.zs.

22 Department of Foreign Affairs and Trade, 'Statistics on who invests in Australia', 2019.

23 Department of Foreign Affairs and Trade, 'Statistics on who invests in Australia', 2019; Ian
Satchwell, 'Trumping trade: Understanding the Australia–United States economic
relationship', Perth USAsia Centre, 2017.

24 Malcolm Cook, 'Between Japan and Southeast Asia: Australia and US–China economic
rivalry', *Insight*, Australian Strategic Policy Institute, 28 June 2019.

25 Rory Medcalf (ed.), 'China's economic leverage: Perception and reality', Policy Options
Paper No. 2, National Security College, Australian National University, Canberra, March
2017.

26 John Garnaut, 'Australia's China reset', *The Monthly*, August 2018.

27 John Garnaut, 'How China interferences in Australia', *Foreign Affairs* online, 9 March
2018.

28 Rory Medcalf, 'Australia and China: Understanding the reality check', *Australian Journal
of International Affairs*, Vol. 73, No. 2, 2019.

29 National Development and Reform Commission, Ministry of Foreign Affairs and Ministry of Commerce, People's Republic of China, with State Council authorisation, 'Vision and actions on jointly building Silk Road Economic Belt and 21st Century Maritime Silk Road', 28 March 2015.

30 David Wroe, '"How Empires Begin"'.

31 Elizabeth Pisani, *Indonesia Etc.: Exploring the Improbable Nation*, Lontar, Jakarta, 2014, p. 9.

32 Evan A. Laksmana, 'Reshuffling the deck? Military corporatism, promotional logjams and post-authoritarian civil military relations in Indonesia', *Journal of Contemporary Asia*, 2019.

33 Matthew Hanzel (trans.), 'Jokowi's inauguration speech in English', 20 October 2014.

34 Lyle J. Morris and Giacomo Persi Paoli, 'A preliminary assessment of Indonesia's maritime security threats and capabilities', Rand Corporation, 2018, p. vii.

35 Jun Suzuki, 'Japanese-Indonesian team to take on Java port project', *Nikkei Asian Review*, 21 May 2018.

36 Lyle J. Morris, 'Indonesia–China tensions in the Natuna Sea: Evidence of naval efficacy over coast guards?' *The Diplomat*, 28 June 2016.

37 Vibhanshu Shekhar, 'Is Indonesia's "Indo-Pacific Cooperation" strategy a weak play?' Pacnet No. 47, Pacific Forum, Honolulu, July 2018; Donald E. Weatherbee, 'Indonesia, ASEAN and the Indo-Pacific cooperation concept', ISEAS Perspective No. 47, Institute of Southeast Asian Studies, Singapore, June 2019.

38 Wilda Asmarini and Maikel Jefriando, 'Indonesia asks China for special fund under Belt and Road: ministers', *Reuters*, 3 July 2019.

39 Jessica Jaganathan and Wilda Asmarini, 'Indonesia's push to nationalize energy assets could chill foreign investment', *Reuters*, 29 August 2018.

40 Park Chan-kyong, 'Seoul eyes intelligence sharing pact with Bangkok as President Moon Jae-in seeks pivot to ASEAN', *South China Morning Post*, 1 September 2019.

41 Siddharth Vinayak Patankar, 'Hyundai India market share hits all time high', NDTV, 20 August 2019; Manu Pubby, 'India, South Korea extend logistical support to navies', *Economic Times*, 7 September 2019; Ju-min Park, 'Samsung ends mobile phone production in China as it expands facility in India', *Livemint*, 2 October 2019.

42 Ramon Pancheo Pardo, 'South Korea holds the key to the Indo-Pacific', *The Hill*, 18 August 2019.

43 Bobo Lo, *A Wary Embrace: What the China–Russia Relationship Means for the World*, Lowy Institute Paper/Penguin, Sydney, 2017, pp. 70, 138.

44 'Russia is helping China build a missile defence system, Putin says', *The Guardian*, 4 October 2019.

45 Nadège Rolland, 'A China–Russia condominium over Eurasia', *Survival*, Vol. 61, No. 1, February–March 2019.

46 Bobo Lo, *A Wary Embrace*, p. 125.

47 'Brothers in arms', *The Economist*, 27 July–2 August 2019.

48 World Bank, 'Gross domestic product 2018', World Bank Data, https://databank. worldbank.org/data/download/GDP.pdf.

49 Paul Goble, 'Russia's demographic decline accelerates increasingly because of Moscow's own policies', *Eurasia Daily Monitor*, Vol. 15, Issue 140, 4 October 2018.

50 'French strategy in the Indo-Pacific: "For an inclusive Indo-Pacific"', French Ministry of Foreign Affairs (*France Diplomatie*), August 2019, https://www.diplomatie.gouv.fr/en/ country-files/asia-and-oceania/the-indo-pacific-region-a-priority-for-france.

51 'France and security in the Indo-Pacific', French Ministry of Defence, 2019, https://www. defense.gouv.fr/content/download/532754/9176250/file/France%20and%20Security%20 in%20the%20Indo-Pacific%20-%202019.pdf.

52 'French President Emmanuel Macron vows to stand against Chinese "hegemony"
    in Asia-Pacific during trip to Australia', *South China Morning Post*, 2 May 2018.
53 Author's private discussion with UK foreign policy officials, October 2019.
54 Ricard Aidoo, 'African countries have started to push back against Chinese development
    aid: Here's why', *The Washington Post*, 16 October 2018.
55 Anthony Bergin, David Brewster, François Gemenne and Paul Barnes, 'Environmental
    security in the eastern Indian Ocean, Antarctica and the Southern Ocean: A risk-
    mapping approach', National Security College, Australian National University and
    Institute de Relations Internationales et Strategiques, 2019, pp. 25–27.
56 Pacific Islands Forum Secretariat, 'Boe Declaration on Regional Security', 6 September 2018.
57 David Brewster, 'Bangladesh's road to the BRI', *The Interpreter* (Lowy Institute blog),
    30 May 2019.
58 Arshad Mahmud, 'New Bangladesh sub base could revive India tensions', *Asia Times*,
    23 July 2019.
59 Khurram Husain, 'Exclusive: CPEC master plan revealed', *Dawn*, 21 June 2017; Andrew
    McCormick, 'Is Pakistani agriculture ready for CPEC?' *The Diplomat*, 17 May 2018.
60 Shem Oirere, 'Tanzania suspends $10b Bagamoyo port project', *Engineering News Record*,
    25 June 2019.
61 Jack A. Goldstone, 'Africa 2050: Demographic truth and consequences', Hoover
    Institution, Governance in an Emerging World project, 14 January 2019.
62 'Who was buying Iranian oil and what happens next?', *Oilprice.com*, 9 May 2018.
63 Euan Graham, 'Should China help secure the Strait of Hormuz?', *The Strategist*, 2 July 2019.
64 Simon Watkins, 'China and Iran flesh out strategic partnership', *The Petroleum Economist*,
    3 September 2019; Jacopo Scita, 'No, China isn't giving Iran $400 billion', *Bourse and
    Bazaar*, 20 September 2019.
65 Michelle Nichols, 'Saudi Arabia defends letter backing China's Xinjiang policy', *Reuters*,
    19 July 2019.
66 Farida Deif, 'China's treatment of Muslims a defining moment for the organization
    of Islamic Cooperation', *Al-Quds* (English translation published by Human Rights
    Watch), 25 February 2019.

Chapter 7: Covering the Waterfront

1 Lisa Martin, 'Australian pilots hit with lasers during South China Sea military exercise',
   The Guardian, 29 May 2019.
2 Homi Kharas and Kristofer Hamel, 'A global tipping point: Half the world is now middle
   class or wealthier', Brookings Institution blog, 27 September 2018.
3 David Scott, 'Naval deployments, exercises and the geometry of strategic partnerships in
   the Indo-Pacific', 8 July 2019, Center for International Maritime Security.
4 Christopher R. O'Dea, 'How China weaponized the global supply chain', *The National
   Review*, 20 June 2019.
5 Adam Smith, cited in Robert D. Blackwill and Jennifer M. Harris, *War by Other Means:
   Geoeconomics and Statecraft*, Harvard University Press, Cambridge Massachusetts, 2016, p. 31.
6 See, for instance, Sam Costello, 'Where is the iPhone made?', *Lifewire.com*, 8 April 2019.
7 World Trade Organization, 'China Trade Profile', 2018.
8 Edward N. Luttwak, 'From geopolitics to geo-economics: Logic of conflict, grammar of
   commerce', *The National Interest*, No. 20, 1990.
9 Anthea Roberts, Henrique Choer Moraes and Victor Ferguson, 'The geoeconomic world
   order', *Lawfare* blog, 19 November 2018.

10 Thomas J. Wright, *All Measures Short of War*, p. 127.

11 Henry Farrell and Abraham L. Newman, 'Weaponized interdependence: How global economic networks shape state coercion', *International Security*, Vol. 44, No. 1, 2019.

12 Michael Wesley, 'Australia and the rise of geoeconomics', Centre of Gravity paper No. 29, Strategic and Defence Studies Centre, Australian National University, 2016.

13 Laurence Dodds, 'Huawei's employee ownership claims are a sham covering up possible communist control, research finds', *The Telegraph*, 16 April 2018.

14 *The New York Times* editorial board, 'China's Canadian hostages', *The New York Times*, 23 December 2018.

15 Peter Harrell, Elizabeth Rosenberg and Edoardo Saravalle, 'China's use of coercive economic measures', Center for a New American Security, June 2018; Rory Medcalf (ed.), 'China's economic leverage'.

16 House of Commons Foreign Affairs Committee, 'China and the rules-based international system', Sixteenth Report of session 2017–2019, 26 March 2019, pp. 41–42.

17 Kibe Hidemitsu, 'Tanker attack shows Asia's vulnerability as "world's workshop"', *Nikkei Asian Review*, 14 June 2019.

18 Sean Mirski, 'Stranglehold: The context, conduct and consequences of an American naval blockade of China', *Journal of Strategic Studies*, Vol. 36, No. 3, 2013.

19 Isabelle Saint-Mézard, 'India's energy security: An assessment of India's international quest for energy sources', in Sumit Ganguly, Nicolas Blarel and Manjeet S. Pardesi (eds), *The Oxford Handbook of India's National Security*, Oxford University Press, New Delhi, 2018, p. 490.

20 Calvin Chen, 'China and India's quest for resources and its impact on the rivalry', in T.V. Paul (ed.), *The China–India Rivalry in the Globalization Era*, Georgetown University Press, 2018, p. 125.

21 Dinakar Peri, 'Vietnam briefs India on standoff with China in South China Sea', *The Hindu*, 30 July 2019; Bennett Murray, 'Vietnam's strange ally in its fight with China', *Foreign Policy*, 1 August 2019.

22 Dominic Dudley, 'China is set to become the world's renewable energy superpower, according to a new report', *Forbes*, 11 January 2019.

23 'How is China managing its greenhouse gas emissions?' China Power, Center for Strategic and International Studies, accessed 6 October 2019, https://chinapower.csis.org/china-greenhouse-gas-emissions.

24 Andrew Erickson and Gabe Collins, 'Beijing's energy security strategy: The significance of a Chinese state-owned tanker fleet', *Orbis*, Vol. 51, No. 4, 2007; David Shambaugh, *China Goes Global: The Partial Power*, Oxford University Press, Oxford, 2013, p. 162.

25 Andrew S. Erickson and Gabriel B. Collins, 'China's oil security pipe dream: The reality, and strategic consequences, of seaborne imports', *Naval War College Review*, Vol. 63, No. 3, 2010; Aaron L. Friedberg, *A Contest for Supremacy*, p. 229.

26 Sean Mirski, 'How a massive naval blockade could bring China to its knees in a war', *The National Interest* online, 6 April 2019.

27 'Official spokesperson's response to a query on participation of India in OBOR/BRI forum', Ministry of External Affairs, Government of India, 13 May 2017.

28 'Memorandum of arrangement on strengthening cooperation on the Belt and Road Initiative between the government of New Zealand and the government of the People's Republic of China', March 2017. In late 2018, Victoria broke ranks with the federal government and, without consulting Canberra, signed a similar document which appeared largely drafted by Chinese officials, 'welcoming and supporting' China's geoeconomic

strategy. Then, in late 2019, the Victorian government claimed to be taking China relations to the next level with a further framework agreement on the BRI that would deliver 'tangible benefits'. It remains unclear whether such documents will alter the commercial calculations of Chinese and Australian corporations in doing business with one another.

29 Nitin Pai, 'Towards many belts and many roads', *Business Standard*, 1 June 2017.

30 Marwaan Macan-Markar, 'Maldives election paves way for China deals investigations', *Nikkei Asian Review*, 15 April 2019; Indrani Bagchi, 'How did "India first" turn into "China first" in the Maldives?' *The Times of India*, 11 February 2018.

31 European Commission and the High Representative of the Union for Foreign Affairs and Security Policy, 'EU–China – a strategic outlook', 12 March 2019, p. 1.

32 Thorsten Benner et al., 'Authoritarian advance: Responding to China's growing political influence in Europe', February 2018, Global Public Policy Institute and Mercator Institute for Chinese Studies.

33 Stuart Lau, 'Is Italy experiencing buyer's remorse after signing up to China's Belt and Road scheme?', *South China Morning Post*, 30 July 2018.

34 Keith Johnson, 'China gets a British bedfellow', *Foreign Policy*, 26 April 2019.

35 House of Commons Foreign Affairs Committee, 'China and the rules-based international system', Sixteenth Report of session 2017–2019, 26 March 2019, p. 3.

36 Michelle Jamrisko, 'China no match for Japan in southeast Asia infrastructure race', *Bloomberg*, 23 June 2019.

37 'Japan and India to develop Colombo Port, countering Belt and Road', *Nikkei Asian Review*, 20 May 2019.

38 Xi Jinping, 'Working together to deliver a brighter future for Belt and Road cooperation', Keynote speech at the opening of the Belt and Road forum for international cooperation, Beijing, Chinese Ministry of Foreign Affairs, 26 April 2019.

39 A claim made in Parag Khanna, *The Future Is Asian*, Simon & Schuster, New York, 2019, p. 110. Other commentators have reached entirely the opposite view, that BRI projects lack commercial logic; see Peter Frankopan, *The New Silk Roads: The Present and Future of the World*, Bloomsbury, London, 2018, p. 119.

40 Daniel Kliman and Abigail Grace, 'Power play: Addressing China's Belt and Road strategy', Center for a New American Security, 2018, p. 2; Nadège Rolland, *China's Eurasian Century? Political and Strategic Implications of the Belt and Road Initiative*, National Bureau of Asian Research, Seattle, 2017, p. xi; George Magnus, *Red Flags: Why Xi's China Is in Jeopardy*, Yale University Press, New Haven, 2018, pp. 175–184.

41 Nadège Rolland reaches a similar conclusion in *China's Eurasian Century?*, but focused more on Eurasia. For the 'world order' claim, see Bruno Maçães, *Belt and Road*, p. 5.

42 Agatha Kratz, Allan Feng and Logan Wright, 'New data on the "debt trap" question', Rhodium Group report, 29 April 2019.

43 Joe Bavier, 'IMF approves Congo Republic bailout after China debt deal', *Reuters*, 12 July 2019.

44 Peter Frankopan, *The New Silk Roads: The Present and Future of the World*, Bloomsbury, London, 2018, p. 127.

45 Nizar Manek, 'Djibouti needed help, China had money, and now the US and France are worried', *Bloomberg*, 6 April 2019.

46 Kate Lyons, 'Papua New Guinea asks China to refinance its national debt as Beijing influence grows', *The Guardian*, 7 August 2019.

47 Ben Packham, 'China and West not everything: Marape backtracks on loan', *The Australian*, 9 August 2019.

48 'Chinese redevelopment of Solomon Islands Gold Ridge mine dubbed "way over the top"', ABC News, 30 October 2019; 'Solomons government vetoes China's attempt to lease an island', *The Guardian*, 26 October 2019.

49 Roland Rajah, Alexandre Dayant and Jonathan Pryke, 'Oceans of debt? Belt and Road and debt diplomacy in the Pacific', Lowy Institute Analysis, October 2019.

50 'China to deepen military cooperation with Caribbean countries, Pacific island countries', *Xinhua*, 8 July 2019.

Chapter 8: Far-flung Battle Lines

1 Sutirtho Patranobis, 'Be ready to fight and win wars, Pres Xi Jinping tell's China's military', *Hindustan Times*, 4 November 2017; 'Xi instructs army to improve its combat readiness', *Xinhua*, 3 November 2017.

2 The data here draws on the two most reputable sources on global military spending, the Stockholm International Peace Research Institute and the International Institute for Strategic Studies. For the underestimation of China's budget, see Meia Nouwens, 'China's defence spending: A question of perspective?' International Institute of Strategic Studies blog, 24 May 2019.

3 Andrew S. Erickson, 'Power vs. distance: China's global maritime interests and investments in the far seas', in Ashley J. Tellis, Alison Szalwinski and Michael Willis (eds), *Strategic Asia 2019: China's Expanding Strategic Ambitions*, National Bureau of Asian Research, Seattle, 2019, p. 247.

4 International Institute of Strategic Studies (IISS), *The Military Balance 2018*, IISS, London, 2018, pp. 252–253.

5 Sebastien Roblin, 'How China got its hands on its first aircraft carrier', *The National Interest* online, 28 July 2018, https://nationalinterest.org/blog/buzz/how-china-got-its-hands-its-first-aircraft-carrier-27122.

6 You Ji, 'The Indian Ocean: a grand Sino-Indian game of "Go"', pp. 98–99.

7 Office of the Secretary of Defense, 'Annual report to Congress: Military and security developments involving the People's Republic of China', 2019, pp. 35, 37–38; Andrew S. Erickson, 'Power vs. distance: China's global maritime interests and investments in the far seas', p. 255; citing Peng Guangqian and Yao Youzhi (eds), *The Science of Military Strategy*, PLA Academy of Military Sciences, Beijing, English translation 2005, pp. 213–215.

8 Michael Beckley, *Unrivaled*, pp. 67, 164.

9 Sam Roggeveen, 'China's new aircraft carrier is already obsolete', *Foreign Policy*, 25 April 2018.

10 Helena Legarda, 'Chinese mercenaries are tightening security on the Belt and Road', East Asia Forum, 16 October 2018; David Brewster, 'The forces needed to protect the Belt and Road', *The Interpreter* (Lowy Institute blog), 28 November 2018.

11 Jeffrey Lin and P.W. Singer, 'A Chinese shipbuilder accidentally revealed its major navy plans', China Aerospace Studies Institute, 15 March 2018.

12 Andrew S. Erickson, 'Power vs. distance', p. 252; citing Academy of Military Sciences, The Science of Military Strategy, pp. 102, 106, 109.

13 You Ji, 'The Indian Ocean: A grand Sino-Indian game of "Go"', pp. 96–97.

14 Timothy R. Heath, 'The ramifications of China's reported naval base in Cambodia', *World Politics Review*, 5 August 2019.

15 David Tweed, 'China's clandestine submarine caves extend Xi's naval reach', *Bloomberg*, 31 October 2014.

16 'China's "maritime road" looks more defensive than imperialist', *The Economist*, 28 September 2019.

17 David Brewster, 'Indian Ocean base race: India responds', *The Interpreter* (Lowy Institute blog), 15 February 2018.

18 Brad Lendon, 'A British military base on the South China Sea is not a far-fetched idea', *CNN*, 4 January 2019.

19 Wilson Vorndick, 'China's reach has grown: So should the island chains', Asia Maritime Transparency Initiative, 22 October 2018.

20 'Global military spending at new post-Cold War high, fuelled by U.S., China: Think tank', *Reuters*, 29 April 2019.

21 'The Soviet Union: Military spending', Nintil, 31 May 2016, https://nintil.com/the-soviet-union-military-spending.

22 'Military spending: % of GDP', The World Bank data, accessed 22 August 2019, https://data.worldbank.org/indicator/MS.MIL.XPND.GD.ZS.

23 'N. Korea ranks No. 1 for military spending relative to GDP: State Department report', Yonhap news agency, 23 December 2016.

24 Tara Copp, 'Japan surges new weapons, military roles to meet China's rise', *Military Times*, 15 January 2019.

25 Ashley Townshend, Brendan Thomas-Noone and Matilda Stewart, 'Averting crisis: American strategy, military spending and collective defence in the Indo-Pacific', United States Studies Centre, University of Sydney, 2019, pp. 27–28.

26 Ibid., pp. 6–7.

27 The incident was brought to public attention by Duan Dang and other Vietnamese social media users. It was also reported by naval analyst H.I. Sutton; see H.I. Sutton, 'Chinese submarine may have been involved in incident in South China Sea', *Forbes*, 16 October 2019. The sudden-surfacing rumour was dispelled by former Royal Australian Navy rear admiral James Goldrick.

28 Greg Torode and David Lague, 'China's furtive fleet of nuclear missile-laden submarines tests the Pentagon', *The Japan Times/Reuters*, 7 May 2019.

29 Brendan Thomas-Noone, 'India's rivalry with China, from the mountains to the sea', *The Interpreter* (Lowy Institute blog), 23 February 2018.

30 Michael Peck, 'North Korea's new submarine-launched missile: Where was it fired from?' *The National Interest* online, 5 October 2019.

31 Brendan Thomas-Noone, 'Nuclear-armed submarines: The Indo-Pacific's great destabiliser', *The National Interest* online, 7 September 2015.

32 Owen R. Cote, 'Invisible nuclear-armed submarines, or transparent oceans? Are ballistic missile submarines still the best deterrent for the United States?' *Bulletin of the Atomic Scientists*, 2 January 2019.

33 For an authoritative survey of the Indo-Pacific's nuclear dynamics, see Ashley J. Tellis, Abraham M. Denmark and Travis Tanner, *Strategic Asia 2013–14: Asia in the Second Nuclear Age*, National Bureau of Asian Research, Seattle, 2015; Muthiah Alagappa, *The Long Shadow: Nuclear Weapons and Security in 21st Century Asia*, Stanford University Press, Stanford, 2008.

34 Minnie Chan and Liu Zhen, 'China rolls out new weapon systems, nuclear-capable missiles in military parade', *South China Morning Post*, 1 October 2019.

35 Elizabeth Roche, 'India's no first use policy may change: Rajnath Singh', *Livemint*, 16 August 2019.

36 Robert Jervis, *The Illogic of American Nuclear Strategy*, Cornell University Press, Ithaca, 1984; Michael Krepon, 'The stability–instability paradox', *Arms Control Wonk*, 2 November 2010.

37 Governments of ASEAN and China, 'Declaration on the conduct of parties in the South China Sea', 4 November 2002.

38 Ashley Townshend and Rory Medcalf, 'Shifting waters: China's new passive assertiveness in Asian maritime security', Lowy Institute Analysis, 2016.

39 Western Pacific Naval Symposium, 'Code for unplanned encounters at sea, version 1.0', 2014.

40 'Japan and China agree on security hotline after a decade of talks', *Reuters*, 9 May 2018.

41 Ministry of External Affairs, Republic of India, 'Media release: Second India-China maritime affairs dialogue', 13 July 2018.

42 David Shambaugh, 'China's soft power push: The search for respect', *Foreign Affairs*, July/August 2015.

43 Ross Babbage, 'Winning without fighting: Chinese and Russian political warfare campaigns and how the West can prevail', Center for Strategic and Budgetary Assessments, 2019, p. 3.

44 Roger Faligot, *Chinese Spies: From Chairman Mao to Xi Jinping*, Scribe, Melbourne, 2019, pp. 2–3.

45 John Garnaut, 'Australia's China reset', *The Monthly*, August 2018.

46 Quentin McDermott, 'Sam Dastyari defended China's policy in South China Sea in defiance of Labor policy, secret recording reveals', ABC News, 29 November 2017.

47 Nick McKenzie and Chris Uhlmann, '"A man of many dimensions": The big Chinese donor now in Canberra's sights', *The Sydney Morning Herald*, 6 February 2019.

48 Dastyari later acknowledged he had been 'too close' to Huang, and had 'paid a very, very high price', ultimately resigning from parliament. See transcript of 'Interference', *Four Corners*, ABC TV, 8 April 2019.

49 Amy Searight, 'Chinese influence activities with US allies and partners in Southeast Asia', testimony before the US–China Economic and Security Review Commission, 6 April 2018.

50 Throughout this book the author's references to 'Chinese influence' are intended to describe not Chinese people in general, but in particular the activities of the Chinese party-state: the People's Republic of China (PRC) as controlled by the Chinese Communist Party (CCP). The motives and elements of CCP influence and interference in Australia are outlined in more detail in Rory Medcalf, 'Australia and China: Understanding the reality check', *Australian Journal of International Affairs*, Vol. 73, No. 2, 2019. On sharp power, see Christopher Walker and Jessica Ludwig, 'Sharp power: Rising authoritarian influence', National Endowment for Democracy, December 2017.

51 Andrew Greene, 'Chongyi Feng's detention in China a blunt warning to Chinese Australians', ABC News, 2 April 2017; Chongyi Feng, 'Why "democracy peddler" Yang Henjun has been detained in China and why he must be released', *The Conversation*, 23 July 2019; Fergus Hunter, 'A student attended a protest at an Australian uni. Days later Chinese officials visited his family', *The Sydney Morning Herald*, 7 August 2019; Nick Bonyhady, 'Outspoken journalist in Australia and father in China harassed online', *The Sydney Morning Herald*, 6 September 2019.

52 Nick McKenzie, Sashka Koloff and Mary Fallon, 'China pressured Sydney council into banning media company critical of Communist Party', ABC News, 19 April 2019.

53 Vicky Xiuzhong Xu, 'Blinkered Chinese nationalists are trolling me – but once I was one of them', *The Sydney Morning Herald*, 20 August 2019; 'Australian warns diplomats after China praises "patriotic" clashes with pro-Hong Kong protesters', *The Guardian*, 27 July 2019.

54 Nick Bonyhady, 'Australia's anti-foreign interference laws a model for Singapore', *The Sydney Morning Herald*, 5 March 2019.

55 Chris Horton, 'China uses Taiwan as R&D lab to disrupt democracies', *Nikkei Asian Review*, 28 December 2018.

56 Anne-Marie Brady, 'Magic weapons: China's political influence activities under Xi Jinping', Wilson Center, 18 September 2017.

57 John Gapper, 'Business in Hong Kong needs to stay strong', *Financial Times*, 21 August 2019.

58 As a consequence of this decision, the children's film in question, aptly titled *Abominable*, was banned in Malaysia and Vietnam: China is not the only party to regional maritime disputes willing to use illiberal means to wage the narrative battle. See Bethany Allen-Ebrahimian, 'Hollywood is paying an "abominable" price for China access', *Foreign Policy*, 23 October 2019.

59 Jordan Valinksi, 'How one tweet snowballed into the NBA's worst nightmare', *CNN Business*, 9 October 2019.

60 Eyck Freymann, '"One Belt One Road" is just a marketing campaign', *The Atlantic*, 17 August 2019.

61 Kate Lyons, 'Fiji PM accuses Scott Morrison of "insulting" and alienating Pacific leaders', *The Guardian*, 17 August 2019.

62 See for instance Ross Babbage, 'Winning without fighting', pp. 3–10.

63 See, especially, 'Power and influence', *Four Corners*, ABC TV, 5 June 2017; Michael Pelly, 'High court appeal on defamation tactics', *Australian Financial Review*, 8 September 2019.

64 Vivienne Chow, 'I've been waiting for a song like "Glory to Hong Kong" my whole life', *The New York Times*, 16 September 2019.

65 Kelsey Munro, 'Australian attitudes to China shift: 2019 Lowy poll', *The Interpreter* (Lowy Institute blog), 27 June 2019.

66 Rekha Bhattacharjee, 'Chinese students, expats are now flexing muscle over Doklam in Australia', *Business Standard* (India Abroad News Service), 31 August 2017.

Chapter 9: Navigating Mistrust

1 Nassim Nicholas Taleb, *The Black Swan: The Impact of the Highly Improbable*, Random House, New York, 2007. To be fair to Taleb, and to the swans, he acknowledges that 'black swan events' are not necessarily calamitous, just high in impact.

2 Peter Ho, 'The black elephant challenge for governments', *The Straits Times*, 7 April 2017.

3 United States National Intelligence Council, *Paradox of Progress*, Global Trends report 2017, p. 21.

4 Ibid., p. 10.

5 Global Military Advisory Council on Climate Change, 'Climate change and security in South Asia', GMACC paper no. 2, May 2016; Intergovernmental Panel on Climate Change (IPCC), 'AR5 Climate change 2014: Impacts, adaptation and vulnerability', Chapter 12, 'Human security'.

6 A scenario for the year 2033 in the US National Intelligence Council's Global Trends report involves a country using aircraft to release vast quantities of sulphate aerosol into the upper atmosphere to reduce the warming effects of solar radiation, provoking an outcry from other countries concerned about side-effects such as acid rain and ozone depletion (ibid., p. 24). See also Adam Lockyer and Jonathan Symons, 'The national security implications of solar geoengineering: An Australian perspective', *Australian Journal of International Affairs*, Vol. 23, No. 5, 2019.

7 'China could be the first country to exploit deep sea minerals', *South China Morning Post*, 23 October 2019.

8   Anthony Bergin and David Brewster, 'Environmental security in the eastern Indian Ocean, Antarctica and the Southern Ocean: A risk mapping approach', ANU National Security College, 2019, p. 32.

9   Elizabeth Buchanan, 'Antarctica: A cold, hard reality check', *The Strategist*, 17 September 2019; Klaus Dodds, 'In 30 years the Antarctic Treaty becomes modifiable, and the fate of a continent could hang in the balance', *The Conversation*, 12 July 2018.

10 One of the most respected thinkers about international order, the Australian scholar Hedley Bull, argued that modern international order combined several elements of a 'society', including power struggle, conflict, solidarity and cooperation, and that in particular circumstances one would predominate; see Hedley Bull, *The Anarchical Society: A Study of Order in World Politics*, Columbia University Press, New York, 1977, p. 39.

11 Kurt M. Campbell and Jake Sullivan, 'Competition without catastrophe: How America can both challenge and coexist with China', *Foreign Affairs*, September/October 2019.

12 Todd S. Sechser and Matthew Fuhrmann, *Nuclear Weapons and Coercive Diplomacy*, Cambridge University Press, Cambridge, 2017, pp. 22–23. It is important to note that, ideally, a coercer seeks 'to change the target's behaviour without actually having to execute threat', since doing so can be costly for both sides – a key point to remember when considering whether smaller nations can afford to resist Chinese pressure.

13 Robert J. Art and Kelly M. Greenhill, 'Coercion: An analytical overview', in Kelly M. Greenhill and Peter Krause (eds), *Coercion: The Power to Hurt in International Politics*, Oxford University Press, New York, 2018, p. 4.

14 Richard Heydarian, 'Rodrigo Duterte thought he had an understanding with China, then came the Reed Bank collision', *South China Morning Post*, 23 June 2019.

15 For instance, Graham Allison, *Destined for War: Can China and American Escape Thucydides's Trap?*, Houghton Mifflin Harcourt, Boston, 2017.

16 Lawrence Freedman, *Strategy: A History*, Oxford University Press, Oxford, 2013, p. xi.

17 Some of China's more moderate and worldly foreign policy thinkers have similarly observed that trust is not a realistic early objective in China's relations with the United States. See, for example, Yan Xuetong, 'Strategic cooperation without mutual trust: A path forward for China and the United States', *Asia Policy*, No. 15, 2013.

18 Andrew Erickson, 'Competitive coexistence: An American concept for managing US–China relations', *The National Interest* online, 30 January 2019.

19 Rory Medcalf and Ashley Townshend, 'India and China: Competitive coexistence in the Asian century', in Amitendu Palit and Gloria Spittel (eds), *South Asia in the New Decade: Challenges and Prospects*, World Scientific, Singapore, 2013. Chinese analyst Cuiping Zhu has likewise noted that coexistence is a realistic and worthy goal for relations between the two giants of the two-ocean region; see Cuiping Zhu, *India's Ocean: Can China and India Coexist?* Springer/Social Sciences Academic Press, Singapore, 2018, pp. 142–143.

20 Lawrence Freedman, *Strategy*, pp. 157–159.

21 Elbridge Colby, 'The implications of China developing a world-class military: First and foremost a regional challenge', Testimony to the US–China Economic and Security Review Commission, 20 June 2019, p. 5.

22 Andrew Kepinevich Jr., 'The eroding balance of terror: The decline of deterrence', *Foreign Affairs*, January/February 2019, p. 62.

23 Ashley Townshend, Brendan Thomas-Noone and Matilda Stewart, 'Averting crisis', pp. 27–28.

24 This was a conclusion from a workshop series involving about seventy Australian and American security analysts conducted by the National Security College at the Australian

National University in mid-2018. Similar conclusions have emerged from other studies, notably the December 2018 US–Australia deterrence dialogue led by the US Studies Centre at the University of Sydney. See Ashley Townshend, Brendan Thomas-Noone and Matilda Stewart, 'Averting crisis', pp. 65–66, 70.

25 Andrew Kepinevich Jr., 'The eroding balance of terror', p. 73; Michael O'Hanlon, 'Can America still protect its allies? How to make deterrence work', *Foreign Affairs*, September/ October 2019.

26 For instance, Hugh White, *The China Choice*.

27 Malcolm Cook, Raoul Heinrichs, Rory Medcalf and Andrew Shearer, 'Power and choice: Asian security futures', Lowy Institute, 2010, pp. 48–49.

28 Such confidence-building measures need to extend to relations between the Chinese and Taiwanese militaries also, given that the Taiwan Strait remains a key flashpoint. See Brendan Taylor, *Dangerous Decade: Taiwan's Security and Crisis Management*, International Institute for Strategic Studies, London, 2019, pp. 113–120.

29 Laura Zhou, 'Vietnam demands Chinese ship leave disputed waters as end of fishing ban threatens to inflame tensions', *South China Morning Post*, 17 August 2019.

30 Similar views on the need for an enhanced East Asia Summit have been put by a distinguished Indonesian scholar-diplomat: Dino Patti Djalal, 'Are we ready for Indo-Pacific 2.0?' *The Jakarta Post*, 25 February 2019.

31 Lyle J. Goldstein, *Meeting China Halfway: How to Defuse the Emerging US–China Rivalry*, Georgetown University Press, Washington, 2015; Brendan Taylor, *The Four Flashpoints: How Asia Goes to War*, Black Inc., Melbourne, 2018.

32 US Overseas Private Investment Corporation (OPIC), 'The launch of multi-stakeholder Blue Dot Network', media release, 4 November 2019.

33 David Wroe, 'China "behind" huge ANU hack amid fears government employees could be compromised', *The Sydney Morning Herald*, 5 June 2019; Ben Doherty, 'Universities to work with security agencies to combat foreign interference', *The Guardian*, 28 August 2019.

34 Ewelina U. Ochab, 'The Magnitsky law is taking over the European Union', *Forbes*, 10 December 2018.

35 'Germany says link between China govt, hackers credible', *Associated Press*, 21 December 2018.

36 Ben Bland, 'China's demands for loyalty are bad for business', *Bloomberg Opinion*, 24 August 2019.

37 Kori Schake, *America vs the West*, pp. 83–95.

38 'Germany, France to launch multilateralism alliance', *Deutsche Welle*, 3 April 2019.

39 Author's meeting with Vietnamese officials and Australian academics, October 2019.

40 Penny Wong and Kimberley Kitching, 'Engaging the parliament on China', Joint media release, Australian Labor Party, 6 September 2019.

41 Steven Stashwick, 'China's South China Sea militarization has peaked', *Foreign Policy*, 19 August 2019.

42 Linda Jakobson, 'New Foreign Policy Actors in China', Stockholm Peace Research Institute, 2010.

43 Lyle J. Goldstein, *Meeting China Halfway*, pp. 336–340.

44 In the words of Howard French, former *New York Times* correspondent in Beijing, 'A China that is treated as an equal with much to contribute … but met with understated but resolute firmness when need be … will mellow as it advances … and then most likely plateau.' See Howard W. French, *Everything Under the Heavens*, p. 284.

45 Peter Hancock, 'Ancient tales of Perth's fascinating birds', *The Sydney Morning Herald*, 5 April 2014.

INDEX